"Tony Kriz engages the missional realities of North American, urban, post-modern culture with a frankness and vigor fed by real data about real people and by a love for the ancient rites and principles of worship preserved in Anglican liturgy."

—**George Hemingway**
Priest-in-Residence
St. Catherine of Alexandria Episcopal Church

"I am a pastor at a liturgical church. I am often asked by people of all sorts, 'why liturgy? What does it matter'? This current and insightful work of Tony Kriz examines the compelling nature of ancient liturgy, the beauty that draws our culture and the proclamation of the Gospel that happens through worship in the Anglican tradition. Tony offers a true church-man's understanding of God's work through the sacraments and how he can woo a post-Christian culture with the song of liturgy. I recommend this book wholeheartedly to the curious, and especially to the hungry."

—**Trish Nelson**
Christ Church Anglican
Overland Park, Kansas

Welcome to the Table

# Welcome to the Table

*Post-Christian Culture Saves a Seat for Ancient Liturgy*

TONY KRIZ

Foreword by
BISHOP TODD HUNTER

WIPF & STOCK · Eugene, Oregon

WELCOME TO THE TABLE
Post-Christian Culture Saves a Seat for Ancient Liturgy

Wipf & Stock
An Imprint of Wipf and Stock Publishers
199 W. 8th Ave., Suite 3
Eugene, OR 97401

www.wipfandstock.com

ISBN 13: 978-1-61097-679-4

Manufactured in the U.S.A.

# Contents

# Foreword

JESUS LOVES ALL THE *children of world* as the old song goes—children from one to one hundred. More profoundly, Jesus' love is not de-cultured. While I'm sure Jesus can accurately discern the good, ethical and righteous parts of American culture from the bad, wrong or evil parts, this discernment does not lead him to hate the creators of culture: us. It important to catch that *us* part. Bashing Hollywood, The Silicon Valley, Madison Avenue or Wall Street is not on my mind. With few exceptions all of us either create or enable the culture around us. And Jesus loves *us*. He loves and remains in solidarity with his broken world. Jesus is not afraid of the cities of America. Nor is he stumped about what to do, how to communicate with them, with us.

Sometimes, though, *we* are afraid. We do get overwhelmed with what appears to be runaway evil and corruption. Lots of us are stumped. I know I could easily fall into the "frustrated evangelist" category. My whole time in ministry—35 years—I've wanted to be fruitful and effective in helping people come to faith in Christ. Most of this evangelistic effort has come in the form of church planting. At this writing I am an Anglican bishop charged with the task of planting Anglican churches on the West Coast (see www.c4so.org). I was engaged in this task when I met Tony.

I was holding a church-planting interest meeting at my alma mater, George Fox University, scouting for church planters in the Portland, Oregon area. Tony came to this "free pizza" lunch not because he likes cheap pizza, but because, as he later told me, "no one plants a church in my city without me knowing about it. I love my city and I want to know what God is doing…" Tony, like his Master Jesus, has stayed connected to his city—its culture and its people.

I am impressed with the quality of Tony's mind. You will be too as you follow him in the pages of this book. But I am even more impressed with the heart he has for his city, with his passion to reinvent almost every important part of his life to connect with his neighbors. His comment that day after pizza showed me for the first time—but not for the last—that his heart was prepared to write this book long before it became clear and practical in him mind.

In one important way my heart and mind have been on the same voyage as Tony: that is finding ancient ways, tools, means and paths with which to engage current culture in gospel dialog. A couple of years ahead of Tony I became an Anglican. Each new day using the Daily Offices, and every Sunday that passes worshipping with my faith-community in a liturgical and sacramental way, I find increasingly profound meaning in these ancient ways. They sneak up on us with God-life; like Jesus walking with discouraged disciples on the Road to Emmaus. They open windows of revelation that take even the most confirmed religious cynics by surprise.

I've already come out as a frustrated evangelist. Now, and especially with the reading of *Welcome to the Table*, I want to come out as a hopeful conversation partner with current culture. Why? I have tools now that were missing from my toolbox in the first decades of my ministry. I am no longer limited to arguing about the inspiration of the Bible—I can now also invite people to come hear it being read in public and let them and the Holy Sprit, who inspired the text, hash it out. I am also no longer restricted to merely arguing about the ontological nature of Jesus, the Christ. I can now invite people who will put their faith in him and begin to follow him, to come to the table at which he is both host and spiritual meal, and help them understand how to feed on him in their hearts by faith.

There is one last thing I would like to say before I turn you over to Tony. Liturgy is frequently misunderstood. Liturgy is not the deluxe or heavyweight version of Christian worship and discipleship. It is not particularly for deep Christians, the especially intellectual, those oriented to literature, to church history or to high forms of church. The liturgy and *The Book of Common Prayer* are precisely the opposite. They are for beginners, for the barely or only culturally churched. Liturgy feeds the spiritually hungry and those seeking training in obedience. They—the Prayer Book and its liturgy—are designed to help people understand and follow Jesus.

Tony Kriz knows how this works in practice, in cities that are often written off as "culturally closed to the Gospel". I commend his head and heart to you, for *Post-Christian Culture* [has indeed] *Saved a Seat for Ancient Liturgy at Its Table.* Tony is already seated there. He knows the players and their tendencies. Come now and sit with him. Let him tell you his story.

—Bishop Todd Hunter

# Abstract

THIS BOOK ADDRESSES THE following question: What hope does Eucharistic liturgy bring to the future of church planting within the increasingly post-Christian urban centers of the Pacific Northwest and beyond? According to my research of a sample zip code of inner-city Portland, Oregon, only one in four people self-identify with Christianity and fewer than one in five attend church. Churches are shrinking rapidly and closing their doors. Our culture is increasingly defined as post-Christian. The plans of the recent church-planting efforts are losing ground. There is no one-size-fits-all solution, but there is significant evidence that the Anglican Eucharistic liturgy will speak today in certain places where other strategies have not.

Section 1 describes the cultural reality of the Pacific Northwest in greater detail and includes the specifics of our unique and localized research (which shows the spiritual state in shocking detail). Within this context we will also explore the Anglican Eucharist as we foreshadow the conclusions to come.

Sections 2 and 3 lay the global-historical continuity of liturgical worship and forms., By the leading of God, the people of Jehovah have voted again and again across generations and cultures—throughout biblical times (section 2) and church history (section 3)—and have concluded that liturgy is meaningful and transcendent

In section 4 we define the essential dance of contextualization. As the church continues to serve and love into post-Christian culture, it must strive to keep the forms and passions of consistent church history while incarnating the unique and particular voice of each localized context. Out of this, section 5 provides a critique of existing church-planting methods.

Section 6 contains my primary conclusions. It considers the structural viability of birthing liturgical communities in post-Christian localities throughout North America, including a discussion of the Eucharistic liturgy in light of a post-Christian encounter with truth, experience of community, and spirituality. Section 7 further applies the liturgy within this new context.

# Acknowledgments

*Thank you to my family:*
    My wife, Aimee
    My boys, Malachi, Hudson, and Tristan
    My parents, Skip and Susie
    My grandmother Ellen

*Thank you to the communities upon which I depend:*
    Sabbath Dinner
    Friday Morning
    Thursday Breakfast
    Churches for the Sake of Others
    The Abbey
    The Parish Collective

*Thank you to the minds that made this book possible:*
    The Right Reverend Dr. Todd Hunter
    Rev. Canon George Hemingway
    Elizabeth Chapin and Laura Denise White
    James Swanson, Jamie Worley, and Denys Hartsfield
    My fellow doctoral students
    The faculty and staff of George Fox Seminary
    My generous survey volunteers

# Introduction

THIS WORK WAS ORIGINALLY completed as the culmination document of a Doctor of Ministry degree in spiritual formation from George Fox University. It was received with enthusiasm and awarded distinction from both the faculty and my academic advisors, most specifically The Right Reverend Dr. Todd Hunter (bishop in the Anglican Mission) and Rev. Canon George Hemingway (Episcopal priest, retired).

Originally this work was not composed with an eye toward publication, at least not in this form, but since its completion there has been demand for its content far beyond my hopes or expectations. I am honored to partner with Wipf and Stock to make it more widely available.

The original title of the dissertation was "Anglican Eucharistic Liturgy: A Church-Planting Hope for the Post-Christian Culture of the Pacific Northwest" (the need for a new title for this publication is self-evident). The topic was originally selected in hope that it would be a gift to my generation, most specifically to my friends and colleagues who are dreaming and cultivating new churches from within the Anglican/ Episcopal stream, as well as leaders of liturgical churches from other traditions. Ultimately though, my hope is for the gospel of Jesus Christ and its proclamation. The Eucharistic liturgy is a beautiful language that provides stage, score, and script for the gospel of the kingdom. May we declare it boldly.

In the spirit of complete disclosure, I, along with my community here in Portland, am a relatively recent convert to the Anglican Way after a life spent in free-church forms. In light of this, I am confident that some may find me ignorantly cavalier about many nuances of tradition, script, and practice. Similarly, others may find me elementary and narrow in my understandings. Any such critiques will find me an enthusiastic ally. I embrace my shortcomings. This work is not a destination, nor is it a final word. It is, at least for me (and I hope for you), a great leap forward in an understanding of the missional dream contained in the ancient Eucharistic way.

Finally, this missional dream within these pages rests inside the increasingly post-Christian culture of North America. This post-Christian culture is in fact *my* culture. It is the culture I was born into. It is the water in which I have swum for forty-plus years. And it is the culture in which my family contentedly missions forward, learning to love more fully and to be more fully loved. I realize this use of the term "post-Christian" creates a linguistic challenge, even a conflict, to many within Christendom. However, I see it and feel it no differently then my Albanian brother who fully lives in, loves, and longs for his Albanian culture for the sake of Christ. My aspiration is to introduce my friend and master Jesus to my friend and neighbor post-Christian culture.

Will you make it your aspiration as well?

# SECTION 1

# Setting the Stage

Let us not give up meeting together, as some are in the habit of doing, but let us encourage one another—and all the more as you see the Day approaching.

Hebrews 10:25

# Chapter 1

# Clint and Kelli

CLINT AND KELLI ARE your typical young Portlanders. Both of them love the city and have chosen to put down roots and raise their family in Portland's inner eastside. They have been married for ten years. They live in the increasingly popular Alberta district. Their home is characteristic of that Portland early-twentieth-century style with its heavy features, shuttered windows, and a wide covered front porch.

They have three young kids ages six, four, and two. It is a growing trend among these young "hipsters" to have good-sized families. It seems the "me first" orientation of the 1980s has given way to a desire for greater rootedness. They are choosing to send their older kids to public school and their younger to the city-owned community center for preschool. They know full well that the schools in Portland rank very low nationally and that their kids may receive less than if they sent them to a private school or charter school, but they also realize that their children are an extension of their family and leaving their kids in public schools helps them to stay engaged and serve their neighborhood.

Clint and Kelli love their neighborhood. In fact, when they say "neighborhood," they mean the walking village, which extends just eight blocks in either direction. They live, shop, entertain, and recreate in this comparatively small space (at least for an educated, middle-class, urban American family). They love that there are six restaurants and four coffee shops within a five-minute walk, all of which are literally owned by Clint and Kelli's neighbors. There is only one limitation to their local lifestyle: the closest decent grocery store is twenty blocks away on Martin Luther King Jr. Boulevard. They buy as much as they can at the local food co-op (preferably organic and locally grown), but unfortunately they still need to take at least one trip each week to a "chain grocery." For the most part their money stays in the community. Clint is always quick to say, "The average dollar spent in a local business will circulate within that local economy an average of five times, while money in a big-box store is lucky to circulate twice before it gets siphoned away."

Religiously, both Clint and Kelli were raised in Christian homes. They attended church all their developmental years, both attending free-church, evangelical-modeled gatherings. Their memories of church are mixed, but they would both say they strongly value their religious roots. Clint puts it simply as, "No matter how much I struggle with institutional belief, my soul was just made for religion. I can't help myself." In college and after, both Clint and Kelli only attended church when some additional motivation prevailed: a popular author/speaker was in town, a friend was involved in a service, or they had a moment of church nostalgia. Their attendance was sporadic at best.

After they got married though, they felt like they needed to give church "commitment" another chance. They began to attend a young but growing emergent[1] church in their area. The pastor was smart and funny and the music was hip, integrating secular tunes with rearranged histori-cal hymns. They were encouraged (and surprised) by the repeated return to themes of justice and social care, and they found themselves often discussing how those themes could be spiritually applied to their neigh-borhood. They also enjoyed the regular references to "sister" churches in India and Mexico. Kelli's big thing was the integration of art into the ser-vice, including the presence of Orthodox icons and locally made pottery for Communion. Church was enjoyable again. The pastor was talented and entertaining. The music was inspiring.

But it didn't last. Even though they had gotten involved in a home group and volunteered in child care, a couple of years ago they just stopped attending. They still loved the church. The pastor was still inspir-ing and hysterical. The music had actually become more and more profes-sional. And the breadth of social outreach and artistic expressions had only grown. To put it in their words, "It just sort of lost its meaning." So, after six years of loyal (though waning) commitment, they said good-bye

---

1. Emergent is a Christian movement of the late twentieth and early twenty-first centuries that crosses a number of theological boundaries and envelops people from a number of traditions. I discuss the emergent movement in more detail in chapter 5.

to what they call "institutional" church. Their weekends are now full of hiking and trips to the beach. Even when in town, they spend their time as a family, walking to the local park or just playing at home.

When friends come over for dinner, the conversation occasionally drifts to religious themes. Clint likes to talk about his interest in Russian Orthodoxy. Kelli's faith is stronger than ever but defined more by daily rhythms and neighborhood relationships than by any specific Christian tradition. They say they believe they will go back to church again someday. When will that day come? No one is sure. They simply believe "they will know it when they feel it."

# Chapter 2

# Context Is a Local Phenomenon

OVER MY ADULT LIFE I have lived in a half dozen countries and along the way I have lived in dozens of cultures. Certainly there was a dramatic cultural shift when I moved from Albania to Yugoslavia in my mid-twenties. However, an equally real cultural shift took place when I moved just three miles from Southeast Portland to North Portland.

Culture is an utterly local phenomenon. As a boy, I was shocked to hear Professor Henry Higgins in the movie *My Fair Lady* declare that he could place a person's accent within two blocks of their London home. The church today needs to raise leaders who are cultural exegetes as passionate as Professor Higgins in articulating their unique time and space.

In this chapter we will zoom the camera, like an telescope from space, down upon North America's western states, onto Oregon, into Portland, further focusing on her urban center, and eventually landing in a single neighborhood: zip code 97217. This localizing will illustrate the insights available from a local and embodied ministry focus.

Localization is also important as we conceptualize the development of post-Christian culture. Like any cultural meta-trend, post-Christendom will have a unique personality in each locality. Locality is like friendship: each personality requires us to love and communicate in a particular way.

As you read this section on context (and the chapters that follow), consider your own unique context with its particular personality. Focus the camera of your heart on your neighborhood as I focus these writings on mine.

## MY CONTEXT: URBAN PORTLAND

Clint and Kelli are a very typical young couple living in an urban center of the Pacific Northwest. The only atypical thing about them is that they articulate a longing to attend a Christian church (we will get to that later). However, if one were to imagine a quintessential young Northwestern family in the city center, it would look very much like Clint and Kelli's (except one might replace the adult church attendance part of their story with a more self-construed faith lifestyle—one that might incorporate personal meditation, qi-gong studies, and justice activism).

Acts 1 says that Jesus "presented Himself alive, after His suffering, by many convincing proofs, appearing to them over a period of forty days, and speaking of the things concerning the kingdom of God."[1] And in that context he spoke these words:

> It is not for you to know the times or epochs which the Father has fixed by His own authority; but you shall receive power when the Holy Spirit has come upon you; and you shall be my witnesses both in Jerusalem, and in all Judea and Samaria, and even to the remotest part of the earth.[2]

If, as he spoke the words "remotest part of the earth," Jesus had risen up in his mind's eye and imagined the story of humanity playing out like ripples on a pond—beginning in Jerusalem and across Judea and Samaria—his gaze could have very easily soared across a vastly unexplored ocean to an "undiscovered"[3] continent, casting across its mountains and plains to its far side and resting on what is now the Pacific Northwest.

Two thousand years later, the Pacific Northwest is a unique and fascinating cultural phenomenon. In the story of Western civilization, the Northwest represents the last dissipating ripple of expansion. It is for Jesus, "the remotest part of the earth."

Native Peoples (First Nations) have been in the area for centuries, if not millennia. They gathered along the coast and in the fertile valleys. "Mild climate, heavy rainfall, lush forests, an abundance of food and leisure time, a rich and varied material culture, and home sites on sheltered bays and harbors characterized their habitat. Physically isolated by

---

1. Acts 1:3 (NASB).

2. Acts 1:7–8 (NASB).

3. At least as far as "Western" history plays out, though at Jesus' time there had long been peoples from Asian tribal migrations on the North American continent.

mountain ranges from other native peoples, their orientation was toward the sea."[4] These words by Carlos Schwantes, the great historian of western North America, express tenacious attributes born far before American frontierism: rich food, lush nature, leisure time, varied material culture, and geographic isolation. These same attributes made it a fascination for later explorers and pioneers, and eventually urban hipsters.

Though many explorers, pirates, and adventurers had come before, Lewis and Clark are remembered as the most influential icons of the birthing of what was then called "The Oregon Territory." "Pacific Northwesterners honor the names of Lewis and Clark above all others. Cities and counties, rivers and peaks, streets and schools, all testify to the importance of the two explorers who have long symbolized the westering impulse of American life."[5] This westering impulse led to the great migration of the pioneer generations along the Oregon/California Trails.

Pioneers, and the pioneer spirit, are the seedbed of Northwest culture. It attracted independent adventurers, some of them running from the law or their past and many running in search of a dream, be it land or wealth (most dramatically gold, in terms of the California Trail). But whatever the draw, these strong-willed, independently minded often people-of-the-land were the first generations, and they laid a cultural pattern that still reigns today. This westerly migration along the Oregon Trail and California Trail illustrates why, in many ways, a city like San Francisco is more culturally related to Portland and Seattle than to Los Angeles and San Diego. Northern California is not geographically identified as the Pacific Northwest, but it does share a cultural affinity. Within the conversation of this book, it will be helpful to see it as a part of this cultural region.

In addition to the pioneer spirit, the Pacific Northwest has been marked by unprecedented isolation. Figures 2 and 3 show population density of the United States in 1890 and 2007. While on both maps there is a "dark spot" of population around Seattle and Portland, one must travel a significant distance to find similar regions of density (let your eyes wander east from the Northwest seaboard and notice how far they travel before finding a comparable color concentration). This isolation is

4. Schwantes, *Pacific Northwest: Interpretive History*.

5. Ibid., 53.

shocking and, however amusing, you get the feeling that Northwesterners like it that way.

Figure 1. United States Population Density 1890. Source: Rand McNally & Co. "United States Population Density 1890." David Rumsey Map Collection. Chicago: Rand McNally, 1897. Online: http://www.davidrumsey.com/maps4338.html.

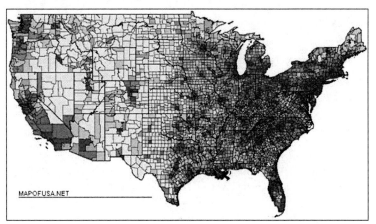

Figure 2. United States Population Density 2007. Source: mapofus.net. "US Population Density Map." Online: http://www.mapofusa.net/us-population-density-map.htm.

Certainly with the travel advances of the last couple of generations this geographical gap does not feel so insurmountable, but those formative generations must have felt like they were alone in Eden.

These themes have led the Northwest region to write a story all its own. Today, the cities of the Pacific Northwest are among the most distinctive and dramatic in the country. To illustrate this distinctiveness, I will highlight my hometown, Portland, Oregon, which will also be the primary location for applying the conclusions of this book.

It is easy to itemize the unique and lovely things about Portland, and as a passionate Portland apologist I often do just that. However, it is also important to remember that Portland is America's most "unhappy" city according to a recent study by *Bloomberg Businessweek*.[6] Economically there is an ongoing struggle. Oregon is one of only seven states with unemployment at 10 percent or higher[7] (which is saying something even in these challenging economic times).[8] However, even while struggling in these ways, Portland is also consistently ranked as America's "Greenest City" considering factors like clean air and clean water, renewable energy, reliable public transportation, a growing number of parks and greenbelts, farmers' markets and, very importantly, opportunities for community involvement.[9] Portland is also America's second "Safest City" according to *Forbes*.[10] It is America's "Best City for Summer Travel" according to *Travel and Leisure*.[11] It is the second-best "Bike City" in America according to *Bicycling Magazine*[12] and the "Best Running City" according to *Runner's World*.[13] Portland can boast America's "Best Street Food"[14] and multiple sources declare it the best beer town in America,[15] if not the world.

Environment, recreation, safety, leisure, rich food, identification with nature—these are factors that mark Northwest culture, in both her rich history and her diverse present.

---

6. Gopal, "America's Unhappiest Cities." This study of fifty US cities by *Bloomberg Businessweek* was based on a compilation of factors including depression rates, suicide rates, divorce rates, crime, unemployment, population loss, job loss, weather, and green space. Portland received the highest composite score including first in depression rank, twelfth in suicide rank, and fourth in divorce rate.

7. Based on 2010 statistics.

8. Bureau of Labor Statistics, "Employment and Unemployment Summary."

9. Kipen, "Top Ten Greenest Cities."

10. Levy, "America's Safest Cities."

11. Pramis, "America's Best Cities for Summer Travel."

12. "America's Top 50 Bike-Friendly Cities."

13. Flax, "Best of Running."

14. Robertson-Textor, "World's Best Street Food."

15. Marchetti, "DRAFT Beer Town: Portland."

Politically and culturally, the Pacific Northwest is known as one of the most liberal and progressive areas of the United States, and in light of its independent and isolated history, that is hardly surprising. San Francisco (considered a part of Northwest culture in this book) is infamous for its progressive politics including gay marriage and social care. In recent history, Oregon was the first state to legalize doctor-assisted suicide. A friend of mine recently came into town and made the comment, "I knew I was in Oregon because I saw an advertisement for medical marijuana."

It is worth noting that while a state like Oregon is considered so politically progressive that presidential campaigns hardly focus election energy on this assumed-Democratic voting block, the Democratic counties are by far the minority. In the 2004 Presidential General Election, only eight counties (out of thirty-six) voted with a Democratic majority. All eight of those counties are found within and around Oregon's two largest cities: Portland and Eugene.

If we could zoom into a block-by-block analysis of the city of Portland (and surroundings), we would discover concentric circles of political "color", with the most heavily Democratic voting block at the center of Portland's inner eastside (Multnomah County) slowly transitioning to lighter shades of "blue" and then to "reds" (Republican) as the city gives way to suburbs and eventually flowing across farmlands.

I remember seeing a map of the 2010 gubernatorial race for Portland's urban and suburban populations.[16] The voting was illustrated with precinct-by-precinct colored identification. The precincts in darkest blue were found along the east side of the Willamette River in Portland, showing voting at 70-plus percent for the Democratic candidate, Kitzhaber, versus only 49 percent for the state as a whole.

This map accurately illustrated the "concentric circles" concept. The city's center was dominated by dark blue neighborhoods along the Willamette River's east bank and downtown. With shocking uniformity those dark blue neighborhoods gave way to lighter blue precincts like ripples from a stone thrown into a still pond. Lighter blue released into lighter red and those into darker and darker crimson shades. Outside the "city" there were virtually no blue precincts to be found.

While this concentric circles phenomenon is not wholly surprising as a population trend, it will be important to understand that the

16. OregonLive.com, "Results by Precinct for the 2010 Oregon Governor Election."

inner-urban context is notably different than that of the suburbs and is often in radical contrast to the rural counties (more on this later).

These analyses are primarily used here not to make a political observation, but to illustrate cultural and sociological trends (using political data) and the reality of the distinctness of the urban phenomenon. They will also help explain my discoveries in the following section, which contrast with those of the data juggernaut Barna Group.

## FAITH AND SPIRITUALITY

The distinctness of the urban phenomenon helps explain some of the demographic data concerning the spiritual dynamics of the cities of the Pacific Northwest. The Barna Group, one of America's most prolific, most quoted, and most respected polling organizations, has just released its impressive *Barna Report: Markets 2011*,[17] in which many significant and well documented statistics are listed regarding US cities. The Barna Group refers to themselves as "a visionary research and resource company located in Ventura, California. The firm is widely considered to be the leading research organization focused on the intersection of faith and culture."[18] According to *Markets 2011* in their research on "Christian identity," they found the US cities with the lowest share of self-identified Christians to be "San Francisco (68%), Portland, Oregon (71%), Portland, Maine (72%), Seattle (73%), and Sacramento (73%)."[19] As you can see, only one of the top five is not on the West Coast and all four of the major population centers of the Pacific Northwest/Northern California make the top five. Similarly, the top five markets that tend toward skepticism about religion in general are "Portland, Maine (19% of the population identify as being atheist or agnostic), Seattle (19%), Portland, Oregon (16%), Sacramento (16%), and Spokane (16%)."[20] And finally, while not as Northwest-centric but still noteworthy, the cities with the highest proportion of faiths other than Christianity are "New York (12%), San Francisco (11%), West Palm Beach (10%), Baltimore (8%), Denver (8%), Los Angeles (8%), and Portland, Oregon (8%)."[21]

---

17. Barna Group, *Markets 2011*.

18. Barna Group, "About Barna Group."

19. Barna Group, "Diversity of Faith."

20. Ibid.

21. Ibid.

The rankings listed in the Barna report are stark and say something of great importance about the distinctiveness of the Pacific Northwest/Northern California region all by themselves; however, I am still surprised by one aspect of their conclusions. According to these numbers, 71 percent of Portlanders self-identify as Christians and only 16 percent see themselves as agnostic or atheist, and finally, only 8 percent identify with faith traditions other than Christianity. These numbers are a far cry from my daily experience in my neighborhood, where it seems like I rarely encounter a self-declared Christian. This brings back the "concentric circles" dynamic from earlier in our discussion. I do not doubt that Portland is among the "least Christian" cities in America. I do, however, doubt that my neighborhood reflects these 71 percent, 16 percent, and 8 percent statistics.

## THE RESEARCH

The religious statistics for the Pacific Northwest are widely chronicled. They are regionally based, state based, and in the case of Barna's *Markets 2011*,[22] even city based. My intent is to dial the discussion of religious identification, church attendance, and perceptions of the Christian church into tight focus. Here is my research, focused on a single zip code.[23]

I live in the 97217 zip code in the inner eastside of Portland. These addresses are technically in North Portland, but the cultural dynamics are more defined by which side of the river you live on and how far your home is from the downtown waterfront. To determine how well the Barna numbers above (71 percent, 16 percent, and 8 percent) apply to my neighborhood, I decided to gather specific data. I initiated an independent survey of residents of the 97217 zip code.[24] For those with familiarity of Portland, this zip code covers the Overlook Neighborhood to the south

22. Barna Group, *Markets 2011*.

23. I corresponded with David Kinnaman, President of Barna Group, regarding our research results. In his brief comments, he explained that our results were different from Barna not only because of their geographic focus, but also because of our less sophisticated research methodology. He stated, "Typically intercept or face-to-face interviews even if done what appears to be a random manner, does not always generate a representative sample." David Kinnaman, email correspondence with author, February 13, 2011.

24. According to my research, there is nothing currently in existence that identifies statistics to this tight a focus and on a population as small and specified as a single zip code. These numbers are a unique contribution to the understanding of urban Northwest culture and the emerging reality of a post-Christian nation.

and the Kenton Neighborhood to the north. It traverses Interstate 5 north of the Rose Quarter from Williams Avenue to the east and past Denver Avenue to the west.

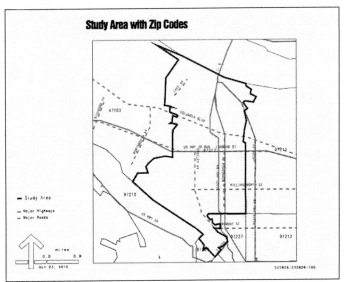

Figure 3. Study Area Definition Zip Code 97217. Source: First View 2010 prepared for Anglican Mission in America.

One hundred and ninety-three individuals were surveyed within zip code 97217. Each short interview was conducted face to face. Each volunteer interviewer was specifically trained in how to administer an objective interview, including polling rules such as read the survey explanation and each question in a neutral way; read each question in the same tone, avoiding inserting personal emphasis or import; let the questions stand for themselves; and avoid "explaining further" as each interviewer risks inserting biased interpretations. (For instance, interviewers were coached not to define "spiritual" in the question, "Do you consider yourself a spiritual person?") Zip code 97217 has a total population of about thirty-one thousand. One hundred and ninety-three surveys represent a plus/minus 7 percent confidence interval with a 95 percent confidence level.[25]

25. Creative Research Systems, "Sample Size Calculator." According to CRS, the "confidence interval" (also called margin of error) is the plus-or-minus figure usually reported in newspaper or television opinion poll results. For example, if you use a confidence interval of four and 47 percent of your sample picks an answer, you can be "sure" that if you had asked the question of the entire relevant population, between 43 percent

Individuals were surveyed on three important topics. The first topic dealt with how the respondent self-identifies religiously. (For example, "What, if any, religion or spiritual tradition do you currently claim or practice?") The second topic dealt with further understanding if the respondent has ever attended a Christian church (worship) service. (For example, "Have you attended a Christian church in the last 6 months?") The third topic dealt with discovering whether the respondent has negative or positive perceptions of a selection of Christian traditions and was measured using the following scale and list:

> This study is collecting observations and critiques of contemporary Christian traditions. In this last section, I will name several religious denominations/traditions and ask you to respond in the following way:
>
> On a scale of 1–5 how positive or negative are your impressions of each denomination/tradition?
>   1. strongly negative impressions
>   2. moderately negative impressions
>   3. equal number of negative and positive impressions
>   4. moderately positive impressions
>   5. strongly positive impressions
> OR: no real impressions one way or the other.
>
> Reminder: this list is only a sampling.

| Roman Catholicism | 1 | 2 | 3 | 4 | 5 | No impression |
|---|---|---|---|---|---|---|
| Charismatic churches | | | | | | |
| "Emergent" churches | | | | | | |
| Lutheran | | | | | | |
| Evangelical | | | | | | |
| Anglican | | | | | | |
| Baptist | | | | | | |
| Methodist | | | | | | |

---

(47-4) and 51 percent (47+4) would have picked that answer.

The "confidence level" tells you how sure you can be. It is expressed as a percentage and represents how often the true percentage of the population who would pick an answer lies within the confidence interval. The 95% confidence level means you can be 95% certain; the 99% confidence level means you can be 99% certain. Most researchers use the 95% confidence level.

The full survey and results can be found in the appendix.

| | | | | | |
|---|---|---|---|---|---|
| Eastern Orthodoxy (Russian, Greek, etc.) | | | | | |
| Pentecostal | | | | | |
| Latter Day Saints (Mormons) | | | | | |
| Presbyterian | | | | | |

Results of the survey are printed in full in the appendix, as well as referenced throughout this book. Here are a few of the discoveries appropriate for this place in our discussion.

According to our results, only 24.8 percent of respondents consider themselves "religious," while 74.6 percent self-identify as "spiritual." When asked to rate the importance of the "spiritual dimension of life on a scale of one to ten,"[26] the responses show an average of 6.6.

Now, this is where the numbers get really fascinating. When asked, "What, if any, religion or spiritual tradition do you currently claim or practice?" only 25.8 percent of respondents claimed "Christian" of any sort or flavor (shattering Barna's 71 percent rating).[27] Only 19.2 percent of whites identify as "Christian," in contrast to 78.6 percent of blacks. Conversely, only 5.7 percent of respondents self-identify as "atheist" or "agnostic" (compared to Barna's 16 percent) and 12.4 percent identify with religious systems other than Christianity (compared to Barna's 8 percent). And most shockingly, eighty respondents said they don't claim or practice any religion or spiritual tradition, and nineteen others define their faith  in such individualistic terms as to not fall under any faith category.[28] That equals an alarming 51.3 percent of respondents as simply non-religious. (Gallup says that Oregon is the most "non-religious" state with 18 percent identifying as such statewide.)[29] Over 50 percent of respondents simply said they have no religious tradition or claim!

26. Actual responses ranged from zero to ten.

27. I corresponded with David Kinnaman, President of Barna Group, regarding our research results. In his brief comments, he explained that our results were different from Barna not only because of their geographic focus, but also because of our less sophisticated research methodology. He stated, "Typically intercept or face-to-face interviews even if done what appears to be a random manner, does not always generate a representative sample." David Kinnaman, email correspondence with author, February 13, 2011.

28. "Atheists" and "agnostics" were not included here, nor were any responses that included any references to a deity of any sort.

29. Jones, "Tracking Religious Affiliation." Gallup is another highly regarded polling

When asked about Christian church attendance, only thirty-eight respondents (19.7 percent) claim to attend church,[30] which is not a surprising number, especially after reading the religious affiliation numbers listed above. (Note: within that number, Blacks and Latinos attend church at a rate of about 65 percent, according to this survey.) However, when those same thirty-eight respondents were asked if they attend regularly (defined as "once a month"), all thirty-eight said they attend at least that often. Why is this important? There is one reason that jumps out at me. It appears there is no cultural pull to pretend like one is a "good Christian." There is zero sense of obligation to claim something is true that is not. If there were, it seems there would have been at least a few people who would claim to attend church and then when asked to clarify would say, "No, not that often" or "I know I should go more often" or would just admit their attendance is irregular. Instead, even though the number is small, every church attendee seems to be devout. I would not have predicted this. Of the 80.4 percent of respondents who said they do not attend church, 66 percent said they had attended regularly at some point in their life (usually childhood).[31] This number was higher than I would have predicted.

To summarize, in addition to being freethinking, independent, isolated, pioneering, recreational, tied to the land, and liberal, these urban Northwesterners (specifically those in zip code 97217) are religiously independent, non-Christian, and non-church attending (though most have attended church at one time).

---

organization. 18 percent as "Non-Religious" is a 2004 statistic.

30. Thirteen percent of those were of faiths other than "Christian." Therefore those attending a "Christian church" is seemingly closer to 17 percent.

31. This observation is anecdotal, based on how people responded to the question, "If 'no,' have you ever regularly attended a Christian church?" Many people said something like "Yes, back when I was a kid."

# Chapter 3

# Liturgy Is a Tradition-Based Phenomenon

I T IS IMPORTANT TO define a few terms in regards to liturgy and tradition.

## LITURGICAL

The word *liturgical* means being done "according to the liturgy." *Liturgy* is defined as a particular "form of public worship, a ritual, a collection of formularies for public worship," or "a particular form or type of Eucharistic service."[1] A liturgy is an ordered form of worship (usually written down and static), which guides a group in a shared, predictable, and participatory religious experience.

Many different religious movements and traditions have established and vetted liturgies that are distinct to their tradition. Historical Christian liturgies share many common elements such as the regular and planned reading of biblical Scriptures, praying written prayers, and the taking of Holy Communion (see chapter 11). In an attempt to protect against overgeneralization, this book will make specific observations based on the Anglican (or Episcopal) Eucharistic liturgy. I encourage you to apply these observations to your particular tradition.

Anglican liturgy, also known as the Eucharist, clearly has roots in the Roman Catholic Mass, but when it was first written six hundred years ago, some passionate distinctions set it apart—and continue to do so today. Thomas Cranmer (1489–1556) "loomed large"[2] in the early Anglican liturgical formation. "Cranmer's main aims were: a wholly vernacular liturgy, a simplification of ceremonies, participation by the people (including

1. Dictionary.com, "Liturgy."
2. Holmes, *What is Anglicanism?*

18

receiving communion regularly) . . . His purpose was far more to write a liturgy embodying receptionism . . . "[3]

## EUCHARIST OR HOLY EUCHARIST

*Eucharist* or *Holy Eucharist* is the Anglican name for its liturgical worship service. The word *Eucharist* is in many contexts synonymous with "Communion," as the name for the holy supper when Christian people come together at the table to break bread, share the cup, and answer Jesus' call to "remember me," but in Anglicanism it refers to the entire liturgy culminating in Holy Communion. (See the step-by-step description of Holy Eucharist below.) It is the ongoing echo instituted by Christ in the upper room where his disciples were specifically exhorted to "do this in remembrance of me"[4] and to do it "until he comes,"[5] a reference to his future return.

This book will be pointing specifically toward the Anglican expression of liturgical worship. Here are the basic elements of an Anglican service.[6] Keep in mind that each of these elements has specific liturgical wording in the Book of Common Prayer:[7]

- The *salutation* begins the conversation between God and his worshiping people. "The Salutation begins the service by drawing priest and people into a dialogue and establishing our reason for being here." For example, "Blessed be God: Father, Son, and Holy Spirit. And blessed be his kingdom, now and forever. Amen."

- The *Gloria*, *Kyrie*, or *Trisagion* is the opening movement of the worship service in praise. "Lord, have mercy. Christ, have mercy. Lord, have mercy."

- The *Collect* is the "theme prayer of the day . . . and is intended to *collect* (hence the name) the prayers of the congregation around a single subject."[8]

3. Davies, *Dictionary of Liturgy and Worship*, 322.

4. Luke 22:19.

5. 1 Cor 11:26.

6. Webber, *Holy Eucharist*. This section was taken from the Rite II organization. Note: Section 7 will express each of these elements in greater detail along with some post-Christian cultural commentary.

7. This section was taken from *The Holy Eucharist, Rite II*.

8. Webber, *Holy Eucharist*, 20.

- *Lessons* (Old Testament, Psalm, and Epistle) are the scriptural readings assigned to each Sunday on a three-year rotation. This ensures a thorough community review of the entire Bible every three years, and it is from these readings that the sermon is most often themed.

- The *Gospel reading* is the same as the lessons above, only it is the weekly reading from the Gospels. This reading "is given the highest honor"[9] of the lessons, is intended to be read by an ordained person, and is often read from within the congregation.

- The *sermon* is located in this first part of the liturgy and is intended to "bring the Word of God to bear on our lives."[10] While the unmistakable climax of the Anglican service is Communion, the sermon still holds an important role.

- The *Creed* is recited as our response to the Word that has been read and proclaimed. It affirms in common voice the belief that we have. Most often the Nicene Creed is read and it begins with the words, "We believe."[11]

- The *Prayers of the People*, which are usually led by a deacon or layperson, are often based upon some system of collecting the actual prayer needs of the gathered community.

- The *Confession* is most often read together as a community. There are several historic examples. One of the most widely used includes, "Most merciful God, we confess what we have sinned against you in thought, word, and deed, by what we have done, and by what we

9. Ibid.

10. Ibid., 21.

11. Nicene Creed: We believe in one God, the Father, the Almighty, maker of heaven and earth, of all that is, seen and unseen. We believe in one Lord, Jesus Christ, the only Son of God, eternally begotten of the Father, God from God, Light from Light, true God from true God, begotten, not made, of one Being with the Father. Through him all things were made. For us and for our salvation he came down from heaven: by the power of the Holy Spirit he became incarnate from the Virgin Mary, and was made man. For our sake he was crucified under Pontius Pilate; he suffered death and was buried. On the third day he rose again in accordance with the Scriptures; he ascended into heaven and is seated at the right hand of the Father. He will come again in glory to judge the living and the dead, and his kingdom will have no end. We believe in the Holy Spirit, the Lord, the giver of life, who proceeds from the Father and the Son. With the Father and the Son he is worshiped and glorified. He has spoken through the Prophets. We believe in one holy catholic and apostolic Church. We acknowledge one baptism for the forgiveness of sins. We look for the resurrection of the dead, and the life of the world to come. Amen.

have left undone." It is followed by a spoken absolution.

- The *Peace* often begins, "Freed from sin, we are brought together in unity."[12] It is a ritual of exchange and often includes blessing one another with the words, "Peace be with you."

- *Holy Communion* (which includes Great Thanksgiving, Breaking of Bread, and The Communion) is the unapologetic climax of the service. This section of the service begins with prayers that lead up to the Breaking of the Bread. These prayers include Eucharist prayers and the Lord's Prayer, which is recited by all. The Breaking of the Bread is marked primarily by silence. Then, "as God came to us in flesh and blood in Jesus of Nazareth, so now God comes to us here in the bread and wine."[13] The congregation comes forward to be served the bread and the wine.

- The *blessing and dismissal* is a closing blessing on the congregation and a sending out for the community to return to the world out of the renewal and sustenance of the Holy Eucharist.

## ANGLICAN

"The Latin term 'Ecclesia Anglicana' was used from the earliest days simply to describe the English Church."[14]

> Anglicanism, in its structures, theology, and forms of worship, is commonly understood as a distinct Christian tradition representing a middle ground between what are perceived to be the extremes of the claims of sixteenth-century Roman Catholicism and the Calvinism of that era and its contemporary offshoots, and as such, is often called via media (or middle way) between these traditions. The faith of Anglicans is founded in the Scriptures and the Gospels, the traditions of the apostolic Church, the historic episcopate, the first seven ecumenical councils, and the early Church Fathers.[15]

Today, the Anglican Communion (established in 1867) is a truly global expression of faith. In fact, most Anglicans live in the Southern Hemisphere

12. Webber, *Holy Eucharist*, 25.
13. Ibid., 30.
14. Chapman, *Anglicanism*.
15. Wikipedia, "Anglican."

with the largest concentration residing in Africa where much of the Anglican leadership can be found.

## CHURCHES FOR THE SAKE OF OTHERS (C4SO)

C4SO is "led" by Bishop Todd Hunter. As an initiative of The Anglican Mission in the Americas (The AM), C4SO is launching a church planting movement designed to develop leaders committed to planting kingdom-based, missional churches located primarily, but not exclusively, on the West Coast of the United States."[16] C4SO is the specific missionary network of the Anglican Mission that is seeking to reach the post-Christian communities on which this book is focused.

16. Churches for the Sake of Others, "Hear the Story."

# Chapter 4

# Context Definitions

## POST-CHRISTIAN CULTURE

IT IS WORTH NOTING that reputable dictionaries like Webster's have no entry for *post-Christianity*. Wikipedia offers this: "a post-Christian world is one where Christianity is no longer the dominant civil religion, but one that has, gradually over extended periods, assumed values, culture, and worldviews that are not necessarily Christian (and further may not necessarily reflect any world religion's standpoint). This situation applies to much of Europe, in particular Central and Northern Europe where no more than half of the residents in those lands profess belief in a transcendent, personal, and monotheistically-conceived deity."[1]

The statistics from the 97217 survey show that East Portland (or at least the representative zip code 97217) has joined central and northern Europe among the areas that have moved past a Christian-cultural orientation. Post-Christianity is primarily defined by a broad societal shift; where that shift leads in each context creates a unique cultural personality. For this reason, we will focus our comments to the particular post-Christian reality of the Pacific Northwest, more specifically the city of Portland, Oregon, and more specifically still, a single zip code in the urban center of Portland.

Throughout this book, post-Christian culture will also be called "post-Christianity" and "post-Christendom."

1. Wikipedia, "Postchristianity."

Post-Christian culture, in its broadest terms, is related to post-Modernity, which "signifies the quest to move beyond modernism."[2] Specifically, it involves a rejection of the modern mind-set.[3] One implication is that "we should simply give up the search for truth and be content with interpretation. [Richard Rorty] proposes replacing classic 'systematic philosophy' with 'edifying philosophy,' which 'aims at continuing a conversation rather than at discovering truth.'"[4] Post-Christianity is also related to pluralism, which Lesslie Newbigin describes as "a society in which there is no officially approved pattern of belief or conduct. It is therefore also conceived to be a free society, a society not controlled by accepted dogma but characterized rather by the critical spirit which is ready to subject all dogmas to critical (or even skeptical) examination."[5] To put the concept in more common terms, post-Christianity is a society (or region) that at one point would have been characterized by having a dominant Christian presence but can no longer be defined as such. In fact, there is no assumption within common culture that Christianity is a dominant or even influential player in the process. To be even more dramatic, imagine society as a chessboard. Within a "Christian society," Christianity is viewed as an influential piece on the board of civil and societal life. Most likely she is even the most influential player: the Queen. In a post-Christian society, Christianity is no longer thought of as a player on the board. It is not that she doesn't exist; it is just that her structures and belief systems are relegated to a minority subculture so she isn't a real player in society at large.

There are many implications of this marginalizing process of going from "majority culture" to "minority culture." One sociological implication is this: any "majority culture" (be it national, genetic, religious, or ideological) faces extra critique, which leads to heightened emotions and often disdain. However, when a population eases out of Christian dominance and into post-Christian culture, the societal anger is often softened

---

2. Sweet and Crouch, *Church in Emerging Culture*, 21–22. "Moving beyond modernism" is a complicated and multidimensional issue. One honest expression of this process is offered by Leonard Sweet who says the process involves reorienting the Intellectual problem, Moral problem, Cultural problem, Spiritual problem, Ecclesiastical problem, and Authority problem. Each of these will be addressed throughout this book.

3. Grenz, *Primer on Postmodernism*, 2.

4. Ibid., 6. Quoting from Rorty, *Mirror of Nature*, 393.

5. Newbigin, *Pluralist Society*, 1.

and even dissipates.[6] That is to say, much ink has been spilt in recent decades over how society in general "hates" the church. However, nowadays when I identify myself as a Christian in my post-Christian Portland neighborhood, people do not cringe, question, or distance relationally. In fact, they often lean in. Their energy could be described as intrigued or surprised as if to say, "I didn't know you guys were still around. How amusing to meet one of you."

Many argue that post-Christianity is a good thing. Stuart Murray refers to post-Christianity as "post-Christendom" and in his book *Post-Christendom*[7] he purports a vision of the church freed from Christendom's attempts to impose Christian faith by coercion. He argues that the during last fifteen hundred years (since the time of Emperor Constantine) the church has pursued its mission from a false and domineering paradigm.

## URBAN

"Urban" is a term that typically exists in contrast to the terms "rural" (farmlands or extremely low population areas outside and between cities) and "suburban" (newer communities, subdivisions, neighboring towns, and bedroom communities on the periphery or close to a large historical city center that tend to be designed to create separation from the complications, crime, and poverty of inner-city life). In other contexts "urban" is used euphemistically to refer to areas of a city that have a concentration of a certain minority race (most often African American) and additionally assumes a concentration of violence, drugs, and poverty. In the context of this book, "urban" simply refers to the non-suburban, non-periphery city centers of the Pacific Northwest. While it is true that post-Christian themes exist throughout Northwest culture, they have a particular concentration in the centers of cities like Portland, Seattle, and San Francisco. The concentric circles begin in these areas closest to the city centers, and in these inner circles is the greatest concentration of post-Christian unchurched and de-churched peoples.

---

6. Kinnaman and Lyons, *UnChristian*, 45. "The hypocritical perception is most acute not when a religion is on the fringes of society, but when it has become a dominant part of the culture."

7. Murray, *Post-Christendom*.

# Chapter 5

# Looking Forward

PHYLLIS TICKLE STATES THAT every five hundred years the people of God need to go through the birth pangs of a major cultural transition. It happened five hundred years ago with the Reformation. It happened one thousand years ago with the Great Schism[1] separating the church East from West. It happened fifteen hundred years ago when "the Apostolic Church . . . gave way to an organized monasticism as the true keeper and promulgator of the faith."[2] It happened two thousand years ago with the life, words, and ministry of Christ himself. It also happened twenty-five hundred years ago with the Babylonian captivity and destruction of Solomon's Temple and three thousand years ago with the end of the Age of Judges.[3]

Today is another one of those transitions. Parts of Europe have already experienced the distancing from Christendom and it is now

---

1. Wikipedia, "Great Schism." "The East–West Schism, sometimes known as the Great Schism,[1] formally divided medieval Christianity into Eastern (Greek) and Western (Latin) branches, which later became known as the Eastern Orthodox Church and the Roman Catholic Church, respectively. Relations between East and West had long been embittered by political and ecclesiastical differences and theological disputes. Prominent among these were the issues of "filioque," whether leavened or unleavened bread should be used in the eucharist, the Pope's claim to universal jurisdiction, and the place of Constantinople in relation to the Pentarchy. Pope Leo IX and Patriarch of Constantinople Michael Cerularius heightened the conflict by suppressing Greek and Latin in their respective domains. In 1054, Roman legates traveled to Cerularius to deny him the title Ecumenical Patriarch and to insist that he recognize the Church of Rome's claim to be the head and mother of the churches."

2. Tickle, *Great Emergence*, 27.

3. Ibid., 26–31.

transforming North America. Perhaps it's not so noticeable in places like the South and Midwest, but it is glaringly evident in the urban centers of cities like Portland, Oregon.

As has already been shown, the presence and influence of the Christian church is waning at best and at worst has already become obsolete. This is a time of incredible opportunity. Change rarely happens in a timely, evolutionary, and incremental way. It happens out of necessity, often because crisis has forced the hand of circumstance (e.g., the Reformation, fall of the "wall" in the Eastern Block, or end of slavery in the United States). We are in a time of necessary transition if we believe that Christ and his church are for service and salvation of this time and place.

Throughout this book, I will suggest and provide evidence for a highly constructive solution, even in the face of cataclysmic cultural change that has left some with little hope (I, for one, am not among them). I hope to illumine the very real need at hand and suggest some conclusions as to how to approach post-Christian culture in an effective, Christ-centered, and historically consistent way.

Section 2 will examine the context of Holy Scriptures, both Old and New Testaments. It will build a biblical case for historical liturgical worship, showing that liturgical themes have always marked the worship life of the people of Jehovah. As a follower of Jesus, it would be utterly inappropriate to suggest a missional quest that is not in line with the Scriptures, which are God's breath.[4] We will see that within the people of Jehovah there has been, since ancient times, a draw to a worshiping structure and specifically a ceremonial invitation to the table of fellowship with God.

Section 3 shows the overwhelming trend in church history for liturgical and structured worship expressions, which culminate in the Lord's Table. This section walks through many influential historical seasons of Christian gathering and expression and shows that the worship systems are thematically harmonious with the Anglican Holy Eucharist. It is tempting to think that "progressive" forms are always the dominant solution regarding culture (a reality that is defended by incarnational theology). It is, however, impossible to deny that throughout church history—and the vast cultural spectrum in which it has grown, lived, and transformed—there has been an ever-present gravitation to liturgy and

4. 2 Tim 3:16.

Eucharist. It would be arrogant to assume that suddenly in the twenty-first century we would discover some new adaptive form of Christian worship. Even more so, the stillness, structure, and transcendence of a liturgical and Eucharistic service encases many of the creation longings of the human soul and ever draws humanity back to her like a migrating salmon is drawn back to its historical and nourishing waters.

Section 4 argues for the absolute necessity of a contextualized and incarnational mindset regarding Christ's mandate and the church's calling. This section also shows how this ever-localized necessity (incarnational mission) is not in conflict with a liturgical orientation.

Section 5 explores many church philosophies that have tried to "solve" the post-Christian problem and honestly states their strengths and weaknesses within a post-Christian culture like Portland's inner eastside. No single "solution" can reach the entirety of our rapidly de-churching society. This is a fact that the Christian church must accept. Honest and open evaluation and critique, in a spirit of shared mission and collaboration (something the people of Jesus have been shamefully poor at during most of her history), are necessary for the continuation of the Great Commission.[5]

Section 6 argues that the Anglican Eucharistic liturgy offers a constructive and attractive church offering in a post-Christian setting like Portland, Oregon. We will illustrate the power of liturgy, but in that show the unique opportunity of the Anglican voice in our culture today. We will share how this church-planting mission has been born out of tested virtue and profound passion. Finally, we will show that the Anglican Eucharistic liturgy can speak specifically and meaningfully to the post-Christian encounter with truth, experience of community, and spirituality.

Finally, section 7 makes some specific suggestions about how to creatively administer the individual steps and themes of the liturgy in ways that might communicate their greatest meaning within post-Christian culture.

The appendix contains the survey used to examine the religious trends and perceptions of zip code 97217 in Portland's inner eastside. It also shows the raw data from that survey (compiled for easy observation) and an itemization of the facts and trends acquired from the 193 respondents.

5. Matt 28:19–20.

# Liturgy in the Context of Scripture

"They devoted themselves to the apostles' teaching and to the fellowship, to the breaking of bread and to prayer."

Acts 2:42

The purpose of this section is to explore what Scripture has to say about liturgical worship. I argue that liturgy, such as the Anglican form of worship described in section 1, is consistent with the teachings and the encouragements of the Holy Scriptures, Old Testament and New Testament. We will ask four core questions as we derive the Bible's position on worship—as it pertains both broadly to the major governing parameters of the liturgy and specifically to the Anglican Eucharist:

- Do the Scriptures support the idea of gathering for worship of Jehovah?

- Do the Scriptures support the idea of structured worship with consistent and repeatable patterns?

- Do the Scriptures support and model written prayers, and are those prayers to be shared within the worship gathering?

- Do the Scriptures defend a coming to the Table of Worship to commemorate the sacrifice for sin, and is that Table the center place of that worship experience?

# Chapter 6

# The Old Testament

## DO THE SCRIPTURES SUPPORT THE IDEA OF GATHERING FOR WORSHIP OF JEHOVAH?

THE HEBREW SCRIPTURES, ACCUMULATED over hundreds of years, reflect rather haphazardly the practices of worship from various localities and from the successive forms of society. While, upon review, the expression and example of public worship is not as consistent as I was originally led to believe, it is clear from the Scriptures' earliest pages that Jehovah called and longed for his people to be a worshiping people and that much of that worshipful calling was in the collective.

The making and carrying of the Tabernacle[1] and later the building of the Temple (first by Solomon) brought "place" to the expression of worship in the Old Testament, as well as the assumed and obeyed rhythm of public gathering. From here came the regular practice of feast, festival, and sacrifice so the people might gather before Jehovah. "And King Solomon and *all the congregation of Israel, who were assembled* to him, were with him before the ark, sacrificing so many sheep and oxen they could not be counted or numbered."[2]

"Certainly from the standpoint of those who held the Yahweh faith, the most significant single aspect of worship was Yahweh himself. Ultimately, every word and act of worship was fraught with the reality of his presence, and gained its meaning only from that fact."[3] This place

1. Exod. 25–31.

2. 1 Kgs 8:5 (italics mine).

3. Weil, "The Holy Spirit," 9.

31

of gathering, sacrifice, and worship was so central to the Old Testament that even war, destruction, and captivity could not deter the people of Israel from returning to the place of divine meeting, even at the profound risk of life and personal destruction. Ezra and Nehemiah tell the story of worshiping people rebuilding the Temple.

"The Temple was primarily concerned with sacrifice, which was normally permitted nowhere else; but, because of God's promise to meet Israel there, it was also the place at which . . . the Jews said their prayers."[4] First Kings 8:28–30 says, "Yet give attention to your servant's prayer and his plea for mercy, O LORD my God. Hear the cry and the prayer that your servant is praying in your presence this day. May your eyes be open toward this temple night and day, this place of which you said, 'My Name shall be there,' so that you will hear the prayer your servant prays toward this place. Hear the supplication of your servant and of your people Israel when they pray toward this place. Hear from heaven, your dwelling place, and when you hear, forgive."

While there is such a dominant Temple tradition in the Old Testament concerning the worshiping people and the rhythms of gathering it requires, note that for much of the Old Testament story the Temple lay in ruins. It is in these times for the people of Yahweh that "the sacrificial law was spiritualized"[5] to maintain its continuity. It is as if the people could not imagine life without the place of gathering and sacrifice.[6] To support this spiritualized continuity, the people heralded passages such as Psalms 50:13 and 51:16 and Isaiah 66:20. This tradition laid the profound and enduring foundation from which sprung the synagogue and the weekly Passover meal.

## DO THE SCRIPTURES SUPPORT THE IDEA OF STRUCTURED WORSHIP WITH CONSISTENT AND REPEATABLE PATTERNS?

"Worship in the Old Testament is inseparable from the matter of how Israel formally acknowledged the Lordship of Yahweh, and how they expressed their response to his Lordship. And this turns out to have been an enormously complex and constantly changing affair. It turns out to

---

4. Jones et al., *Study of Liturgy*, 41-42.

5. Ibid., 41.

6. Segal, *Hebrew Passover*. Segal speaks of how the worship gathering became less about an animal and more about the domestic or family occasion.

be inseparable from the whole pilgrimage through which the people of Yahweh moved during their thousand-year history reflected in the Old Testament."[7] At the very least, the early festival system, initially set up in Exodus, sets the pattern of community worship in the Old Testament. These early public festivals included Unleavened Bread, Weeks (or Harvest), and the Ingathering.[8] In Deuteronomy 16, Passover was added to this list[9] and became a "centralized public observance."[10] Passover played an important role as the reliving of the Exodus from Egypt at the hand of the loving God who had not forgotten them and of whom they were not to forget. "Observe the month of Abib and celebrate the Passover to the Lord your God, for in the month of Abib the Lord your God brought you out of Egypt by night. And you shall sacrifice the Passover to the Lord your God from the flock and the herd, in the place where the Lord chooses to establish His name."[11] These festivals are important aspects of the annual structure in Old Testament worship. The following figures show a simple example of a Jewish worshiping year[12] and an Anglican worshiping year.

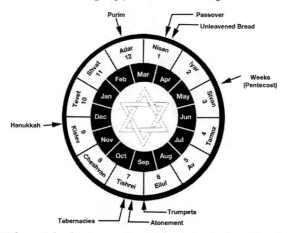

Figure 4. Hebrew Calendar. Source: Created for author by James Standridge.

7. Wharton, "Obedience and Sacrifice," 7.

8. Exod 23:14–17, 34:18–23.

9. Many assume the later addition of Passover was because previously Passover had been celebrated in the home—perhaps because the mark of the blood was on the home's door posts.

10. Davies, *New Westminster Dictionary*, 397.

11. Deut 16:1–2.

12. This Jewish calendar includes the extra-biblical Hanukkah.

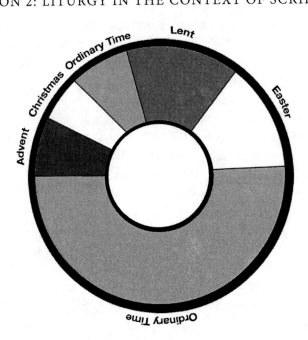

Figure 5. Liturgical Calendar. Source: Created for author by James Standridge.

Weekly worship patterns were typical as well, exemplified in the Sabbath. The Law stated, "Remember the Sabbath day by keeping it holy. Six days you shall labor and do all your work, but the seventh day is a Sabbath to the LORD your God. On it you shall not do any work, neither you, nor your son or daughter, nor your manservant or maidservant, nor your animals, nor the alien within your gates. For in six days the LORD made the heavens and the earth, the sea, and all that is in them, but he rested on the seventh day. Therefore the LORD blessed the Sabbath day and made it holy."[13] These people of Yahweh were privileged to unite themselves to God by participating in his rest.[14] "The Sabbath became the primary day of worship for the Jews, especially after the Babylonian exile. It was observed by meetings in the synagogues to read and study the Torah . . . It is certain that elements of the Jewish Sabbath were later absorbed into the Christian Lord's Day, and that Christian worship was also held on the weekly fixed day."[15]

13. Exod 20:8–11.

14. Gen 2:1–3.

15. Senn, *Christian Liturgy*, 20.

Finally, there was also a daily rhythm of worship in the Old Testament. In fact, there seems to be a specific pattern of praying three times a day: a pattern we observe in both the Psalms and the Prophets. "Evening, morning and noon I cry out in distress, and he hears my voice."[16] In Daniel we read, "Now when Daniel learned that the decree had been published, he went home to his upstairs room where the windows opened toward Jerusalem. Three times a day he got down on his knees and prayed, giving thanks to his God, just as he had done before."[17] The three daily hours for saying the *Tefillah*[18] and the two for saying the *Shema*[19] were of course also observed on the Sabbath.

The Old Testament models regular worship in annual, weekly, and daily patterns. These patterns have been defended and reflected throughout church history and are expressly practiced in the Anglican way through the church calendar, weekly Eucharist, and daily prayers (as found in the Book of Common Prayer).

## DO THE SCRIPTURES SUPPORT AND MODEL WRITTEN PRAYERS, AND ARE THOSE PRAYERS TO BE SHARED WITHIN THE WORSHIP GATHERING?

It seems appropriate to begin this answer with *The Shema Israel*, originally taken from Deuteronomy 6:4:

> Shema Yisrael Adonai Eloheinu Adonai Echad
> Hear, O Israel: the Lord is our God, the Lord is One

Later expressions of this prayer, which was also a declaration of faith, came from Deuteronomy 6:4–9 and 11:13–21 and Numbers 15:37–41. There are varying beliefs as to how early this prayer was integrated into regular and ubiquitous Jewish worship, but by the time of the synagogue system, one found "the *Shema* at both morning and evening services."[20]

The Psalms are a virtual library of written prayers. It is easy to see the Psalms' place in personal worship as it is often taught in Western churches.

---

16. Ps 55:17.

17. Dan 6:10–11.

18. *Tefillah* is the prayer recitations that form part of the observance of Judaism. These prayers, often with instructions and commentary, are found in the *siddur*, the traditional Jewish prayer book.

19. *The Shema* will be explained in the next section.

20. Senn, *Christian Liturgy*, 69.

However, as Frank Senn writes, the "Psalms, which were originally part of the temple liturgy . . . are sung at the beginning of the synagogue service and between readings."[21] The Psalms were corporate in their application.

"The Old Testament narrative itself reminds us that ritual acts are normally accompanied by vocal reciting. 'I will offer in his tent sacrifices and shouts of joy; I will sing and make melody to the Lord.'[22] 'There shall be heard again . . . the voice of those who sing, as they bring thank offerings to the house of the Lord.'"[23]

Let's take one particular sort of written (liturgical) prayer as an example: the prayer of confession. As stated in section 1, the Confession is an essential element of the Anglican liturgy. This emphasis is pulled from the Scriptures themselves. Psalms 51 is perhaps the most famous example—here are its first twelve verses:

> Have mercy on me, O God,
> according to your unfailing love;
> according to your great compassion
> blot out my transgressions.
> Wash away all my iniquity
> and cleanse me from my sin.
>
> For I know my transgressions,
> and my sin is always before me.
> Against you, you only, have I sinned
> and done what is evil in your sight,
> so that you are proved right when you speak
> and justified when you judge.
> Surely I was sinful at birth,
> sinful from the time my mother conceived me.
> Surely you desire truth in the inner parts;
> you teach me wisdom in the inmost place.
>
> Cleanse me with hyssop, and I will be clean;
> wash me, and I will be whiter than snow.
> Let me hear joy and gladness;
> let the bones you have crushed rejoice.
> Hide your face from my sins and blot out all my iniquity.

21. Ibid., 70.

22. Ps 27:6.

23. Also see Hustad, "Psalms," 409. The verse quoted is Jer 33:10b–11a.

Create in me a pure heart, O God,
and renew a steadfast spirit within me.
Do not cast me from your presence
or take your Holy Spirit from me.
Restore to me the joy of your salvation
and grant me a willing spirit, to sustain me.

This calling to embrace prayers of confession exists throughout the Old Testament. Numbers 5:5–8 says, "The LORD said to Moses, 'Say to the Israelites: When a man or woman wrongs another in any way and so is unfaithful to the LORD, that person is guilty and must confess the sin he has committed. He must make full restitution for his wrong, add one fifth to it and give it all to the person he has wronged.'" And Leviticus 16 shows an example of the community pleading for forgiveness as the chief priest prays on behalf of the people. This theme extends into the books of history. Both Ezra, chapter 9, and Nehemiah, chapters 1 and 9, have prayers of public confession. And finally in the Prophets is possibly the most famous example, the prayer of Daniel in chapter 9. Here are a couple of excerpts from his long and meaningful communal prayer.

I prayed to the LORD my God and confessed: "O Lord, the great and awesome God, who keeps his covenant of love with all who love him and obey his commands, we have sinned and done wrong. We have been wicked and have rebelled; we have turned away from your commands and laws. We have not listened to your servants the prophets, who spoke in your name to our kings, our princes and our fathers, and to all the people of the land . . . O Lord, listen! O Lord, forgive! O Lord, hear and act! For your sake, O my God, do not delay, because your city and your people bear your Name."[24]

Other examples of written prayers include David's canticle[25] in 1 Chronicles 16:9 and Deborah's canticle in Judges 5. Old Testament books of history, psalms, and prophets all model written prayers and use them in the public worship.

24. Dan 9:4–6, 19.

25. A canticle is a hymn or song primarily used for worship. It is related to psalms in style, but is found apart from the book of Psalms.

## DO THE SCRIPTURES DEFEND A COMING TO THE TABLE OF WORSHIP TO COMMEMORATE THE SACRIFICE FOR SIN, AND IS THAT TABLE THE CENTER PLACE OF THAT WORSHIP EXPERIENCE?

The prefiguring of the table has the earliest of roots. It can be argued that it begins with the sacrifice of Abel, but most assuredly it is linked to Melchizedek, King of Salem, who "brought out bread and wine; now he was a priest of God Most High."[26] "The bread and wine offered by Melchisedech were considered from a very ancient date to be a figure of the Eucharist. Clement of Alexandria (late second century) specifically wrote 'Melchisedec, who offered bread and wine, the consecrated food as a figure of the Eucharist.'"[27] And Saint Cyprian (middle third century) wrote:

> Also in the priest Melchizedek we see prefigured the sacrament of the sacrifice of the Lord, according to what divine Scripture testifies, and says, "And Melchizedek, king of Salem, brought forth bread and wine." Now he was a priest of the most high God . . . In Genesis, therefore, that the benediction, in respect of Abraham by Melchizedek the priest, might be duly celebrated, the figure of Christ's sacrifice precedes, namely, as ordained in bread and wine; which thing the Lord, completing and fulfilling, offered bread and the cup mixed with wine, and so He who is the fullness of truth fulfilled the truth of the image prefigured.[28]

The predominant image that sets the "table" for the sacrificial feast shared by Jehovah and his beloved is found in Genesis 18. This is the same scene from which Andrei Rublev (the fourteenth-century Russian iconographer) drew when he created his most famous icon: *The Icon of The Holy Trinity*. This piece "constitutes his masterpiece, an unexcelled jewel of iconography. The grace of its line and the delicate finesse of its colors not only portray an intense spiritual beauty, but manifest to us that which the most beautiful theological texts could never convey."[29]

---

26. Gen 14:18.
27. Daniélou, *Bible and Liturgy*, 143.
28. Cyprian, "Epistle LXII," 777–78.
29. Quenot, *The Icon*, 31.

Figure 3. Rublev's Icon: *The Holy Trinity.* Source: Image owned by author. Photo by Steve Harmon.

The three figures seated at the table are from Genesis 18:1–16, the story of the three messengers who appear to Abraham under the oak of Mamre to tell him and Sarah of the forthcoming birth of their son. In response to the second commandment, icons do not depict the unseen, even as they reveal the unseen. Rublev evokes this historical moment in the Old Testament as a symbolic representation of the Divine: three seated together in eternal and still communion around a table. This table represents the invitation of the Divine Triune to eat—initially with Abraham at his home, but through analogical extension, ultimately with all of Jehovah's people both now and into eternity. Other versions of this icon include Abraham and Sarah at the table, further emphasizing the invitation of the Divine to share the table.

The food at the table is also prefigured in the manna in Exodus, chapter 16. In reference to manna, Jean Danielou writes, "But this nourishment that you receive, the Bread descended from heaven, communicates to you the substance of eternal life. It is the Body of Christ. As the light is greater than the shadow, the truth than the figure, so the Body of the Creator is greater than the manna from heaven."[30] He is working off the same truth as Jesus when Jesus said:

> I tell you the truth, it is not Moses who has given you the bread from heaven, but it is my Father who gives you the true bread from heaven. For the bread of God is he who comes down from heaven and gives life to the world . . . I am the bread of life. Your forefathers ate the manna in the desert, yet they died. But here is the bread that comes down from heaven, which a man may eat and not die. I am the living bread that came down from heaven. If anyone eats of this bread, he will live forever. This bread is my flesh, which I will give for the life of the world.[31]

In Exodus 24, we are given the "meal of the Covenant on Mount Sinai" as expounded by John Witvliet.[32] "And Moses wrote down all the words of the Lord. Then he arose early in the morning and built an altar at the foot of the mountain with twelve pillars for the twelve tribes of Israel. And he sent young men of the sons of Israel, and they offered burnt offerings and sacrificed young bulls as peace offerings to the Lord."[33]

The next major movement of Eucharistic prefiguring in the Old Testament is in the Passover. "A fair reading of Leviticus emphasizes the spiritual dimension of the act of sacrifice. The word for 'body' has multiple references as microcosm for the temple and for God's universe. We have also to take into account the interchangeability in the Bible of words for spiritual and material food, bread and flesh, wine, blood, life and soul. Even the reference to the covenant is the same . . . Compare the wording with the altar of the show bread."[34]

| Luke 22:17, 20 | Leviticus 24:8 |
|---|---|
| This is my body, which is given for you. Do this in remembrance of me . . . This cup which is poured out for you is the new covenant in my blood . . . | Every Sabbath day Aaron shall set it in order before the Lord continually on behalf of the people of Israel as a covenant forever. |

---

30. Daniélou, *Bible and Liturgy*, 149.

31. John 6:32–34, 48–51.

32. Witvliet, "Former Prophets," 88.

33. Exod 24:4–5.

34. Douglas, "Eucharist," 210.

Then, "just as the people of Israel gathered together to renew their covenant with God, so we Christians gather to renew the new covenant God has made with us in Christ."[35] One example of this can be found in Joshua 24, when Joshua presses his famous declaration, "Choose for yourselves today whom you will serve."[36] And to which the people responded, "As for me and my house, we will serve the Lord."[37]

In Proverbs 9, wisdom calls out and invites the reader, "Come, eat of my food and drink of the wine I have mixed."[38] The early church fathers[39] referenced the following passages as figuring both the eschatological meal and the Eucharistic banquet: "Ho! Everyone who thirsts, come to the waters; and you who have no money, come, buy and eat . . . Listen carefully to Me, and eat what is good, and delight yourself in abundance."[40] Also, and here we have the additional theme of how *all peoples* are invited to the table of God, "And the Lord of hosts will prepare a lavish banquet for all peoples, on this mountain; a banquet of aged wine, choice pieces of marrow, and refined, aged wine."[41]

35. Witvliet, "Former Prophets," 88.

36. Josh 24:15.

37. Ibid.

38. Prov 9:5.

39. Daniélou, *Bible and Liturgy*, 153–54. Danielou draws from the writings of St. Ambrose and the Book of Enoch when referencing these passages.

40. Isa 55:1–2.

41. Isa 25:6.

# Chapter 7

# The New Testament

WITH THE INCARNATION OF Jesus the entire map of Jehovah-focused faith and practice went through a massive metamorphosis: a fuller revelation. Having established that the Old Testament does have ample space for the continuity of liturgical worship through its epochs, will Jesus and his renewed way redirect or affirm these examples and exhortations of liturgical worship? Here are some New Testament responses to the same four questions we examined from the Old Testament.

## DO THE SCRIPTURES SUPPORT THE IDEA OF GATHERING FOR WORSHIP OF JEHOVAH?

It seems that in the specific season of Jesus' life and ministry the Jewish habit of gathering was practiced and affirmed. From Jesus' earliest years, there is clear evidence of worship gathering, and the Scriptures seem to laud these behaviors. "And when the days for the purification according to the law of Moses were completed, they brought Him [Jesus] up to Jerusalem to present Him to the Lord . . . and to offer a sacrifice according to what was said in the Law of the Lord."[1] In his childhood, "His parents used to go to Jerusalem every year at the Feast of the Passover. And when He [Jesus] became twelve, they went up there according to the custom of the Feast."[2] And while Jesus' family's dedication seems undeniable, Jesus' personal dedication exceeded even that: "And when He [Jesus] became twelve, they went up there [Jerusalem] according to the custom of the

1. Luke 2:22, 24.
2. Luke 2:41.

Feast; and as they [Jesus' parents] were returning, after spending the full number of days, the boy Jesus stayed behind in Jerusalem. And His parents were unaware of it, but supposed Him to be in the caravan, and went a day's journey; and they began looking for Him among their relatives and acquaintances. And when they did not find Him, they returned to Jerusalem, looking for Him."[3] Jesus' response when they finally found their escaped twelve-year-old, "Why is it that you were looking for Me? Did you not know that I had to be in My Father's house [the temple]?"[4] Jesus' dedication to gathering was not just a Jerusalem-based (temple-based) expression. Luke explains, "He went to Nazareth, where He had been brought up; and as *was His custom* [emphasis added] He entered the synagogue on the Sabbath."[5]

Luke also explains in his Gospel how Jesus began his ministry. "He entered the synagogue on the Sabbath, and stood up to read. And the book of the prophet Isaiah was handed to Him. And He opened the book and found the place where it was written, 'The Spirit of the Lord is upon Me . . .'"[6]

Throughout Jesus' ministry he visited the synagogue. Mark, the writer of the shortest Gospel account, tells us that Jesus went to the synagogue in Capernaum to teach in the earliest part of his ministry.[7] He went into a synagogue and performed healings.[8] Upon a trip to Nazareth he taught in the synagogue.[9] Jesus seemed drawn time and again to the temple courts. Mark says that Jesus visited the temple on three different occasions in just one chapter: after his "Triumphal Entry,"[10] before turning over the money changers' tables,[11] and when confronted by the chief priests, scribes, and elders.[12]

This pattern of Jesus was observed and echoed by his earliest followers. In the book of Acts, the Apostle Paul is said to have entered

3. Luke 2:42–45.
4. Luke 2:49.
5. Luke 4:16.
6. Isa 61:1 and Luke 4:16–18.
7. Mark 1:21.
8. Mark 3:1.
9. Mark 6:1–2.
10. Mark 11:11.
11. Mark 11:15.
12. Mark 11:27.

the synagogues of the cities he visited no less than nine times.[13] As the Scriptures say, "When they had passed through Amphipolis and Apollonia, they came to Thessalonica, where there was a Jewish synagogue. *As his custom was*, Paul went into the synagogue, and on three Sabbath days he reasoned with them from the Scriptures."[14]

From the very inception of the church, the people of Jesus were marked by their custom to meet. "So then, those who had received his [Peter's] word were baptized; and there were added that day about three thousand souls. And they were continually devoting themselves to the apostles' teaching and to fellowship, to the breaking of bread and to prayer."[15] "And all those who had believed were together, and had all things in common . . . And day by day continuing with one mind in the temple, and breaking bread from house to house."[16]

The very organization of the New Testament supports a gathering people. Each epistle is a letter written to a gathering community, supposedly to be read before that community. "Paul, called as an apostle of Jesus Christ by the will of God, and Sosthenes our brother, to the church of God which is at Corinth . . . "[17] " . . . to the churches of Galatia,"[18] " . . . to the saints who are at Ephesus,"[19] "to all the saints in Christ Jesus who are in Philippi,"[20] and " . . . to the church of the Thessalonians."[21]

There are many points in the New Testament where the writers assume the regular gathering of Christians. When the Apostle Paul wrote to a church like Corinth (a church whose conduct in the assembly Paul had particular concern about), his language is telling: "When you are assembled in the name of our Lord Jesus,"[22] and "for *your meetings* do more harm than good. In the first place, I hear that *when you come together as*

---

13. Passages starting with Acts 13:14; 14:1; 17:1, 10, 16; 18:4, 19, 26; and 19:8.

14. Acts 17:1–2 (italics mine).

15. Acts 2:41–42.

16. Acts 2:44, 46.

17. 1 Cor 1:1–2.

18. Gal 1:2b.

19. Eph 1:1b.

20. Phil 1:1b.

21. 1 Thess 1:1b.

22. 1 Cor 5:4.

*a church . . .* "[23] The writer of Hebrews says, "Let us not give up meeting together, as some are in the habit of doing."[24]

"We must never forget that almost all of St. Paul's letters are directed to communities of Christians. When, therefore, he spoke of offering prayers, material gifts and sacrifices, he was thinking of communal offerings. Since the great act of communal worship in the early Church was the celebration of the Eucharist, this would be the most propitious time to present these offerings."[25]

John's Revelation also reveals the commitment to seeing the people of God as worshiping communities, and not from a perspective that exists solely "under the sun" as the Revelation comes from Jesus Christ and is "communicated by His angel."[26] The Revelation reads, "Write in a book what you see, and send it to the seven churches: to Ephesus and to Smyrna and to Pergamum and to Thyatira and to Sardis and to Philadelphia and to Laodicea."[27]

## DO THE SCRIPTURES SUPPORT THE IDEA OF STRUCTURED WORSHIP WITH CONSISTENT AND REPEATABLE PATTERNS?

The New Testament period was a time of discovery for the Christian church. Many of the most important norms of Christian life and worship were just finding their first voices amongst the church leadership and within the assembly. For instance, the full equality of Jews and Gentiles within the Christian family was still being debated at least into the mid-first century.[28] Likewise, it is not surprising that many of the worship norms were still finding their structure and system.

We have already noted those first chronicled worship norms from the earliest paragraphs in the Acts of the Apostles, "They devoted themselves to the apostles' teaching and to the fellowship, to the breaking of bread and to prayer."[29] And while this is not equivalent to full-fledged

---

23. 1 Cor 11:17b–18a (italics mine).

24. Heb 10:25a.

25. Grassi, "St. Paul," 612–13.

26. Rev 1:1b.

27. Rev 1:11.

28. The Epistles to the Galatians and the Ephesians offer commentary on the ongoing tension over integrating Gentiles into the Christian church.

29. Acts 2:42.

liturgical worship order, it is indicative of the early normative behavior within Jesus' church.

So much of the church's early life was an extension/transition of the Jewish worship system. As listed above, visiting the temple and synagogues maintained a place in Christian practice. So Christian worship "would have been shaped to some extent by the Jewish lectionary,"[30] and would therefore have been liturgical in nature. It has even been suggested that Jesus' teachings are linked to the synagogue lectionary.[31]

In this same heart, some scholars have suggested that much of the New Testament itself was organized in a lectionary way. "G.D. Kilpatrick suggested that Matthew was intended for public reading at worship . . . Michael Goulder went further, and regarded all three Gospels as lectionary books—Mark for half a year, Matthew for a full year following the festal cycle, and Luke for a full year following the Sabbath cycle."[32]

The use of the Lord's Supper in worship was a normative, structured, and regular expression of worship. It was used from the earliest days of the Christian church and expressed in the New Testament. For more on this read ahead in the section titled, "Do the Scriptures defend a coming to the Table of Worship to commemorate the sacrifice for sin, and is that Table the center place of that worship experience?"

"In Romans 15:16, St. Paul describes himself as a *leitourgos*, literally, one who performs service at the altar."[33] This priestly role, mentioned in numerous places in the New Testament, is reflective of both the continuity with the priestly office and, according to Joseph Grassi's work cited here and in the case of Paul, performing the "service."

## DO THE SCRIPTURES SUPPORT AND MODEL WRITTEN PRAYERS, AND ARE THOSE PRAYERS TO BE SHARED WITHIN THE WORSHIP GATHERING?

The single most famous written prayer in the Christian tradition is found in Matthew, chapter 6 and is often called the "Lord's Prayer." Jesus commands his followers,

---

30. Bradshaw, *Christian Worship*, 30.

31. Finch, *Synagogue Lectionary*.

32. Bradshaw, *Christian Worship*, 31.

33. Grassi, "St. Paul," 611.

Pray, then, in this way:
"Our Father who is in heaven,
Hallowed be Your name.
Your kingdom come.
Your will be done,
On earth as it is in heaven.
Give us this day our daily bread.
And forgive us our debts, as we also have forgiven our debtors.
And do not lead us into temptation, but deliver us from evil.
[For Thine is the kingdom, and the power, and the glory forever. Amen.]"[34]

Jesus' command to "pray in this way" has been taken to heart and adopted in public and private worship for two thousand years.

There are other examples of "actual liturgical texts, and especially hymns, within the New Testament books themselves."[35] Here are some of the more obvious examples:[36]

My soul glorifies the Lord
and my spirit rejoices in God my Savior,
for he has been mindful
of the humble state of his servant.
From now on all generations will call me blessed,
for the Mighty One has done great things for me—
holy is his name.
His mercy extends to those who fear him,
from generation to generation.
He has performed mighty deeds with his arm;
he has scattered those who are proud in their inmost thoughts.
He has brought down rulers from their thrones
but has lifted up the humble.
He has filled the hungry with good things
but has sent the rich away empty.
He has helped his servant Israel,
remembering to be merciful
to Abraham and his descendants forever,
even as he said to our fathers.[37]

34. Matt 6:9–13 (NASB).

35. Bradshaw, *Origins of Christian Worship*, 42.

36. Ibid., 42–43. This particular list of written prayers and hymns was taken from Paul Bradshaw's text. Bradshaw is compiling his arguments from Brown, *Birth of the Messiah*; Martin, *Carmen Christi*; and Schnackenburg, *Gospel According to St. John*.

37. Luke 1:46–55.

Praise be to the Lord, the God of Israel,
because he has come and has redeemed his people.
He has raised up a horn of salvation for us
in the house of his servant David
(as he said through his holy prophets of long ago),
salvation from our enemies
and from the hand of all who hate us—
to show mercy to our fathers
and to remember his holy covenant,
the oath he swore to our father Abraham:
to rescue us from the hand of our enemies,
and to enable us to serve him without fear
in holiness and righteousness before him all our days.
And you, my child, will be called a prophet of the Most High;
for you will go on before the Lord to prepare the way for him,
to give his people the knowledge of salvation
through the forgiveness of their sins,
because of the tender mercy of our God,
by which the rising sun will come to us from heaven
to shine on those living in darkness
and in the shadow of death,
to guide our feet into the path of peace.[38]

Sovereign Lord, as you have promised,
you now dismiss your servant in peace.
For my eyes have seen your salvation,
which you have prepared in the sight of all people,
a light for revelation to the Gentiles
and for glory to your people Israel.[39]

In the beginning was the Word, and the Word was with God, and the Word was God. He was with God in the beginning. Through him all things were made; without him nothing was made that has been made. In him was life, and that life was the light of men. The light shines in the darkness, but the darkness has not understood it. There came a man who was sent from God; his name was John. He came as a witness to testify concerning that light, so that through him all men might believe. He himself was not the light; he came only as a witness to the light. The true light that gives light to every man was coming into the world. He was in the world, and though the world was made through him, the world

38. Luke 1:68–79.
39. Luke 2:29–32.

did not recognize him. He came to that which was his own, but his own did not receive him. Yet to all who received him, to those who believed in his name, he gave the right to become children of God—children born not of natural descent, nor of human decision or a husband's will, but born of God. The Word became flesh and made his dwelling among us. We have seen his glory, the glory of the One and Only, who came from the Father, full of grace and truth. John testifies concerning him. He cries out, saying, "This was he of whom I said, 'He who comes after me has surpassed me because he was before me.'" From the fullness of his grace we have all received one blessing after another.[40]

Who, being in very nature God,
did not consider equality with God something to be grasped,
but made himself nothing,
taking the very nature of a servant,
being made in human likeness.
And being found in appearance as a man,
he humbled himself
and became obedient to death—even death on a cross!
Therefore God exalted him to the highest place
and gave him the name that is above every name,
that at the name of Jesus every knee should bow,
in heaven and on earth and under the earth,
and every tongue confess that Jesus Christ is Lord,
to the glory of God the Father.[41]

He is the image of the invisible God, the firstborn over all creation. For by him all things were created: things in heaven and on earth, visible and invisible, whether thrones or powers or rulers or authorities; all things were created by him and for him. He is before all things, and in him all things hold together. And he is the head of the body, the church; he is the beginning and the firstborn from among the dead, so that in everything he might have the supremacy. For God was pleased to have all his fullness dwell in him, and through him to reconcile to himself all things, whether things on earth or things in heaven, by making peace through his blood, shed on the cross.[42]

40. John 1:1–16.
41. Phil 2:6–11.
42. Col 1:15–20.

DO THE SCRIPTURES DEFEND A COMING TO THE TABLE
OF WORSHIP TO COMMEMORATE THE SACRIFICE FOR SIN,
AND IS THAT TABLE THE CENTER PLACE OF THAT WORSHIP
EXPERIENCE?

The absolute centrality of the Eucharist is based unapologetically on the direct example and exhortation of Jesus. The Gospel writers Matthew, Mark, and Luke each recall the story of Jesus in the upper room with his disciples the night before his crucifixion and sharing the bread and wine.[43] The setting is more than simply another transcendent moment between Jesus and his followers, and its uniqueness is betrayed by Jesus' own words. According to Paul Bradshaw, "Of the four versions, Luke 22:7–38 provides the most fully developed form."[44]

> And when the hour had come He reclined at the table, and the apostles with Him. And He said to them, "I have *earnestly desired* to eat this Passover with you before I suffer; for I say to you, *I shall never again eat it until it is fulfilled in the kingdom of God.*" And when He had taken a cup and given thanks, He said, "Take this and share it among yourselves; for I say to you, I will not drink of the fruit of the vine from now on until the kingdom of God comes." And when He had taken some bread and given thanks, He broke it, and gave it to them, saying, "This is My body which is given for you; *do this in remembrance of Me.*" And in the same way He took the cup after they had eaten, saying, "This cup which is poured out for you is *the new covenant in My blood.*"[45]

Jesus seemed to have a unique anticipation for this particular moment in his ministry with his closest friends and followers. Jesus said that he "earnestly desired" for this moment. He spoke of its eschatological implication: "I shall never again eat it until it is fulfilled in the kingdom of God." And he even dares to interpret and edit the understanding of "covenant," which now appears located within Jesus' own blood.[46] All of these observations begin the conversation for this passage's uniqueness in Jesus' ministry and in the story of his people/church.

---

43. Matt 26:20–29, Mark 14:17–25, and Luke 22:14–20.

44. Bradshaw, *Eucharistic Origins*, 7.

45. Luke 22:14–20 (italics mine).

46. Luke 22:20.

This uniqueness is picked up on by the earliest expressions of the Christian church. There is an allusion to it as early as Acts, chapter 2, "They devoted themselves to the apostles' teaching and to the fellowship, to the breaking of bread and to prayer."[47] And there is undeniable normalization of the Supper by the time of Paul's letter to the Corinthians, in chapter 11:

> For I received from the Lord what I also passed on to you: The Lord Jesus, on the night he was betrayed, took bread, and when he had given thanks, he broke it and said, "This is my body, which is for you; do this in remembrance of me." In the same way, after supper he took the cup, saying, "This cup is the new covenant in my blood; do this, whenever you drink it, in remembrance of me." For whenever you eat this bread and drink this cup, you proclaim the Lord's death until he comes.[48]

This passage, written within a generation of the original event, faithfully maintains the language and foci of the original meal, but even more interesting are Paul's words leading up to the restatement of the Eucharistic liturgy:

> In the following directives I have no praise for you, for *your meetings* do more harm than good. In the first place, I hear that when you *come together as a church*, there are divisions among you, and to some extent I believe it. No doubt there have to be differences among you to show which of you have God's approval. *When* you come together, it is not the *Lord's Supper* you eat, for as you eat, each of you goes ahead without waiting for anybody else. One remains hungry, another gets drunk. Don't you have homes to eat and drink in? Or do you despise the church of God and humiliate those who have nothing? What shall I say to you? Shall I praise you for this? Certainly not![49]

If we can look past the pejorative language in this introductory paragraph, we can see some very significant themes—themes that give strong evidence of the central liturgical space afforded the Eucharist. Not only does Paul seem to express the normalized (liturgical) language reflective of the upper-room experience of Jesus and his disciples, but he also shows the central place the meal has inhabited. The community is having

---

47. Acts 2:42.

48. 1 Cor 11:23–26.

49. 1 Cor 11:17–22 (italics mine).

"meetings" where they "come together as a church" showing the normative practice of gathering. Furthermore, Paul says, "when" these meeting
occur, the "Lord's Supper" is practiced. And to press even deeper into
the evolution of communal norms, this upper-room experience had been
so important to warrant a community-shared (branded) name: "Lord's
Supper." This name maintained its place in the church's vernacular right
into the Patristic period with the likes of Hippolytus[50] and even into contemporary times.

## SUMMARY

Old Testament and New Testament agree. The Judeo-Christian model is
gathering for worship, and it is regularly practicing structured worship
according to consistent and predictable patterns. There is evidence that
written liturgy, particularly written prayers, populate those worship experiences. And the Table of Sacrifice is the centerpiece of the worship
gathering.

In biblical times, this was the reality. Will this reality continue and
experience greater definition in the post-biblical age of the church?

50. Davies, *Liturgy and Worship*, 340.

# SECTION 3

# Liturgy in Christian History

This section examines church history and the consistent embrace of liturgical/Eucharistic worship throughout the first two millennia of the Christian church. However, before we jump specifically into "Christian" thought there is another historical bridge that needs to be considered and crossed.

# Chapter 8

# The First-Century Jewish Bridge

A S WE ENTER THIS section of Christian history and thought, I will pause for just a few moments to bridge the era of biblical history (dominated by Jewish life, thought, and worship) and the era of Christian (church) history. To do this, we will spend a few moments in extra-biblical Jewish practices that existed in the first century and beyond.

This link is essential. According to my studies, scholars focus on either the biblical data (as I have in section 2) or the evidence from church history, mistakenly missing the very waters out of which the church originally sprung to life. This bridge not only shows that the liturgy is a Judeo-Christian reality, it also demonstrates the unbroken story of the liturgical life as the very stage of the worship gathering.

## SYNAGOGUE LITURGY

Here is a short reflection on the synagogue liturgy as it surfaced and crystallized in the common era of the first century. First, let's observe the synagogue liturgy (as listed by Frank Senn)[1] alongside the Anglican liturgy.[2] (See chapter 3 for further descriptions of the Anglican liturgical categories.)

1. Senn, *Christian Liturgy*, 68–71.
2. Webber, *Holy Eucharist*, 18–31.

| Synagogue Liturgy | Anglican Liturgy |
|---|---|
| **Invocation:** "Bless the Lord who is to be blessed." | **Salutation:** Begins the conversation between God and His worshiping people. |
| The *Shema Israel*: "Hear, O Israel" and its blessings. | **The Gloria, Kyrie, or Trisagion:** Opening movement of praise, e.g., "Lord, have mercy . . . " |
| **The Eighteen Benedictions:** Also known as the *Amidah* (Standing Prayer) or simply *Tefillah* (The Prayer). The first three blessings are called "praises," and the last three are called "thanksgivings" including the *Shalom* or prayer for peace. | **The Collect:** The theme prayer of the day. |
| | **The Lessons:** Read from the Old Testament, Epistles, and Psalms. |
| | **The Gospel Reading** |
| | **The Sermon:** Usually delivered by clergy. |
| **The Priestly Blessing:** The Great Prayer and the Aaronic Benediction were viewed as a single liturgical unit, and the Prayer was regarded as *a substitute for the material sacrifice [italics mine]*. | **The Creed** |
| | **Prayers of the People** |
| | **Confession** |
| **Readings from the Torah and the Prophets:** Scholarly opinion held that it specified a three- year lectionary cycle. | **The Peace** |
| | **Holy Communion:** Includes the Great Thanksgiving, Breaking of Bread, and the Communion. |
| **Psalms:** Originally apart of the Temple liturgy. Sung at the beginning and between readings. | **Concluded with the Blessing and Dismissal:** The sending of the congregation into the world in the renewal and sustenance of the Holy Eucharist. |
| **Homily:** Delivered often by a visiting rabbi. | |
| **Concluded with "Alenu leshabeah":** "We must praise the ruler of all." A prayer that anticipates God's rulership over all. | |

Table 2

While there are obvious variances in the worship order, it only takes a moment to see the numerous overlaps between the two liturgical practices. No doubt, some elements like the Gospel reading and the prayers of the people are unique to the Anglican liturgy; however, other apparent discrepancies are not as divergent as one might initially think. For instance, the Anglican emphasis on "Creed" echoes the Jewish use of the *Shema,* and the Holy Communion is enveloped in the sacrificial harkening in the priestly blessing.

## SHABBAT LITURGY

The other dominant liturgical practice in first-century Jewish worshipful expression and into the centuries that followed was the Sabbath (Shabbat) liturgy. That Shabbat meal was shared at the family table on Friday evening (the beginning of the Shabbat, which ran from sunset on Friday through sunset Saturday). The meal was as formal a gathering as a family could afford and constituted a weekly repeated liturgy of worship. This liturgy included written prayers, blessings, Scripture reading, and "congregational" prayers. The most striking portions of the Shabbat liturgy (for a twenty-first-century Eucharist Christ-follower like me) are the blessings for the wine (Kiddush) and for the bread, which seem so prefiguring of Jesus' own words in the upper room (and consequently the words of his church throughout the centuries): "And he took bread, gave thanks and broke it, and gave it to them, saying, 'This is my body given for you; do this in remembrance of me.' In the same way, after the supper he took the cup, saying, 'This cup is the new covenant in my blood, which is poured out for you.'"[3]

The following is an English translation of some of that Shabbat liturgy as translated by the Bat Kol Institute,[4] a community of scholars that exists to teach, train, and help contemporary believers integrate Jewish practices and thought. It is a simplified adaptation of the Shabbat liturgy, but for our purposes here it does illustrate some of the many themes shared by Christian liturgical worship and this long-held Jewish sacred tradition.

A Sabbath Evening Table Celebration[5]

1. Gathering hymn

2. One participant reads:
   Thus, the heavens and the earth were finished, and all their multitude.
   And on the seventh day God finished the work that he had done,
   and he rested on the seventh day from all the work that he had done.
   So God blessed the seventh day and hallowed it, because on it God
   rested from all the work that he had done in creation.[6]

3. Another leads in lighting the Sabbath table candles:

---

3. Luke 22:19–20.
4. Bat Kol Institute, "Home Page."
5. Bat Kol Institute, "Sabbath Evening."
6. Gen 2:1–3.

Blessed are you Lord God, Sovereign of the Universe,
who has sanctified us with your commandments,
and ordained that we kindle the Sabbath lights.

4. All of the participants read:
   The week has ended. The Sabbath with its peace has come. Together
   let us pause and allow its meaning to enlarge our lives: Be praised,
   O YHWH, our God, who has blessed us with the gift of Sabbath. May
   the light of these Sabbath candles reflect the love and devotion that
   brighten our lives. May this light inspire us toward the fulfillment of
   our sacred aspirations. May we be guided by your law of love, and
   love one another as we have been commanded. Bless us, YHWH, with
   Sabbath joy, with Sabbath holiness, and with Sabbath peace.

5. The presider or host introduces the blessing of the table companions, or you may use Aaron's Blessing.

6. A participant leads in the blessing of the wine:
   . . . Blessed are you Lord God, Sovereign of the Universe,
   who creates the fruit of the vine . . .

7. Another leads in the blessing of the bread:
   . . . Blessed are you Lord God, Sovereign of the Universe,
   who brings forth bread from the earth . . .

8. All then enjoy the Sabbath dinner.

I am not arguing that Christian liturgy is a direct adaptation of these two
forms of Jewish liturgy. Nor am I arguing that the Christian Eucharist is
an evolution of the Shabbat and synagogue service and language (though
I am sure they were profound influences, at least culturally if not ecclesias-
tically). What I do want to affirm and argue is that throughout the history
of the people of Jehovah (Old Testament, inter-testamental period, New
Testament, and beyond), these people of faith have found a meaningful
worship home in the secure walls of liturgical forms and around the sacred meal. Through these times of massive change, cultural breadth, and
theological transformation and upheaval, time and time again the rhythm
and lyrics of the liturgical life has consistently provided the soundtrack
to the communal life of faith. That is to say, Christian liturgical and
Eucharistic worship stands on a very thick foundation. This foundation
has been poured over many centuries and its footers were being dug by
her Jewish ancestors even before the invention of the Christian church
with her unique and shared practices of life, gathering, and worship.

# Chapter 9

# Liturgy in the First Centuries

IN THIS CHAPTER WE will survey formative high points of liturgical and Eucharistic practice and scholarship. Our goal is to show that from the earliest days of the church, structured and patterned worship, which climaxed in the sharing of the Lord's Supper, has been the consistent and ubiquitous practice and dedication of the gathered followers of Jesus Christ.

"A group of churches which identifies and unifies itself around an authorized liturgy expresses a conviction that worship holds a central place in the Christian community. The church is not primarily a forum for thought and reflection; it is not primarily a league for mutual help, charitable works, or social action. It may be all of those things rightly if, before, and with all else, it is a community of acknowledgment, doxology and prayer."[1]

Once again, in lieu of our study of Scripture, we are looking for consistent liturgical practices from church history. Liturgical practice in this space contains the following themes: regular (rhythmic) gathering, structure (even regiment) in the worship gathering, use of written prayers and blessings, and the commitment to the Lord's Supper (Eucharist). However, we will also observe the solidifying of not just these themes but also the specific forms, schedule, and wordings of Christian liturgy, and that those specifics have been consistently affirmed and reaffirmed across times, cultures, and traditions.

On some levels, this feels like the "obvious" chapter of this book. Catholic Mass, Eastern Orthodox Eucharist, Luther, Zwingli, Calvin, and

---

1. Wolf, *Anglican Spirituality*, 105.

Knox have all been liturgical and so have their traditions. Certainly since the legalization of Christianity, following the conversion of Constantine in AD 312, the Christian Mass has dominated Christian worship and communal practice. Later, liturgies modified and refocused but maintained a liturgical center. In fact, it is the "free-church" model that is the stark minority report in church history.

I will focus most of my studies on the first centuries of church history to construct a bridge from the biblical and first-century practices (section 2) and the more well-known realities of post-Constantinian Christendom (a time, at least regarding liturgy(s), that is little known by most Christians). Let's begin about as early in church history as one can go.

## THE *DIDACHE*

The *Didache* is a very early church document. "Estimates of its date have varied widely. Some place it in the second century, others assign it to the first century, and some argue that it antedates many of the New Testament writings."[2] It is widely accepted as a document from Syria. It is one of the earliest existing testaments to the life of the Christian church and worship in a time just a few generations removed from events and personalities of the New Testament period. The *Didache* is a wonderful and fascinating document both because of its ancient roots and also because of the clarity of commentary it makes about church life.

The *Didache* contains many very specific practices of Christian life and community worship. These specific practices have noteworthy overlaps with Christian liturgical worship, and specifically for this context, with Anglican liturgical worship as outlined in the Book of Common Prayer. The latter sections of the *Didache* deal specifically with Christian life and worship, for example the practices of twice-weekly fasting (Wednesdays and Fridays) and thrice-daily prayer (chapter 8), forms of prayer for use in either an Agape or a Eucharist (chapters 9–10), and the celebration of the Eucharist on the Lord's Day (chapter 14).

Here is a sample of the text from the *Didache* as the language is continuing to evolve from the New Testament period. This early chapter of church history is undeniably liturgical and Eucharistic:

2. Bradshaw, *Origins of Christian Worship*, 85–86.

Chapter IX

1. And concerning the Eucharist, hold Eucharist thus:

2. First concerning the Cup, "We give thanks to thee, our Father, for the Holy Vine of David thy child, which, thou didst make known to us through Jesus thy Child; to thee be glory forever."

3. And concerning the broken Bread: "We give thee thanks, our Father, for the life and knowledge which thou didst make known to us through Jesus thy Child. To thee be glory forever.

4. As this broken bread was scattered upon the mountains, but was brought together and became one, so let thy Church be gathered together from the ends of the earth into thy kingdom, for thine is the glory and the power through Jesus Christ forever."

5. But let none eat or drink of your Eucharist except those who have been baptised in the Lord's Name. For concerning this also did the Lord say, "Give not that which is holy to the dogs."

Chapter X

1. But after you are satisfied with food, thus give thanks:

2. "We give thanks to thee, O Holy Father, for thy Holy Name which thou didst make to tabernacle in our hearts, and for the knowledge and faith and immortality which thou didst make known to us through Jesus thy Child. To thee be glory forever.

3. Thou, Lord Almighty, didst create all things for thy Name's sake, and didst give food and drink to men for their enjoyment, that they might give thanks to thee, but us hast thou blessed with spiritual food and drink and eternal light through thy Child.

4. Above all we give thanks to thee for that thou art mighty. To thee be glory forever.

5. Remember, Lord, thy Church, to deliver it from all evil and to make it perfect in thy love, and gather it together in its holiness from the four winds to thy kingdom which thou hast prepared for it. For thine is the power and the glory forever.

6. Let grace come and let this world pass away. Hosannah to the God of David. If any man be holy, let him come! If any man be not, let him repent: Maranatha ('Our Lord! Come!'), Amen."

7. But suffer the prophets to hold Eucharist as they will.[3]

3. Bettenson, *Documents*, 90.

The *Didache* was not alone in this very early period of church history in its liturgical voice; Bradshaw says that the early liturgy is "most clearly demonstrated in the *Didache* but with possible parallels in first-century Corinth and in the material in the *Apostolic Tradition*, as well as Papias."[4] Without listing the specific content of each, it is important to note that while the "most clearly demonstrated" material of this time may be found in the *Didache*, these themes have not been preserved by the *Didache* alone.

## JUSTIN MARTYR (103–165)

Justin Martyr is another significant early voice in Christian history. His *First Apology* was written in Rome around AD 150. Most of what is known about the life of Justin Martyr comes from his own writings. He was born at Flavia Neapolis in Judea/Palestine. He called himself a Samaritan. According to the traditional accounts of the church, Martyr suffered martyrdom at Rome under the Emperor Marcus Aurelius between 162 and 168. He was brought up as a pagan, but later converted to Christianity and devoted the rest of his life to teaching the true philosophy, still wearing his philosopher's gown to indicate that he had attained the truth. He probably traveled widely and ultimately settled in Rome as a Christian teacher.[5]

Martyr wrote to some length on Christian gathering and practice—here are a few sections .

Chapter 65

But we, after we have thus washed him who has been convinced and has assented to our teaching, bring him to the place where those who are called brethren are assembled, in order that we *may offer hearty prayers* in common for ourselves and for the baptized [illuminated] person, and for all others in every place, that we may be counted worthy, now that we have learned the truth, by our works also to be found good citizens and keepers of the commandments, so that we may be saved with an everlasting salvation. Having *ended the prayers*, we *salute one another* with a kiss. There is then brought to the president of *the brethren bread and a cup of wine mixed with water*; and he taking them, *gives praise and*

4. Bradshaw, *Eucharistic Origins*, 59.

5. Roberts et al., *Ante-Nicene Fathers*, starting at 295; Bradshaw, *Eucharistic Origins*, 61; and Wikipedia, "Justin Martyr."

glory to the Father of the universe, through the name of the Son and of the Holy Ghost, and offers thanks at considerable length for our being counted worthy to receive these things at His hands. And when he has concluded *the prayers and thanksgivings*, all the people present express their assent by saying Amen. This word Amen answers in the Hebrew language to [so be it]. And when the president has given thanks, and all the people have expressed their assent, those who are called by us deacons give to each of those present *to partake of the bread and wine mixed with water* over which the thanksgiving was pronounced, and to those who are absent they carry away a portion.[6]

Chapter 66 (excerpt)

Of the Eucharist

And this food is called among us Eujcariatia [the Eucharist] ... For the apostles, in the memoirs composed by them, which are called Gospels, have thus delivered unto us what was enjoined upon them; that Jesus took bread, and when He had given thanks, said, "This do ye in remembrance of Me, this is My body;" and that, after the same manner, having taken the cup and given thanks, He said, "This is My blood;" and gave it to them alone.[7]

Chapter 67

Weekly Worship of the Christians

And we afterwards continually remind each other of these things. And the wealthy among us help the needy; and we always keep together; and for all things wherewith we are supplied, we bless the Maker of all through His Son Jesus Christ, and through the Holy Ghost. And *on the day called Sunday*, all who live in cities or in the country *gather together* to one place, *and the memoirs of the apostles or the writings of the prophets are read*, as long as time permits; then, when the reader has ceased, the president *verbally instructs*, and exhorts to the imitation of these good things. Then we *all rise together and pray*, and, as we before said, when our prayer is ended, *bread and wine and water are brought*, and the president in like manner offers prayers and thanksgivings, according to his ability, and the people assent, *saying Amen*; and there is a distribution to each, and a participation of that over which

---

6. Roberts et al., *Ante-Nicene Fathers*, 353–54 (italics mine).
7. Ibid., 354–55 (italics mine).

thanks have been given, and to those who are absent a portion is sent by the deacons. And they who are well to do, and willing, give what each thinks fit; and what is collected is deposited with the president, who succors the orphans and widows and those who, through sickness or any other cause, are in want, and those who are in bonds and the strangers sojourning among us, and in a word takes care of all who are in need. But *Sunday is the day on which we all hold our common assembly*, because it is the first day on which God, having wrought a change in the darkness and matter, made the world; and Jesus Christ our Savior on the same day rose from the dead. For He was crucified on the day before that of Saturn (Saturday); and on the day after that of Saturn, which is the day of the Sun, having appeared to His apostles and disciples, He taught them these things, which we have submitted to you also for your consideration.[8]

In these passages we not only have many liturgical practices in a worship gathering including prayers, blessings, reading from the apostles, "verbal instructions" (homily), and congregational greetings (here called "salute one another with a kiss—and in Anglican language might be called "Passing the Peace"), all of which are articulated at such an early date (AD 150). We also have other significant declarations. There is the repeatedly emphasized breaking of bread and wine (mixed with water), which is specifically tied to the witness of the Gospels. It is also worth noting that the norm is a regular gathering on Sunday ("Chapter 67"). Martyr has provided what appears to be full-form liturgical and Eucharistic life of the church as performed in the church's earliest days.

## ST. HIPPOLYTUS OF ROME

The first and second centuries provide some simple and thematic renderings of church worship order and centrality of the Eucharist, but in the third century we can begin to see liturgical specifics more and more clearly. "For the first time we learn the actual wording of the Eucharistic prayer; for the first time we are given a full description of the daily devotions of the faithful and of the discipline of the sacraments, especially Baptism and Holy Orders."[9]

---

8. Ibid., 355–56 (italics mine).

9. Jungmann, *Early Liturgy*, 52.

St. Hippolytus was a presbyter in the Roman church at the beginning of the third century. He died a martyr. He is believed to have been a disciple of St. Irenaeus. He was an influential writer, and his most famous work on the teachings for the church is most often called *The Apostolic Tradition* (written in 217 or even a few years earlier).[10] This work was so influential that over time it has been found translated in several corners of the Roman world under varying names: *The Egyptian Church Order* (called thus because it was written in languages connected to Egypt), *The Canons of Hippolytus* (Arabic and Ethiopic), *The Apostolic Constitutions* (Syrian origin), *The Epitome* (Greek), and *Testamentum Domini* (Syriac). This apparent widespread dispersal of Hippolytus's writings is important because it is evidence of the universalizing norms that the church was already developing at the beginning of the third century—not just universalized practices, but also universalized specific wording and liturgical order.

The details in Hippolytus's writings are profound and cover a wide range of topics: instructions for ordination and widow care, details for caring for catechumen and a liturgy for baptism, numerous written prayers for ministries such as electing elders and giving of offerings, and even specifics about how a bishop is to "lay hands" (with a wise and amusing assertion that "hands are not laid on a virgin").

Here are some of Hippolytus's instructions for Sunday gathering and the worship.

Chapter 22

On the first day of the week the bishop, if possible, shall deliver the oblation to all the people with his own hand, while the deacons break the bread. When the deacon brings it to the elder, the deacon shall present his platter, and the elder shall take it himself and distribute it to the people by his own hand.[11]

Chapter 25

The Bishop: The Lord be with you.

People: And with thy spirit.

10. Ibid., 57.

11. Hippolytus, "Apostolic Tradition." These excerpts were taken from the translation by Kevin P. Edgecomb of Berkeley, CA, found on his website where he offers his translations for public use.

B.: Lift up your hearts.

P.: We lift them up unto the Lord.

B.: Let us give thanks unto the Lord.

P.: It is meet and right.

B.: We give thee thanks, O God, through thy beloved son Jesus Christ, who thou didst send to us in the last times to be a savior and redeemer and the messenger of thy will; who is thy inseparable Word, through whom thou madest all things, and in whom thou was well pleased. Thou didst send him from Heaven into the Virgin's womb; he was conceived and was incarnate, and was shown to be thy Son, born of the Holy Spirit and the Virgin; Who, fulfilling thy will and preparing for thee a holy people, stretched out his hands in suffering, that he might free from suffering them that believed on thee.

Who when he was being betrayed to his voluntary suffering, that he might destroy death, break the chains of the devil, tread Hell underfoot, bring forth the righteous and set a bound, and that he might manifest his Resurrection, took bread and gave thanks to thee and said: "Take, eat: this is my body which is broken for you." Likewise also the cup, saying: "This is my blood which is shed for you. As oft as ye do this ye shall do it in remembrance of me."

Wherefore we, being mindful of his death and resurrection, do offer unto thee this bread and this cup, giving thanks unto thee for that thou hast deemed us worthy to stand before thee and minister as thy priest. And we beseech thee that thou wouldst send thy Holy Spirit upon the oblation of thy holy Church; and that thou wouldst grant it to all the saints who partake, making them one, for fulfillment of the Holy Spirit and for the confirmation of their faith in truth; that we may praise and glorify thee through thy Son Jesus Christ, through whom be glory and honor to thee, to the Father and to the Son with the Holy Spirit in thy Holy Church, both now and forever. Amen.[12]

These liturgical instructions are specific. They include all the elements for our definition of liturgy: regular and structured gathering, written prayers, congregational responses, and centrality of the Lord's Table.

Take a look at this short excerpt and its comparison to the equivalent liturgical discourse from a contemporary Anglican Book of Common Prayer:[13]

12. Bettenson, *Documents*, 106–7.

13. Anglican Mission in the Americas, *Anglican Prayer Book*, 54.

| Apostolic Tradition by Hippolytus | Anglican Book of Common Prayer |
|---|---|
| The Bishop: The Lord be with you. | Priest: The Lord be with you |
| People: And with thy spirit. | People: And with your spirit. |
| B.: Lift up your hearts. | Priest: Lift up your hearts. |
| P.: We lift them up unto the Lord. | People: We lift them to the Lord. |
| B.: Let us give thanks unto the Lord. | Priest: Let us give thanks to the Lord our |
| P.: It is meet and right. | God |
| | People: It is right to give him thanks and |
| | praise. |

These liturgical themes and even the very wordings have lasted the test of time across continents and through innumerable cultures, and they have been reaffirmed time and time again as meaningful. The continuity, universality, and tenacity of these literary elements extend to the most important parts of the worship service and, as Theodor Klauser asserts about Hippolytus, "In fact the Eucharistic prayer, as those who read it will have sensed, was, in essence, then exactly what it is today."[14] The structure underlying the Eucharistic prayers to come are found in this passage: "The initial dialogue; an introductory formula expressing thanksgiving and an anamnesis of the work of salvation accomplished by Christ, ending with the narrative of the eucharistic institution; a formula of offering, introduced by a paschal anamnesis and followed by a second formula of thanksgiving; an epiclesis of the Holy Spirit on the offerings of the assembly, with the mention of praise; a trinitarian doxology."[15]

14. Klauser, *Western Liturgy*, 17.
15. Metzger, *History of the Liturgy*, 43.

# Chapter 10

# Liturgy in the Middle

THE FOURTH CENTURY BROUGHT about a time of radical change for the church of Jesus Christ. Christians were no longer subject to persecution but were now followers of a legitimate and respectable religion. They had gained the status of *cultus publicus* and with it brought great opportunity.

## LATIN MASS

The end of the third century had been a time of destruction for the church. Eusbius of Caesarea (265–340) wrote of this era, " . . . the houses of prayer, because of which, not being satisfied any longer with the ancient buildings, they built, from the foundations up, spacious churches . . . We saw with our own eyes the houses of prayer cast down to the very foundations from top to bottom, and the inspired and sacred Scriptures given over to flames in the midst of the market places."[1] And so with the church's newly found legitimacy, everything solidified from the standpoint of public face and institutional structure. "Its number grew, as so it occupied larger and grander buildings than before, and consequently its worship became more formal in style and incorporated ritual . . . "[2]

With this newfound freedom, most of the existent writings of this era focus on points of theology, debate, and antiheretical arguments. What we do know is that "Latin Christianity arose in North Africa at the close of the second century and gradually attained pre-eminence over the

1. Ibid., 39–40. Metzger is quoting from Eusebius, *Ecclesiastical History*, 37–38.
2. Bradshaw, *Eucharistic Origins*, 139.

West, informing the liturgy."[3] We also know that the Roman rite, which dominated most of Western church history, almost immediately split into two streams. "The Roman type, which was used in the Eternal City and perhaps in North Africa; and the Gallic type, which prevailed in Milan and beyond the Alps."[4] "The need of the period . . . (from the fourth century to the eighth) was to adapt the old pre-Nicene tradition of Christian worship to its new 'public' conditions and function. But this need was felt by different churches with a different intensity and at different times. And the practical break-up of the Christian empire in the fifth century—it still continued as a theory, so mightily had the universal dominion of Rome impressed the imagination of the world."[5]

"There is reason to believe that the Roman rite evolved in Rome itself . . . Its appearance coincided with the gradual transition of that community from Greek to Latin, which was underway by the pontificate of Cornelius (251–3) . . . The core of the Roman Mass must have been fixed at the beginning of the fifth century. . . the liturgy no longer countenanced the primitive freedom of extempore prayer and unfixed forms, but presented a very definite shape and text . . . [and] elements to accommodate the Church Year."[6]

Once solidified, this Latin Mass was sanctified. I'm shocked to read that the earliest copies of the full Mass available to us are from the seventh century, but as stated above, the church has long assumed that the Mass was established much earlier. An excellent side-by-side translation into English can be found in *The Missal in Latin and English*,[7] which derives its text from the *Missale Romanum*, fully printed from pages 676 through 720.

The Gallic type is less known to most. It could not withstand the tide of history and in an attempt to bring the entire church in closer communion with Rome, it was eventually overtaken by the Roman rite. In summary, here is the basic schedule of worship of the Gallic type, summarized from the writings of Bard Thompson in *Liturgies of the Western Church*:[8]

3. Thompson, *Liturgies of the Western Church*, 27.
4. Ibid.
5. Dix, *Shape of the Liturgy*, 435.
6. Thompson, *Liturgies of the Western Church*, 32.
7. Catholic Church et al., *Missal*.
8. Thompson, *Liturgies of the Western Church*, 30–32.

- Commenced with the antiphon, also called the *Ingressa* or the *Officium*, which accompanied the entrance of the clergy
- Bishop greeted the people
- Three canticles followed: the Trisagion, the Kyrie eleison, and the Benedictus
- Bishop prayer
- Three lessons were read:
  » Old Testament
  » Epistles or Acts
  » The Gospels accompanied by the Benedictus es, a responsorial chant, and the bringing of the Gospel book by solemn procession led by seven torch bearers
- The Trisagion chanted again
- Homily
- The Church Prayers by the Deacons, after each the congregation says "Lord, have mercy"
- The Collect
- Catechumens dismissed
- Procession of Eucharistic gifts (*Sonus* chanted by choir)
- Sacred Song
- Opening address called *praefatio missae* to explain the holy meaning
- The Collect *post nomina*
- The giving of the Kiss of Peace
- The Communion
  » Preface which focused upon thanksgiving for the life and work of the Savior
  » *Sanctus* and collect *post Sanctus*
  » Words of Institution
  » Prayer of Consecration

» The Fraction (breaking of bread)

» Particles of bread arranged elaborately on the altar, often in cruciform (showing the Gallic tendency toward symbolic action)

» Congregational reciting of the *Pater Noster*

» "The high moment of the Mass"[9]

  * People invited to bow their heads for the Benediction, given by the bishop or priest

  * Blessing most often as "Peace, faith, and love, and the communication of the Body and Blood of Christ be with you always"

  * Communion accompanied by the antiphon based on Psalms 33

  * Thanksgiving given and dismissal, "*Missa acta est—in pace.*"

Eastern Orthodoxy (earlier simply known as the Eastern Church) has maintained its own commitment to liturgical life. From the earliest centuries, "the East was inclined toward a type of worship that was timeless and changeless, transfixed in holiness, and celebrated at the threshold of heaven . . . [it] was given to resplendent ceremonial and embellished speech."[10]

"In the Holy Eucharist we offer to God the substance of our life and receive it back as the body and Blood of Christ for the sanctification of our soul and bodies and as the mystery of the Church's unity in Christ."[11]

More than any of the major branches of Christendom, Eastern Orthodoxy has endured a horrifying history. The Balkans, Asia Minor, and Eastern Mediterranean housed much of her history. These lands are also a "highway" for every war-wielding empire in European (and beyond) history. "Actually its position was often a terrible one, and it is impossible to describe all the suffering, humiliation, and outright persecution the

9. Ibid., 31.

10. Ibid., 27.

11. Carlton and Royster, *Understanding Orthodox Christianitu*, 203.

Church was obliged to undergo in this age, which was dark indeed."[12] And yet, it has maintained an uncompromised liturgical tradition.

"When an Anglican cleric asked patriarch Aleksii of Moscow to define the Russian Orthodox Church in a phrase, he received the answer, 'It is the church which celebrates the divine liturgy.'"[13] This statement points to the reality that "the centrality of worship, above all of Eucharistic worship, in the life of the Orthodox Church. For it is in the [E]ucharist that she most fully confirms her identity, integrity, and her vocation."[14] And this liturgy is not transient in its form or expression. "Indeed, the order of this church's elaborate services has remained exceptionally constant over the last millennium or more."[15]

"The Byzantine rite itself, clearly of Antiochene-Syrian derivation, continued to develop along its own lines down to the seventh century and did not become absolutely rigid until the ninth century . . . before that date [seventh century] the East had shown more tendency to innovate in the liturgy than the West."[16] Why did this Eastern liturgy solidify so profoundly from the seventh century onward? Dix insists that it was not because of "'arrested development' . . . It is only a case of completed development."[17]

Distinctive elements of the Eastern Church include a more multisensory worship experience using icons and incense. In addition to this, "actions are expressed in words (liturgy). These words are usually sung or chanted. . . . Services involve a dialogue between the people and the celebrant . . . [they] have distinct and well-established roles to play."[18]

Most of us in the West have little to no connection to the Eastern Church. It is ironic that this second largest tradition in church history should continue to be so ignored. I took a seminary class on church history, and this attempt to survey the breadth of church history dedicated no readings to the Eastern Church and only a small portion of one class lecture. Though the Orthodox Church has lasted along an independent

---

12. Schmemann, *Eastern Orthodoxy*, 273. An excerpt specifically about the life under the Ottoman Empire, but indicative of Orthodox history more broadly.

13. Davies, *Liturgy and Worship*, 421.

14. Ibid., 422.

15. Ibid.

16. Dix, *Shape of the Liturgy*, 547–48.

17. Ibid., 548.

18. Davies, *Liturgy and Worship*.

historical narrative (often isolated from the West), it has independently affirmed and defended the absolute centrality of a liturgical model of worship and the celebration of the Eucharist.

## THE MEDIEVAL AGES

The Roman Catholic Mass reigned all through the medieval ages. Liturgy scholars understandably focus the vast majority of their commentary on liturgical events from the eighth century and before and the sixteenth century and later. The medieval times offer far less data and distinction (which may explain why this era is simply called "middle"). However, that is not to say that liturgical life was static. Throughout these times the on-going liturgical practice of local adaptation continued while maintaining historical continuity.

Local Italian rites sprung up between the sixth and ninth centuries, and the Gelasian Sacramentary rite, which can be pieced together from primarily seventh-century manuscripts, was discovered in France.

A unique "Western Synthesis" (as it is referred to by Dix)[19] appears to be a synthesis of the *Missale Gallicaum* (or the Gallic rite, as discussed above in the section of the Latin Mass) and prayers of the Gregorian Church. "The result is not merely a 'Gelasianised Gregorian' book, less austere and sober in tone than Gregorian as S. Gregory had left it. It can only be described as an ingenious combination of French taste and feeling with the old Roman sense of form."

On Christmas Day in AD 800, the emperor Charlemagne, as a way of consolidating his power and aligning his reign with the imperial legend of Rome, reinstituted the Latin rite (with a few fresh reforms) following his crowning as Roman emperor by the pope in St. Peter's. This liturgical adaptation was an example of universalizing liturgy as an instrument of political power, under which many contextualized liturgies were squashed for the sake of imperial continuity. "One immediate result was the end of the Gallican rite as a rite wherever it still survived. Charlemagne peremptorily forbade its use . . . followed by the slower decline of the sister Mozarabit rite in Spain."[20]

The medieval ages are dramatically illustrative of the greatest battle within a liturgical worship framework. There is an even pull: on the one

19. Dix, *Shape of the Liturgy*, 573–75.
20. Ibid., 581.

side, to allow the liturgy to breathe within each context, to find a freshness of voice while hopefully maintaining its abiding connection and submission to the church, global and historical. On the other side is the seduction of power to use the ways of worship to control people and consolidate authority. When this happens, the liturgy loses its true spirit and becomes a weapon and an abuse. This is a tragic theme of human history: to take something so consistently meaningful and life giving and bastardize it for institutional gain.

# Chapter 11

# Liturgy in the Reformation and Beyond

CHRISTIANITY ENTERED THE LITURGICAL laboratory in the sixteenth century. It is in this century that the Reformation and Counter-Reformation were birthed and overflowed with creative energy. Many liturgies were first penned from this creative laboratory. Each liturgy reflected the personality of the new traditions it represented while also affirming the historic congruence of structured liturgical life.

The Protestant Reformation was a move away from the authority of Rome and established many new (and lasting) Christian traditions, each of which took the best of the Roman Catholic Mass and added/adapted to the local theological and cultural distinctiveness. The influential names from this era of catalytic change and unprecedented theological escalation and communication[1] are well known: Luther, Zwingli, Bucer, Calvin, and Knox. And each of these has a liturgy that bears his name or influence.

## MARTIN LUTHER

Martin Luther's liturgical works were first published in December 1523 under the title *Formula Missae*. Luther had been hesitant in making such a liturgy. "But now the time was ripe for a revision—not that he intended to deal severely with the liturgy, but merely to purge it of its abominable additions."[2] Luther "did not lose sight of the historical character and reli-

---

1. One profound example of the change in communication came from the invention of the printing press in 1440. It forever changed the pace and volume of idea exchange and mass education. By the sixteenth century the press was in mass use, and the Protestant Reformers were the first generation of Christian leaders to utilize its unending channels of influence.

2. Thompson, *Liturgies of the Western Church*, 99.

gious values of the Latin rite . . . he chose to purge and reinterpret rather than destroy. Three of his own contributions were of the highest order: the recovery of the sermon, the introduction of German hymns, and the triumphant restoration of the Communion of the people."[3] In addition to a vernacular liturgy, "Luther advocated the addition of vernacular hymnody."[4] It is also worth noting that Martin Luther himself was aware of the liturgy's import but also the missional mandate of the Church of Jesus Christ. Luther wrote in his introduction to *The German Mass and Order of Service* (1526), "Above all things, I most affectionately and for God's sake beseech all, who see or desire to observe this our Order of Divine Service, on no account to make of it a compulsory law, or to ensnare or make captive thereby any man's conscience; but to use it agreeably to Christian liberty at their good pleasure as, where, when and so long as circumstances favour and demand it. Moreover, we would not have our meaning taken to be that we desire to rule, or by law to compel, any one."[5]

## ZWINGLI

Liturgical adaptation was not always prescribed with such a positive bent. Zwingli's first liturgical work was titled *An Attack on the Canon of the Mass*. However, his policy of revision was conservatism. "He kept the first part of the Mass intact, except to simplify the lectionary, remove the Propers for saints' days, and to insist that the lessons and sermon must be given in the vernacular."[6] Zwingli's other, and perhaps most profound contribution was in the delivery of the elements. "After the assistant had read the Words of Institution (1 Cor. 11), there was no more speaking, and a profound stillness settled over the church. When the clergy had communicated, the assistants carried the elements to the people in wooden utensils. No Words of Delivery were spoken, no music sung or played; but the silence prevailed."[7] It is also worth noting that it appears from the 1525 liturgy that the assistants take the elements to the people and then the people serve themselves by tearing a "mouthful with his own

---

3. Ibid., 104.

4. White, *Introduction to Christian Worship*, 245.

5. Kidd, *Continental Reformation*, 193.

6. Thompson, *Liturgies of the Western Church*, 141.

7. Ibid., 145.

hand"[8] as well as apparently taking the cup themselves to drink. "Thus by a powerful, communal symbol, the congregation realized itself as the Body of Christ."[9]

## MARTIN BUCER

Diabald Schwarz began reading his own liturgy on February 16, 1524, in Strassburg, this beginning the Strassburg liturgical tradition. By 1539, eighteen editions of the liturgy were produced each with varying changes. Martin Bucer, whose name is better known than Schwarz, influenced this tradition greatly. "In the course of time, the word 'Mass' gave way to 'Lord's Supper.' The 'altar' became the 'altar-table' or simply 'table.' The celebrant was no longer described as 'priest' but as 'parson,' and more often as 'minister.' He stood behind the table, facing the people . . . Finally vestments disappeared."[10] Strassburg was known for elevating the congregational confession and pardon. While these changes were radical by sixteenth-century standards, Bucer was adamant that the church remain unified in its worship and that her ways be always liturgical. "By 1534 he began to plead for uniformity. While he still maintained that 'the Spirit of Christ inspires the churches,' he was now dismayed by 'deplorable differences' of practice and 'detestable changes' made upon an unfounded notion of freedom."[11] I am struck by the simultaneous leveling of humanity by limiting the distinctions between clergy and laity (changing titles, vestments, placement during Communion) while still insisting that structure and continuity rule the worship life of the church: tradition and adaptation living hand in hand.

## JOHN CALVIN

John Calvin seemed to have the most passionate desire to condemn the Mass. "Of all the idols, he knew none so grotesque as that in which the priest called down Christ into his hands by 'magical mumblings' and offering him anew on the sacrificial altar, while the people looked on in 'stupid amazement.'"[12] However, he held to and defended much of the Mass's

---

8. Ibid. This entire liturgical text is *Action and Use of the Lord's Supper, Easter, 1525* in Thompson's *Liturgies*. The exact quote is on page 154.

9. Ibid., 145.

10. Ibid., 160.

11. Ibid., 163.

12. Ibid., 185.

forms. When he wrote about his early proposal for the Lord's Supper in his 1536 *Institutes*, he spoke of all these elements: weekly distribution, common prayers, sermon, bread and wine on table, recitation of the Institution of the Supper, excommunication of those excluded from the Supper, the Thanksgiving, sung psalms, breaking of bread and giving of cup, exhortation of sincere faith, and final thanks and dismissal.[13]

Calvin perhaps brought the strongest emphasis on sermon and the Word proclaimed. (Bread and wine were not brought out until the Word was read. "Calvin did not think it appropriate to expose the elements until the Word could be added to validate the sacrament . . . apart from the Word, he said, the Lord's Supper has no power, but remains 'a lifeless and bare phantom.'").[14] He also placed a unique emphasis on excommunication (regarding the Supper) and on the regular reading of the Ten Commandments in order to stimulate the very real guilt of the gathered.

Of what use, then, were the erection in churches of so many crosses of wood and stone, silver and gold, if this doctrine were faithfully and honestly preached, viz., Christ died that he might bear our curse upon the tree and expiate our sins by the sacrifice of his body, wash them in his blood, and, in short, reconcile us to God the Father? From this one doctrine, the people would learn more than from a thousand crosses of wood and stone.[15]

## JOHN KNOX

John Knox wrote his *The Forme of Prayers* liturgy in 1556. His conceptualization birthed from the 1552 English Book of Common Prayer,[16] but adapted along Knox's particular values. Knox infused thoughts taken from Calvin, including the emphasis on the Word, and so believed that it speaks authoritatively that he removed the "consecration of the elements" from his liturgy. One of the most important contributions that Knox brought to the Eucharist was that after the communicants were invited

---

13. For the sake of space, I have summarized the elements listed in a large section of chapter 4 of Calvin's 1536 *Institutes*.

14. Thompson, *Liturgies of the Western Church*, 192.

15. Calvin, *Institutes of the Christian Religion*, 133.

16. English Book of Common Prayer will be discussed in the next section titled, "English Rite."

to the table and the minister delivered the Eucharistic prayer of thanks,[17] the minister would then deliver the bread to the people who divided it among themselves. "By sitting down together and by serving the elements to one another, the people were able to realize their fellowship and mutual priesthood in the Body of Christ."[18]

## ENGLISH RITE

Out of this same period came the English rite. "Neither Cranmer nor Somerset cherished a drastic breach with tradition (the Latin rite). The initial steps were rather designed to encourage sound preaching and to establish men in the English Bible." In fact, the 1549 *Booke of the Common Prayer* kept the structure of the Latin rite, but all agreed that the service ought to be in English. More than in possibly any other Protestant church that birthed in this era, the Englsih reformers had a great desire to maintain the traditions of their Catholic heritage, all the while making no concessions for the papists. For instance, in the Canon (the part of the early liturgy containing the venerable prayers surrounding the Consecration), a portion of the Mass that Luther called a "heap of filth," the English reformers chose—instead of abolishing the Canon—to carefully purify it of its sacrificial doctrine. This spirit is what gave birth to the popular Anglican slogan *via media* or "middle way." "This phrase was popularized in the nineteenth century by John Henry Newman, to refer to Anglicanism's position between Roman Catholicism on the one hand and Protestantism on the other. We have often said, somewhat smugly, that we are 'fully catholic and fully reformed.'"[19]

"The principles (of the English rite) were set out in the 1549 BCP[20] in the preface and in the tract entitled *Of Ceremonies* . . . [First] a single 'use' for the whole country . . . Second, all services were to be in English instead of Latin . . . Third, there was an emphasis on edification, particularly through scripture . . . Fourth, the central act of public worship was to be

17. " . . . using an original prayer that was truly Eucharistic in its scope; it included adoration, thanksgiving for creation and redemption, a brief anamnesis, and a doxology." Thompson, *Liturgies of the Western Church*, 293.

18. Ibid., 294.

19. Schmidt, *Glorious Companions*, xii–xiii.

20. Theology and Worship Ministry Unit for the Presbyterian Church, *Book of Common Worship*.

the eucharist[21] . . . Finally, the liturgy was to be loyal to scripture and loyal to tradition."[22] Even these principles evolved over time as the "Church of England" spread, missionally, to touch other parts of the world. In time, the English language was replaced by the principle of primacy of the vernacular and thus furthered this commitment: "It is now recognized that worship cannot be static; it is affected not only by developments in theology but also by the changing pattern of life in the world . . . [it] cannot be committed to the precise positions of . . . [the] sixteenth and seventeenth centuries . . . it must take into account fresh and contemporary understanding of the gospel."[23] This process of Anglican cultural evolution and adaptation is illustrated in greater detail in section 4.[24]

The reformers certainly initiated and participated in an era of creative transformation. They were contextually driven, focusing much energy on translating the Scriptures and liturgy into the local vernacular. They restarted the necessity of meaning through accurate and thorough explanation of the worshiping acts. They brought their congregants into greater participation in the worship gathering, even encouraging them to participate in the very distribution of the Eucharist elements (Zwingli and Knox). They even localized some elements, as Zwingli did with his wooden utensils. All the while, those changes swam in deep liturgical waters. As Calvin spoke of (above), the major elements of the historical liturgical service were maintained and defended. Even some, like Luther, seemed to fight to defend as much ongoing tradition as possible or, like Bucer, stood strongly against too much freedom in church.

The brilliant men and women of the reformation and their liturgical adaptations have been the lyrics of the church's ecclesial song for five hundred years and for much of Protestantism (particularly those denominations that are called "mainline"). Today's liturgies remain true to those sixteenth-century reforms. For instance, you can hear Calvin's ethos in the introduction to the Lord's Day service from today's Presbyterian *Book*

21. For a fuller discussion of the structure of Anglican worship, see chapter 3 under the subheading "Eucharist." And for a further critique, visit section 7.

22. Davies, *Liturgy and Worship*, 21. To see how Scripture and tradition have been maintained, see chapter 3 subheading "Eucharist."

23. Ibid., 22.

24. For a commentary on how the Anglican Eucharist might be specifically adapted and applied to post-Christian Northwest culture while maintaining its commitment to the sign, symbol, Scriptures, and tradition, see section 7.

of Common Worship. "With its focus upon scripture and sacrament, the main body of the service moves broadly from hearing to doing, from proclamation to thanksgiving, and from Word to table."[25]

Thank you, ancient friends, for your labor, your courage, and your Christ-devoted thoughts in words.

## COMPARING LITURGIES ACROSS TRADITIONS

**The Holy Eucharist — ANGLICAN BOOK OF COMMON PRAYER**
- Salutation and Collect
- Gloria or Kyrie or Trisagion
- Salutation and Collect for the Day
- Lessons
- Old Testament
- Psalm
- New Testament
- Gospel Reading
- Sermon
- Creed
- Prayers of the People
- Confession of Sin
- Absolution
- Passing the Peace
- Offertory
- Preface and Sanctus
- Great Thanksgiving
- Lord's Prayer
- Breaking of the Bread
- Communion (Hymn, Psalm, or Anthem)
- Post-Communion Prayer
- Benediction and Dismissal

**Service for the Lord's Day — PRESBYTERIAN BOOK OF COMMON WORSHIP**
- Call to Worship
- Prayer of the Day
- Hymn of Praise
- Confession and Pardon
- Canticle: Psalm, Hymn, or Spiritual
- Prayer for Illumination
- First Reading
- Psalm
- Second Reading
- Hymn or Psalm
- Gospel Reading
- Sermon
- Affirmation of Faith
- Prayers of the People
- The Peace
- Offering
- Invitation to the Table
- Great Thanksgiving
- Lord's Prayer
- Breaking of Bread
- Communion of the People
- Hymn, Spiritual, Canticle, or Psalm
- Charge and Blessing

**The Holy Communion — LUTHERAN BOOK OF WORSHIP**
- Entrance Hymn
- Apostolic Greeting
- Kyrie, Gloria and/or Hymn
- Salutation and Prayer of the Day
- First Lesson
- Psalm
- Second Lesson
- Gospel
- Sermon
- Creed
- Prayers of the Church
- Confession of Sin
- Greeting of Peace
- Offering
- Offertory
- Preface and Sanctus
- Of Words of Institution
- Great Thanksgiving
- Lord's Prayer
- Communion
- Hymn
- Post-Communion Song
- Post-Communion Prayer
- Silent Reflection
- Benediction and Dismissal

**Service of Word and Table — THE METHODIST HYMNAL**
- Gathering and Greeting
- Hymn of Praise
- Opening Prayer
- Prayer for Illumination
- Scripture Lesson
- Psalm
- Scripture Lesson
- Hymn or Song
- Gospel Lesson
- Sermon
- Creed
- Concerns and Prayers
- Invitation to the Table
- Confession and Pardon
- The Peace
- Offering
- Hymn or Psalm
- Great Thanksgiving
- The Lord's Prayer
- Breaking of Bread
- Giving the Bread and Cup
- Post-Communion Prayer
- Hymn or Song
- Dismissal with Blessing
- Going Forth

**The Order of Mass — ROMAN MISSAL**
- Entrance Psalm
- Invocation and Greeting
- Penitential Rite
- Kyrie and/or Gloria
- Salutation and Collect of the Day
- First Lesson
- Psalmody
- Second Lesson
- Alleluia Verse
- Gospel
- Homily
- Creed
- Intercessions
- Offering
- Preface and Sanctus
- Canon
- Lord's Prayer
- Peace of the Lord
- Lamb of God
- Communion
- Silent Reflection
- Post-communion Prayer
- Benediction and Dismissal

Figure 07. Comparing Liturgies Across Traditions. Source: Created by Author.

25. Theology and Worship Ministry Unit for the Presbyterian Church, *Book of Common Worship*, 33.

## FREE-CHURCH

I want to take just a few moments to acknowledge the free-church paradigm. There are two primary definitions of "free-church" which influence and inform one another. At its birth, free-church was related to churches that were not directly associated with a national government (national church) or at least a national endorsement (as the Roman Church crossed many national boundaries). "[They] began with a radical break from . . . regional territorial pattern of state-church."[26] In England, such churches were called "Dissenting" or "Nonconformist." Because of this rejection of national control or influence, these free-church movements were, well . . . *free*—free to pursue their own forms and patterns. In light of this, these movements transcended the stasis associated with most denominations. These early movements included the Donatists, Waldensians, Lollards, and Anabaptists.[27]

The second definition of "free-church,"[28] which is more applicable specifically to the American experience,[29] is a philosophy of church where her forms, particularly corporate worship forms, are creative, free-flow, and determinable by the local community's desires and tastes. It was initially associated with "Baptists, Quakers, Pentecostals, and a variety of other evangelical and congregational groups."[30] Five traits that define free-church are "1) freedom of governance (non-hierarchical order/congregational polity), 2) freedom of worship (non-prescribed liturgy/spiritual worship), 3) freedom of faith (non-binding confession . . .), 4) freedom of conscience (non-coercive authority/soul liberty), and 5) freedom of religion."[31] This form of church-worship gained its greatest influence in the latter twentieth century. It was linked most often to evangelicalism and more specifically to the "church-growth movement."[32] Within "church growth," marketing philosophy is shrewdly grafted onto church

26. Littell, "Historical Free Church."

27. These movements are cited as early examples by two authors: Murray, *Post-Christendom* and Randall, "Mission in Post-Christendom.

28. Or "Free-Form" or "Free Worship."

29. These movements have flourished in America simply because the United States was founded without a national church and with a foundational commitment to separate church and state.

30. Freeman, "Communion Ecclesiology," 259.

31. Ibid.

32. Also called "seeker-sensitive" or "attractional church."

organization to make the entrance into church as "easy" as possible. Often this means making church like other societal forms (e.g., entertainment forms), while historical church forms are most often antithetical to this philosophy. "We do best when we make evangelism less difficult and recognize that we all naturally share the good things that happen to us best with those we know the best":[33] those who are most *like* us.

This short discussion of free-church is important because it has saturated most of the missional conversation over the last forty years. And it is within this sort of free-flow, entertainment-oriented, and worship-dejour context that our post-Christian world has thrived and accelerated.

33. Zunkel, "Countering Critics," 998.

# SECTION 4

# Contextualization

"The Word became flesh and blood, and moved into the neighborhood."

John 1:14 (The Message)

# Chapter 12

# The Life, the Spirit, the Acts

THROUGH THE FIRST THREE sections, this book has made an argument for the biblical, historical, and theological integrity of a consistent, structured, and traditional worship form. However, inherent to our argument, a case must also be made for the cultural imperative of biblical Christianity. To put it another way, the missional heart of Jesus' invitation to go to "Jerusalem, and in all Judea and Samaria, and even to the remotest part of the earth"[1] demands a theology of cultural integration, meaning that while the expression of Christian life and worship must never submit to the local cultural forms (being "of the world"),[2] they must at the same time be deeply embedded within each unique cultural context (being "into the world").[3]

Missionaries and church planters, at least the good ones, have been practicing contextualization since the beginning. This is seen in the Old Testament where God comes to people in ways and forms that they can understand. The New Testament itself bears witness to this process.

"It provides 'stories of contextualization'—particularly in the Gospels and Acts—in which Jesus and the apostles tailor the gospel message to address different groups of people. The journey of the church from its beginnings as a Jewish sect to becoming a largely Gentile body that proclaimed a universal faith required the gospel to engage new cultural groups and circumstances at each point along the way."[4]

1. Acts 1:8 (NASB).
2. John 17:16.
3. John 17:18.
4. Flemming, *Contextualization*, 15.

Contextualization is more than just "good marketing." This is about more than just presenting the gospel in such a way so that it sells more and more copies. "The idea that one can or could at any time separate out by some process of distillation a pure gospel unadulterated by any cultural accretions is an illusion."[5] The gospel cannot be separated from culture. And with equal strength it can never be equated to any individual cultural expression. "The word of God is to be spoken in every tongue, but it can never be domesticated in any."[6]

Jesus is our ultimate model of contextualization. He is the Word "who became flesh and dwelt among us."[7] From a theology of culture, this simple phrase is more than just a travelogue. This is a foundational truth of Orthodox Christianity throughout all time and space. The Word, coequal with the Father, over and beyond creation, the very Creator (John 1:1), the One who in whom all things are held together,[8] took on human flesh. This does not *simply* mean that Christ became human: simply some sort of generic über-human. Jesus became a human, yes. Jesus also became a man, a first-century man, a Palestinian man, a peasant man, a Jewish man, a resident of the Roman Empire, etc. Jesus' incarnation was particular! It was particular to a very specific time, a very specific geography, a very specific societal dynamic, *and a very specific culture.*

Dr. Paul Metzger writes in his extensive response (and affirmation) to Karl Barth's theology of culture:

> One thing that is required is a model of the Word that is truly incarnational: contextual, affirming the Word's embodiment in culture, and yet, at the same time, dialectical, safeguarding against the syncretistic union of gospel and culture. On the whole, Barth's doctrine of the Word provides such a model of Christ and culture, one that affirms the incarnation of the Word while guarding against the domestication of the gospel, and also against the cultural imperialism that so easily results from such syncretism when the church of one culture offers its supposedly unadulterated gospel to another people. Barth's theology of the Word . . .

5. Newbigin, *Foolishness to the Greeks*, 4.

6. Ibid., 47.

7. John 1:14 (NASB).

8. Col 1:15–17: He is the image of the invisible God, the firstborn over all creation. For by him all things were created: things in heaven and on earth, visible and invisible, whether thrones or powers or rulers or authorities; all things were created by him and for him. He is before all things, and in him all things hold together.

enable[s] him to affirm the incarnation of the divine Word in human history, and to protect the distinction between the divine and human natures in the incarnate life. The Word becomes incarnate as a human, as a Jewish male, in history. However, the Word is not exhausted by that enculturation. For the divine nature ever remains distinct from the human in their union in the person of the Word.[9]

In the book of Acts, we witness the first leaders of the church, as extensions of the ministry of Jesus, wrestling with and ultimately incorporating the themes of contextualization within their formative ministries. They did this as dedicated followers of the Holy Spirit. It can be argued that the "father" of church multiculturalism is the Spirit himself. It was the Spirit who demonstrated that the church could not be domesticated under any single cultural expression, time, or language and thus, splintered and multiplied the church's cultural expressions on the very day of its birth, Pentecost:

> Suddenly a sound like the blowing of a violent wind came from heaven and filled the whole house where they were sitting. They saw what seemed to be tongues of fire that separated and came to rest on each of them. All of them were filled with the Holy Spirit and began to speak in other tongues as the Spirit enabled them. Now there were staying in Jerusalem God-fearing Jews from every nation under heaven. When they heard this sound, a crowd came together in bewilderment, because each one heard them speaking in his own language. Utterly amazed, they asked: "Are not all these men who are speaking Galileans? Then, how is it that each of us hears them in his own native language? Parthians, Medes and Elamites; residents of Mesopotamia, Judea and Cappadocia, Pontus and Asia, Phrygia and Pamphylia, Egypt and the parts of Libya near Cyrene; visitors from Rome (both Jews and converts to Judaism); Cretans and Arabs—we hear them declaring the wonders of God in our own tongues!"[10]

As the apostles followed the Spirit's leading and example, they experienced an incredible transformation in the realm of contextualization. They went on a profound journey from their faith embodied as a "Jewish sect to becoming a largely Gentile body."[11] The Gentile Cornelius was used, in co-

---

9. Metzger, *Word of Christ*, 153.

10. Acts 2:2–11.

11. Flemming, *Contextualization*, 15.

operation with a holy vision from heaven, to convert the Apostle Paul to the multicultural realities of God's plan. Paul grew to master non-Jewish cultural forms to communicate the gospel. In his famous speech on Mars Hill, the apostle used locally valued poets, philosophers, and even religious symbols to missionally woo and confound his audience in Athens.

If we believe the Scriptures, the destiny of the church has been revealed. The angel of Jesus Christ appeared to the Apostle John in his Revelation and showed him a vision, which John described, "I looked, and behold, a great multitude, which on one could count, from every nation and all tribes and peoples and tongues, standing before the throne and before the Lamb, clothed in white robes, and palm branches were in their hands; and they cry out with a loud voice, saying, 'Salvation to our God who sits on the throne, and to the Lamb.'"[12] This picture of heaven is both inspiring and convicting. There are few examples of God's expansive creativity broader and more diverse than human culture(s), and heaven will be populated by the very expanse of its rainbow-expressions. And this revelation begs a central question to the people of Christ: Will we choose to practice for heaven now or will we rebuff the way of heaven and culturally homogenize the expression of Christ's church?

Darrell Whiteman, in his article, "Contextualization: The Theory, the Gap, the Challenge," echoes this perspective saying, "The concern of contextualization is ancient—going back to the early church as it struggled to break loose from its Jewish cultural trappings and enter the Greco-Roman world of the Gentiles."[13] Noting the evolution of the concept, or at least terminology, he sees it a part of an evolving stream of thought that relates the gospel and church to a local context. In the past we have used words such as "adaptation," "accommodation," and "indigenization" to describe this relationship between gospel, church, and culture, but "contextualization" (introduced in 1971), and "inculturation" (a companion term that emerged in literature in 1974) are deeper, more dynamic, and more adequate terms to describe what we are about in mission today.[14]

Essentially, contextualization addresses the challenge of communicating the gospel message in ways and terms that unbelievers understand. Its challenge is avoiding the foreignness of a gospel dressed

---

12. Rev 7:9–10 (NASB).

13. Whiteman, "Contextualization," 2.

14. Ibid.

in Western clothes that characterized the era of non-contextualization. Contextualization seeks to overcome the ethnocentrism of a monocultural approach by taking cultural differences seriously and affirming the good in all cultures.[15]

Critical contextualization leads us to see contextualization as an ongoing process.[16] It requires us to trust the Holy Spirit to direct us in this process. Here, old beliefs and customs are neither rejected nor accepted without careful examination in light of biblical truth.[17]

15. Hiebert, *Anthropological Insights*, 108.
16. Ibid., 92.
17. Ibid., 186.

# Chapter 13

# Colonialism and Insecure Traditionalism

Two counter trends compete with biblical contextualization. One is "religious colonialism," which is born out of power and fueled by a culturally entrenched view of a religious expression. With religious colonialism, a dominant and more powerful culture uses the systems of power to spiritually subjugate a population under its, as of yet, external and foreign religious structure and ultimately demands either the castration or total elimination of the cultural values and means of the preexistent culture and people. Religious colonialism is most often associated with imperial expansion, but it has applications over and beyond mere global-political empire building.[1] African scholar Ngugi Wa Thiong'o, in *Decolonizing the Mind: The Politics of Language in African Literature*, describes this reality from his point of view, the colonized. Thiong'o sees that the way control was introduced and managed was to deconstruct the people's sense of self and replace it with that of the colonizer.

Colonialism imposed its control of the social production of wealth through military conquest and subsequent political dictatorship. But its most important area of domination was the mental universe of the colonized—the control, through culture, of how people perceived themselves and their relationship to the world. To control a people's culture is to control their tools of self-definition in relationship to others. For colonialism this involved two aspects of the same process: destruction and domination

---

1. Webber, *God Still Speaks*, 65. Webber is softer in his description stating, "We tend to communicate our own culturalized view of Christianity. In the case of faith, Western Christians have filtered the notions through a cultural grid. Three more common grids are rationalism, romanticism, and existentialism."

92

of culture. Destruction brought the deliberate undervaluing of a people's culture, including its art, dances, religions, geography, education, history, oral expressions, and literature. Behind this destructive cycle comes the conscious elevation of the language of the colonizer. This domination of a people's language by the languages of the colonizing nations was crucial to the domination of the mental universe of the colonized.[2]

The other countertrend is more of an insecure traditionalism. In this stream, there is most often a geographically embedded historical community (or communities) of faith that cannot let go of the way that they have "always" expressed their faith. This becomes particularly sad and counterproductive as the historical religious population moves from majority culture to minority culture, and though they have lost their "deciding vote" within society, they continue to exist as if they still have it. I sometimes refer to this as the "if you don't want to play by our rules then we will just take our ball and go home" response. The sad thing is that in these times of religious decline, the remnant religious community often does not realize that someone else now owns the court where the game is played. In the most extreme examples, at least within the American story, it has led to the creation of geographically isolated, parallel societies (Amish, commune-cults), but it is more often manifested through subtle religious subcultures where all aspects of cultural expressions are populated by those of similar ideological/religious paradigms.[3] Within Christendom this necessitates the creation of subculture serving education, social, and entertainment structures.

Religious colonialism is most powerful and rears its head when a new (powerful) Christian religious system exerts itself upon a previously pre-Christian culture. The latter phenomenon (insecure traditionalism) most usually occurs as a population transitions from a "Christian culture"[4] into a post-Christian culture.

2. Thiong'o, *Decolonizing the Mind*, 16.

3. Black, *Culturally-Conscious Worship*. Consider this work for a conversation on the place and means of multiculturalism within a worshiping body.

4. Just a reminder, "Christian culture" is in quotes here because it is not referring primarily to a religious or spiritual state of a culture. What it is referring to is more of a societal and sociological reality in which the church is a strong and recognized player on the societal stage and wherein the majority of persons within that society freely recognize the church's voice as such.

# Chapter 14

# Serving the Context

DARRELL WHITEMAN IDENTIFIES TWO distinct characteristics of good contextualization. First, "contextualization attempts to communicate the Gospel in word and deed and to establish the church in ways that makes sense to people within their local cultural context, presenting Christianity in such a way that it meets people's deepest needs and penetrates their worldview, thus allowing them to follow Christ and remain within their own culture."[1] Whiteman also insists that

> . . . another function of contextualization in mission is *to offend—but only for the right reasons, not the wrong ones.* Good contextualization offends people for the right reasons. Bad contextualization, or the lack of it altogether, offends them for the wrong reasons. . . . Unfortunately, when Christianity is not contextualized or is contextualized poorly, then people are culturally offended, turned off to inquiring more about who Jesus is, or view missionaries and their small band of converts with suspicion as cultural misfits and aliens. When people are offended for the wrong reason, the garment of Christianity gets stamped with the label "Made in America [or in another generation] and Proud of It."[2]

This second function is particularly important, because some assume that the contextualizing missionary is just "watering down" the gospel. In fact, the well-contextualized gospel actively proclaims Jesus, who is a stumbling stone, but labors to desperately limit any and all additional stumbling stones to the missional story.

1. Whiteman, "Contextualization," 2.
2. Ibid., 3–4 (italics mine).

94

Additionally, "When the Gospel is presented in word and deed, and the fellowship of believers we call the church is organized along appropriate cultural patterns, then people will more likely be confronted with the offense of the Gospel, exposing their own sinfulness and the tendency toward evil, oppressive structures, and behavior patterns within their culture."[3] Thus, contextualization is not the same as syncretism. In fact, it is just the opposite. Ultimately contextualization, biblically practiced and spiritually discerned, provides the ultimate cultural critique because the contextualized people and voice of the gospel of the kingdom are able to speak freely within the cultural context, unfettered by the additional offenses of religiously clothed cultural dissonance.

This is the same idea that Richard Niebuhr discussed back in 1951 in his classic book *Christ and Culture*.[4] In its pages Niebuhr considers several models of cultural engagement: Christ against culture, Christ of culture, Christ above culture, and Christ and culture in paradox. The final model that he introduces is Christ the transformer of culture. "The transformationist view rests on a positive doctrine of creation and incarnation, while yet admitting the radical corruption of humanity. Corruption is the perversion of the good, not intrinsic evil. Conversion and rebirth are needed."[5] Niebuhr spoke of F.D. Maurice, an Anglican scholar, as a strong example of the "transformer" view. He said, "In Maurice the conversionist idea is more clearly expressed than in any other modern Christian thinker and leader. His attitude toward culture is affirmative throughout, because he takes most seriously the conviction that nothing exists without the Word. It is thoroughly conversionist and never accommodating, because his is most sensitive to the perversion of human culture . . . " Now, Niebuhr was not necessarily advocating any one of the models over the others in his work. In summation he said, "To make our decisions in faith is to make them in view of the fact that no single man or group or historical time is the church; but that there is a church of faith in which we do our partial, relative work and . . . in view of the fact that Christ is risen from the dead, and is not only the head of the church but the redeemer of

---

3. Ibid., 2.

4. Niebuhr, *Christ and Culture*.

5. Jones et al., *Study of Spirituality*, 603. See Wainwright's discussion of Niebuhr's work from part III "Pastoral Spirituality" and section II "Types of Spirituality."

the world . . . in view of the fact that the world of culture—man's achievement—exists within the world of grace—God's kingdom."[6]

## CONTEXTUALIZATION ILLUSTRATED

Here are a couple of examples of contextualization from the history of Christ's missional church.

### James Hudson Taylor (May 21, 1832–June 3, 1905)

When I was a young missionary living in Albania, it was the story of Hudson Taylor that inspired me to embrace a contextualized missiology. "Hudson Taylor was a British Protestant missionary to China, and founder of the China Inland Mission (CIM, now OMF International). Taylor spent fifty-one years in China. The society that he began was responsible for bringing over 800 missionaries to the country who began 125 schools and directly resulted in 18,000 Christian conversions, as well as the establishment of more than 300 stations of work with more than 500 local helpers in all eighteen provinces."[7] Taylor's transformational epiphany was to take the very structure of missions in China away from the missionary ghettos along the affluent eastern seaboard and into the very heart of the Asian continent. Not only was he willing to leave the physical comfort of the Westernized colonial populations, he also left the philosophical comfort of his peers and training. Taylor's contextual brilliance and courage led him to grow his hair, dress in local garb, speak fluently in local language and dialect, and adopt every local custom to speak more completely to the Chinese people, both peasant and aristocrat.[8] He was ridiculed by his peers, but the incarnational mission of Jesus compelled him to do what heretofore had not been attempted. Ruth Tucker wrote, "No other missionary in the nineteen centuries since the Apostle Paul has had a wider vision and has carried out a more systematized plan of evangelizing a broad geographical area than Hudson Taylor."[9]

6. Niebuhr, *Christ and Culture*, 256.

7. Wikipedia, "Hudson Taylor."

8. For more of Hudson Taylor's unprecedented story, consider the biography written by his son: Taylor et al., *Hudson Taylor's Spiritual Secret*.

9. Tucker, *Jerusalem to Irian Jaya*, 73.

*Saints Cyril and Methodius (Ninth Century)*

Another example from a bit further back in the church's story is of two Byzantine Greek brothers born in the ninth century in Thessoloniki. Saints Cyril and Methodius were "missionaries of Christianity among the Slavic peoples of Great Moravia and Pannonia. Through their work they influenced the cultural development of all Slavs, for which they received the title 'Apostles to the Slavs.' They are credited with devising the Glagolitic alphabet, the first alphabet used to transcribe the Old Church Slavonic language. Both brothers are venerated in the Eastern Orthodox Church as saints with the title of 'Equals to the Apostles.'"[10]

In Cyril and Methodius's day, the Greek language was considered sacred, and from their monastery in northern Greece they became scholars of the highest level, masters of theology and language. However, as they looked north into the tribal lands of the Balkans and into what is now Eastern Europe, they saw a land without the gospel of Jesus Christ. From a missionary passion they pressed out into the north as strangers in a strange land. They lived among the Slavic peoples where they created the Glagolitic alphabet (the predecessor of the Cyrillic alphabet) in order to translate the Scriptures into the local tongue and to give the "nations" a chance to read the sacred words in their own language. These brilliant scholars saw the need to take the gospel to the nations, but they also saw the reality that to love another is to also love their culture and to give to that culture its unique language of worship and truth.[11]

---

10. Wikipedia, "Saints Cyril and Methodius."

11. For more of their story and their unequaled influence in the histories of Slavic peoples from Macedonia to Russia, consider Tachiaos, *Cyril and Methodius of Thessalonica.*

# Chapter 15

# Contextual Struggle: An Anglican Story

THE CRITIC COULD CONTEND that my argument thus far is conflicted at best, if not contradictory. Through sections 2 and 3 I argue for the stasis of worship. I have shown that historically worship has been liturgical and that liturgy, at its very definition, is fixed and repeated; on some level those fixed forms transcend the human experience across time and space. And then here in section 4 I argue for the absolute centrality of contextualization in the history and heart of the Jesus-way: embodied by Christ, embraced and defended by the Holy Spirit, and manifested through God's holy apostles and saints through the centuries. So is this a contradiction?

The history of the church, biblical and post-biblical, shows a continuity within liturgical worship. East and West, ancient and modern times, again and again, the people of God have found meaning in liturgical worship. This is a statement of description, *not* prescription. Old Testament, New Testament, first century, church history—the people of God have found meaning in written prayers, structured worship, and the Lord's Table. We can only guess why that might be. Maybe it is the reality that these prayers and practices have been affirmed again and again in echoing ovation across generations, cultures, and times, and so we cannot deny their meaningfulness. Maybe there is a necessary solidarity that the human spirit is looking for to feel unified with universal humanity in the experience of God[1] (as if we intrinsically long to pull ourselves toward the scene in Revelation 7:9–10, or maybe, more accurately, we are being

1. Weil, *Theology of Worship*, 4–8.

pulled toward it).[2,3] Maybe there is a rhythmic, almost meditative sensation in something clear and repeated that centers the human soul and/or soothes mind, heart, and body, much like the singing of the same lullaby every night to my boys leads them from chaos to stillness. And finally, maybe sign and symbol is simply the language of the soul.[4]

Whatever it is (and make no mistake, it *is*) the Anglican Way has found surprising tenacity over its six hundred years. Its liturgy, first penned by Thomas Cranmer but clearly built on the shared worship experiences of church history (see section 3), has found a resonance of meaning across cultural expressions.

However, and about this I want to be very clear, the rhythms of sign and symbol and the comfort and wisdom of structured readings, prayers, and worship are not to be superimposed upon each local cultural context. No, they must be nestled in among the local culture with its unique forms, structures, and aesthetics. It was Thomas Cranmer himself who wrote these words in the Preface to the 1549 Book of Common Prayer:

> Though it be appointed in the afore written preface, that al thinges shalbe read and song in the churche, in the Englishe tongue, to thende yt the congregacion maie be therby edified: yet it is not meant, but when men saye Matins and Evensong privatelye, they maye saie the same in any language that they themselves do understande. Neither that anye man shalbe bound to the saying of them, but suche as from tyme to tyme, in Cathedrall and Collegiate Churches, Parishe Churches, and Chapelles to the same annexed, shall serve the congregacion.[5]

Cranmer launched his lauded book, a book that was specifically written to unify the people of England under a common church experience and, as stated in his preface, to free them from the tyranny of the Latin tongue as the language of the church.[6] Here in the preface's last line, Cranmer

2. Chan, *Liturgical Theology*, 46. "Worship not only distinguishes the church as church, *it also makes or realizes the church* (italics mine). . . In the liturgical tradition, what is realized in the worship is the church as an ontological rather than sociological reality."

3. I am indebted to Joshua Butler for many transformative theological perspectives, including this idea of inverted time, in which the kingdom story is not "unfolding" before us but instead it is being pulled forward, a process that we are experiencing in reverse.

4. Galli, *Beyond Smells and Bells*, 47–54.

5. Prins, *Booke of the Common Prayer* (original spelling retained).

6. Ibid., Preface. "Whereas s. Paule would have suche language spoken to the people

reminds that the use of language is ultimately for one reason: that it "shall serve the congregacion [*sic*]," so much so that he releases the local congregation from the danger that one form of cultural tyranny (Latin and Rome) might be replaced by another.

Perhaps it is for this very reason that Anglicanism has spread so deftly into the cultures of the world.[7] It is the commitment to the declaration of the Father, in Christ. "And whatever you do, whether in word or deed, do it all in the name of the Lord Jesus, giving thanks to God the Father through him."[8] In *Introduction to Liturgical Theology*, Schmemann wrote of the dependence on the Father in this essential though tenuous dynamic:

> In the early Christian understanding, prayer was not opposed to life or the occupations of life. Prayer penetrated life and consisted above all in a new understanding of life and its occupations, in relating them to the central object of faith—to the kingdom of God and the Church . . . Work was controlled, enlightened, and judged by prayer, it was not opposed to prayer . . . Prayer in the spirit meant above all a constant recollection of the relatedness and subordination of everything in life to the reality of the kingdom manifested in this world.[9]

Saturated in this Fatherly dependence and in lieu of Cranmer's directives, I am convinced that the culturally conscious reality of the Anglican Eucharistic liturgy will continue to bring meaning. Even in places where the culture is leaving behind Christian heritage, the drama of her words and Table has a unique opportunity to declare the kingdom.

It would be foolish to claim that there are no dark chapters in the missional story of the Anglican Church[10] wherein cultures were invalidated and even crimes committed. The British Empire fueled much of the early growth of the Anglican Communion and with that colonial impetus came much "religious colonialism" (as discussed and defined above). This

in the churche, as they mighte understande and have profite by hearyng the same; the service in this Churche of England (these many yeares) hath been read in Latin to the people, whiche they understoode not; so that they have heard with theyr eares onely; and their hartes, spirite, and minde, have not been edified thereby."

7. "Thomas Cranmer's prayer book—in whatever version—is no longer the glue holding the identity of the Anglican Communion together."

8. Col 3:17.

9. Schmemann, *Liturgical Theology*, starting at 105.

10. Alan W. Jones, *Common Prayer*. Part 1 of Jones's book is titled, "A Plague on Both Your Houses."

was particularly evident in the global South.[11] There have been "crimes" committed in the global North as well. Lesslie Newbigin, a clergyman who left England as a missionary to India, returned to Britain in the 1970s after forty years of international work in pluralistic lands and found the church of his homeland existing as if England were still a Christian land—while the British culture had long become post-Christian in expression.[12] In this blindness and arrogance, the true spiritual needs and dynamics of the UK were no longer being met (or even considered?) by the clergy. His observations could be defined as a church burdened by "insecure traditionalism."

Despite these realities (and many more), Anglicanism has had a striking ability to adapt and invite other cultures, particularly cultures of the global South, into true ecclesial fellowship (non-hierarchical partnership)—so much so that today there are more Anglicans in the global South than in the North *and* the leaders of those southern expressions are exercising significant, if not majority, authority over all of the Anglican Communion.

The British Broadcasting Company (BBC) did a study in 2008 on the Anglican Communion to understand its statistical foundation and numbers distribution. The following chart compares Anglican membership between the United Kingdom and some nations/regions of Africa:

| Anglican Church Membership | |
|---|---|
| United Kingdom | 13.4 Million |
| Nigeria | 17.5 Million |
| Uganda | 8 Million |
| Sudan | 5 Million |
| Kenya | 2.5 Million |

11. Wikipedia, North-South Divide. "The North-South Divide is a socio-economic and political division that exists between the wealthy developed countries, known collectively as 'the North,' and the poorer developing countries (least developed countries), or 'the South.' Although most nations comprising the 'North' are in fact located in the Northern Hemisphere (with the notable exceptions of Australia and New Zealand), the divide is not wholly defined by geography. The North is home to four of the five permanent members of the United Nations Security Council and all members of the G8. 'The North' mostly covers the West and the First World, with much of the Second World."

12. Lesslie Newbigin's story can be found in his autobiography: Newbigin, *Unfinished Agenda*.

| Tanzania | 2 Million |
|---|---|
| Southern Africa | 2 Million |
| West Africa | 1 Million |
| Central Africa | 600,000 |

Figure 8. Anglican Church Membership Worldwide. Source: Church of England/ Anglican Communion/National Statistics.

The most striking observation is that today there are 13.4 million Anglicans in the UK, and just counting the eight African countries/regions listed here, Africa's numbers exceed 38 million.

But what is the state of those African national churches—are they just colonized extensions of British culture? Esther Mombo writes, "The establishment of Anglicanism in the colonies of eastern Africa had as one of its main resources the 1662 Book of Common Prayer. Written in the context of English tradition, imported and translated for use by the colonized . . . "[13] But it seems that the Anglican Church was served by the loss of Britain's imperial dominance. As nationalistic movements "freed" the countries of places like Africa, it also infused creative and contextualized movements of worship and spirituality. That process of contextualization led Grant LeMarquand to write about the Kenyan liturgy (called *Our Modern Services*):

> *Our Modern Services* is clearly an African book which encourages an African style of language, African prayer, and musical traditions within worship, and seeks to meet the needs of Kenyan realities. Yet it is also a book which in its forms and much of its theological content is clearly a descendant of the Book of Common Prayer.[14]

LeMarquand has expressed a wonderful example of contextualization, in which the traditions (which have been affirmed across cultures and generations) are not rejected but are held with one hand while the other hand is grasping fully the voice and cultural ways of the local, contemporary reality. This breaking from colonialism and embracing contextualized liturgical worship is the norm of the African continent within the Anglican Communion. This balanced evolution harmonizes with Cranmer's words:

> It is a most invaluable part of that blessed "liberty wherewith Christ hath made us free," that in his worship different forms and

13. Hefling and Shattuck, *Oxford Guide*, 277.

14. Ibid., 287.

*usages may without offence be allowed, provided the substance of the Faith be kept entire; and that, in every Church, what cannot be clearly determined to belong to Doctrine must be referred to Discipline; and therefore, by common consent and authority, may be altered, abridged, enlarged, amended, or otherwise disposed of, as may seem most convenient for the edification of the people, "according to the various exigency of times and occasions."*[15]

This two-handed commitment to tradition and context in worship has not been universally applied throughout Anglican history, but it has been so embedded in its DNA that contextualized movements of faith are thriving, growing, and even leading Anglican growth and mission around the world today. So much so that the Province of the Anglican Church of Rwanda, for example, is leading a significant and inspired church planting effort in North America, which is fueled by a commitment to doctrinal tradition and a heart for contextualization. Bishop Todd Hunter writes on his website for Churches for the Sake of Others (C4SO):

> The Most Rev. Emmanuel M. Kolini of the Province of the Anglican Church of Rwanda was inspired to create the Anglican Mission (TheAM) which serves as a missionary outreach of the Province of Rwanda. For decades the church in the West has been sending missionaries to places like Rwanda, but with this shift to an increasingly post-Christian culture in America, kingdom-minded communities like the Anglican Church of Rwanda are now sending missionaries our way . . . The Anglican Mission in the Americas has launched Churches for the Sake of Others . . . We're growing churches from the mission field backward. Which means . . . we recognize that mission fields have unique populations and varying contexts.[16]

This epic story, which crosses two millennia, is inspiring. Now, it seems, the missionary story has come full circle. Just like in the church's first chapter when a subjugated and colonized people (Jews) were the first missionaries, many missionaries today are going from the geographical margins of an empire-dominated world to bring the word of redemption and freedom, the gospel of the kingdom, into our diverse and broken world full of cultures, languages, and spiritual expressions.

---

15. The Book of Common Prayer, "The Book of Common Prayer" (italics mine). From the preface.

16. Churches for the Sake of Others, "Hear the Story and See the Vision."

## Section 5

# Other Contemporary Church Models for Post-Christian Culture

"And pray for us, too, that God may open a door for our message, so that we may proclaim the mystery of Christ, for which I am in chains. Pray that I may proclaim it clearly, as I should. Be wise in the way you act toward outsiders; make the most of every opportunity. Let your conversation be always full of grace, seasoned with salt, so that you may know how to answer everyone."

Colossians 4:3–6

We are in trouble. I just came out of a pastors' roundtable meeting for four hours. I just sat there, listening to the problems that pastors are facing. I was looking around the room and one of the most striking things is that I am the youngest guy in the room. I am forty-two years old. The rest of the room is still worrying about problems like "worship wars" and accommodating worship to keep the big donors happy. We are missing the point, believing, "if we could change our worship style it would save the church . . . should we add an electric guitar?" The really sad thing is that they are missing the rich opportunities all around them.[1]

This opening paragraph came from an interview with Jim Wicks, an influential pastor in the Nazarene denomination. His church, called Adsideo, is located in the Sellwood Neighborhood of Portland's inner eastside. In their own words, "We are a community who seeks to minister

1. Jim Wicks, interview by author, Portland, OR, November 11, 2010.

to an emerging, postmodern neighborhood. We live and gather in the Sellwood neighborhood here in Southeast Portland. We are dedicated to the journey of discovering the fullness of God's redemptive vision for this world."[2] Adsideo has been around for four years and cares for around one hundred and fifty parishioners and more importantly, their neighborhood. Pastor Jim has one of the few thriving and growing young churches in the Nazarene tribe. In light of this, his denomination is looking to him (and a small handful of others) to solve the challenge of raising up next-generation leaders.

According to Jim,

> We are experiencing a 17 percent decline annually in the Northwest within our denomination. To better understand that number, you need to understand that it incorporates the rate of population growth and compares it to church attendance decline. So based on that, I am assuming that our actual interior decline is over 20 percent.[3] The number that I am hearing is 15 percent; we are closing around 15 percent of our churches annually within the US.[4]

So the question is: What is the church's plan for moving into the future? To put it another way: What is our plan to reach and resource our ever-increasing post-Christian culture? How will we point the way to Jesus?

Several strategies are currently in play for accomplishing these essential missional goals. It would be impossible to be exhaustive in examining and evaluating all such strategies, so I will choose a selection that are current in the mainstream Christian world, specifically focusing my comments on strategies that are currently active in Portland's urban center (as opposed to the more culturally "Christian" suburbs or rural areas). I will also evaluate each one from an often (admittedly) subjective position. I am asking an *effectiveness* question. In what ways does (or doesn't) each strategy actually draw citizens in our post-Christian society[5] into faith in Christ and church life? The purpose is not to criticize. In fact, many of my comments will be very complimentary. While this book is moving toward

2. The Community of Asideo, "Welcome to Asideo."

3. To clarify, Pastor Wicks is stating that the 15 percent assumes a static population number; however, when that same 15 percent is related to the growing population, the actual impact (or loss of market share) is even greater (over 20 percent).

4. Jim Wicks, interview by author, Portland, OR, November 11, 2010.

5. As opposed to simply more effectively consolidating the remaining vestiges of "Christian culture."

a proposed solution (section 6), that solution is not exclusive or absolute. Bishop Todd Hunter of the Anglican Mission has often stated, "Moving into the future will require dozens of models of church." Our world is becoming increasingly globalized, pluralized, and diverse. Creativity and courage will be required as we explore and chart these expanding new cultural waters.

# Chapter 16

# "Emergent"

T HE "EMERGENT" PHENOMENON IS not simple to tie down. It includes the Emergent Village, which is most closely associated with
Bryan McLaren. "Emergent Village is a growing, generative friendship
among missional Christians seeking to love our world in the Spirit of
Jesus Christ."[1] However, the emergent movement has been more broadly
defined as

> A Christian movement of the late 20th and early 21st century
> that crosses a number of theological boundaries: participants
> can be described as evangelical, protestant, roman catholic, post-
> evangelical, anabaptist, adventist, liberal, post-liberal, reformed,
> charismatic, neocharismatic, post-charismatic, conservative, and
> post-conservative. Proponents, however, believe the movement
> transcends such "modernist" labels of "conservative" and "liberal,"
> calling the movement a "conversation" to emphasize its develop-
> ing and decentralized nature, its vast range of standpoints, and its
> commitment to dialogue. Participants seek to live their faith in
> what they believe to be a "postmodern" society. What those in-
> volved in the conversation mostly agree on is their disillusionment
> with the organized and institutional church and their support for
> the deconstruction of modern Christian worship, modern evange-
> lism, and the nature of modern Christian community. The emerg-
> ing church favors the use of simple story and narrative. Members
> of the movement often place a high value on good works or social
> activism, including missional living. While some Evangelicals
> emphasize eternal salvation, many in the emerging church em-
> phasize the here and now. Key themes of the emerging church

1. Emergent Village, "Growing, Generative Friendship."

are couched in the language of reform, Praxis-oriented lifestyles, Post-evangelical thought, and incorporation or acknowledgment of political and Postmodern elements. Many of the movement's participants use terminology that originates from postmodern literary theory, social network theory, narrative theology, and other related fields.[2]

## NETWORKS

Emergent networks exist in loose relationship to denominations or are totally independent of denominations. One network that could be lumped into the broadest category of "emergent," which is actively at work in Portland (and other urban centers of the Pacific Northwest), is the Acts 29 Network. "The Mission of Acts 29 is to band together Christian, Evangelical, Missional & Reformed churches, who, for the sake of Jesus and the gospel, plant churches across the United States and the world."[3] In the Portland urban center, Acts 29 was instrumental in planting churches such as Imago Dei Community,[4] Red Sea,[5] Bread and Wine,[6] and The Table.[7],[8] I was a leader of and contributor to Imago Dei during its first ten years and have played an advisor or close observer to each of the other plants listed here. There are several other smaller networks of churches that could be included here, including the church planting efforts of Mosaic Church/Northwest Church Planting[9] and the Evergreen Church.[10]

The goal of these networks is to manifest viable forms of church expression that will continue and thrive in the postmodern world. Naturally, there is a need to critique the modernist forms of church (many of which have been held onto as "sacred cows"), and try to re-envision the church's voice and (to some extent) structure. While many elements remain the

2. Wikipedia, "Emerging Church" (original capitalization retained).

3. Driscoll, "Vision of Acts 29."

4. Imago Dei Community, "Home Page."

5. Red Sea, "Home Page."

6. Bread & Wine, "Home Page."

7. The Table, "Home Page."

8. Note: Imago Dei Community and The Table are no longer affiliated with Acts 29.

9. Mosaic, "Church Planting."

10. The Evergreen Community, "Home Page."

same (as common evangelical church formation of the second half of the twentieth century), there are some distinctive and laudable changes:

- Gospel is perceived as more holistic. As the motto of Imago Dei Community states, "The whole gospel, to the whole person, to the whole world."[11] The gospel is about more than just assuring one's eternal destiny. It is defined by more than a handful of doctrinal propositions. Instead, the gospel has something to say about every aspect of existence and particularly every part of the human experience. The gospel is for the "whole person" and thus ought to transform us more than just spiritually but also psychologically, socially, relationally, communally, economically, and mentally. The gospel is not just about the unseen realms (as Western dualism has been syncretized with the church's view of the "gospel"), but affects all aspects of this "whole world" and therefore has, among other things, social and justice implications.

- Teaching is formed and delivered in narrative. Simply put, ideas are shaped so that the meaning is primary, as opposed to the information being primary. This is not to say that narrative thought and delivery are anti-information. Quite on the contrary. The hope is to free the conceptualization of the gospel and the kingdom of God from a post-Enlightenment, cognitive domination. It is necessary to not just deconstruct Western paradigms, but more importantly, to reconstruct through the mentorship of both global and historical voices. For the congregation, the primary question is not "what?" or even "why?" but instead, "So what? So what for my life? So what for my family? So what for my community? So what for my world?" To accomplish this task, pastors need to use personally impactful story (testimony or personal encounter), and when it is at its best, limit the use of triumphalism (the illusion that the person speaking "has it all figured out"). Thus, communication often includes self-deprecating humor, the centrality of the journey (over arrival), and even, at times, personal struggle and doubt.

- Worship (in its public and corporate, often Sunday morning, manifestation)[12] takes on at least two evolutions within emergent

11. Imago Dei Community, "What We Believe."

12. I acknowledge that "worship" is far broader and all-encompassing, far beyond the singing and actions of a Sunday service. However, for this short section, I am focusing

movements. The first is the freedom to create (or adapt) forms, musically and otherwise. There is a refusal to "baptize" certain worship styles (for instance, "we only use hymns" or "we never use hymns"). The "worship wars" of the latter twentieth century have no value or concern. The church worship experience can integrate "secular" songs or musical styles and can use anything from a keyboard to a didgeridoo. Another distinction is that worship can draw from a far broader pallet. It is typical within an emergent community to see icons, sacred symbols, the centrality of Communion, recited creeds, on-stage painting, prayer stations, or even kinetic and tactile worship using clay or other mediums.

- Social justice is another priority in every emergent church I have witnessed. Significant time, money, and energy are put toward working with those who live outside (homeless), helping those inside struggling schools, or assisting community development initiatives. There is a reaction against the purely proclamational focus of the church, whose end is propagating intellectual assent to a Christian creed or where the work of the church is merely about getting more and more people to come to church. The belief is that the people of God are to manifest goodness, truth, and beauty in all places, and part of that is taking on the care, creation, healing, and provision of Christ in their neighborhoods and world.

In light of the distinctives listed above, emergent churches and movements have provided a profound and important home to thousands of Christians in the urban centers of the Pacific Northwest. The de-churching trend in America and the church exodus, which we have been dramatically witnessing over the last 40 years, has been populated by twenty- and thirty-somethings who are tired of their parents' (or grandparents') worship styles, a purely proclamational gospel, aesthetic reductionism, and dualistic faith application. In light of this reality, emergent churches have actually grown. This would explain why the only category of church that David Olsen says has grown between 2000 and 2005 in Oregon is "non-Baptist, non-Pentecostal evangelical churches."[13]

---

on the popular use of the term "worship" as a corporate act usually performed during a Sunday morning church service.

13. Olson, *American Church in Crisis*, 112.

The main criticism made of many emergent churches is that while they have been an effective way station of faith, they have been little more than the last gasp of the attractional model[14] of church, which so dominated the seeker-sensitive movements of the latter twentieth century. Yes, it was a brilliant move to integrate arts, justice, and broader worship forms into church life. Yes, it was culturally contextualized to see that the old rhetorical philosophy, which churches had artificially held onto, needed to be replaced by more image- and narrative-driven models, which are more consistent with our postmodern world. However, were these changes little more than effective marketing to the already churched? As one pastor of a large and successful suburban Presbyterian mega church lamented to me, "We have all but closed down our adult singles ministry because all our people are now attending Imago Dei." Another influential congregant of a large emergent church in Portland said, "Sometimes I sit back and wonder if at the end of the day our community is little more than a 'mega church that paints.'"

A related critique is that the "tools" of worship and practice are implemented for purely utilitarian reasons. For instance, a Celtic cross might be the symbol of the church (it might even be tattooed on the pastor's shoulder), but it is used primarily because it looks cool and gives the appearance of history and mysticism. However, only a cursory examination will reveal that the church itself is not submitted to the Celtic tradition in any way, nor has it given particular place to Celtic thought or spirituality. In fact, none of its leadership is even Irish or studied in Celtic schools or under Celtic scholars. Can you see how this can unintentionally communicate an insincere spirituality? This post-Christian generation is very intuitive and suspicious of this sort of pragmatism. To give another example, a similar observation can be made about the use of icons. While they make interesting and even inspiring ornaments of worship, any Eastern Orthodox believer would be horrified by their vulgar application. In this sense the very tradition (of icons in this case), which the church is co-opting, is being more plundered than honored.

There is a real question whether or not these churches are reaching the post-Christian city. While their brick-and-mortar expressions

14. "Attractional model" is another way of labeling the "seeker sensitive" church model, also known as the "church growth" movement. The main idea is that marketing philosophy is used to determine why the church does what it does. The goal is to get people in the door.

may exist in the heart of the city and their missions state their purpose as "reaching the city," the reality is a vast majority of their congregants and leaders[15] commute to and from the suburbs. This concept has been echoed by many suburban pastors who now feel the challenge of filling their own over-leveraged properties as their congregations are traveling into the city for church. Some contend that the church of the city has not grown at all; the cards have just been shuffled and redealt to new hands.

Finally, these emergent churches (again, using a fairly broad definition of "emergent") have received a significant amount of press and recognition in the American Christian systems. In fact, large "emergent" churches in Portland and Seattle have received an incongruent percentage of press, even while existing within some of the most challenging post-Christian locations in the country. Here is the challenge: Is the "formula" that created these large new churches truly reproducible? As one smart, committed, and tattooed church planter in Portland recently said to me, "I was sent to Portland by my denomination to plant the next Imago Dei; however, I have come to realize that I can't. Rick McKinley[16] is the funniest guy on the planet."[17] These impressive and wonderful churches are led by the most exceptional sort of people and because of this, many fear, may not be duplicated.[18] All-world personalities are painfully few (which is why they are so significant when they come along).

## NEXT GENERATION ADD-ONS

"Next generation add-ons" is a term unique to this book. The idea that it intends to communicate is more or less an adaption of the emergent strategy above. The difference is that these "add-on" strategies exist deeply embedded within a preexisting historical denomination or tradition that

15. I know of one church that passionately proclaimed its commitment to the city, so much so that they would only consider properties for worship that were within a short distance from the city's center. However, when I surveyed the two pastors and six elders, only one elder lived within the "city boundaries" and he was sixty blocks from the center.

16. Rick McKinley of Imago Dei Community in Portland, Oregon is possibly the most talented and inspiring pastor I have ever encountered. He is truly gifted.

17. Clyde Vernon Hartline III, pastor of Vibrant Covenant Church in Portland, Oregon.

18. Mars Hill in Seattle, led by Marc Driscoll, is another example of a large and impressive church of the "emergent" stream that has received significant national press. The press that Mars Hill, the church, receives though is far less than the press focused on its leader, Mark Driscoll.

is seeking to evolve its ecclesial strategy and create a sub-movement within an existing construct. The goal is to reach the "next generation" and secondarily, ensure the denomination does not die.

The Nazarene tribe is a good example of this strategy.[19] It is a fairly moderate evangelical denomination, which also has the unique fact that one of its first congregations was located in Portland's inner eastside. As stated above, this tribe is in decline. Jason Robertson said about his denomination, "I believe we are already closing churches faster than adding them."

Robertson had been a successful pastor of a next-generation service embedded in a large and growing Nazarene church in Ohio for six years. He was strongly recruited[20] to join the faculty at Olivet Nazarene University as a professor of theology and ministry development. I interviewed Professor Robertson about the future plans of his denomination.[21] "They were looking for someone of the emergent/emerging persuasion who had maintained commitment to a denominational identity. Olivet was particularly drawn to the fact that I had done it in the confines of a traditional, middle-class, and established church context." Olivet spoke of the importance that Professor Robertson was able to build an emergent-like movement inside an existing church, "allowing both to exist within the same building." This appears to be a large part of their leadership and educational strategy.

Pastor Jim Wicks agrees that developing leaders is the hope for his denomination. However, he has real doubts about the viability of institutionally based education, especially from where he sits, deeply entrenched in Portland's post-Christian eastside. "We all recognize that their modern education system is on the decline. We used to boast about it. Today, there is an entire populous of leaders that are rejecting the idea of the old model

19. I have fairly extensive firsthand experience in the Nazarene denomination's attempts to navigate the changing culture. I served as a keynote speaker at the last two Nazarene Emergentia pastors' training conferences. I have been a friend and advisor to one the denomination's flagship next-generation churches, Adsideo. And I have been a friend and mentor to two influential Nazarene leaders.

20. Professor Robertson insisted that he was not looking to teach. He said multiple times, "They called me" and even suggested that no one else was being considered and Olivet would wait for him to finish up his ministry practice.

21. Professor Jason Robertson, Associate Professor of Theology of Olivet Nazarene University, phone interview by author, November 9, 2010.

of education. Part of that is affordability. NNU[22] is one of our cheaper colleges at $25k per year. Here is another issue: there are few students coming from West Oregon. Youth groups are not sending kids to NNU. This plan is losing the next-generation leaders. Three percent of every church's income goes to the college, but the churches are not sending their kids."

Pastor Wicks is an influential leader as his denomination moves forward. When I pressed him for how he (along with others) is leading the way into the future, Jim shared that they are fast-tracking two strategies (as least as fast as denominational evolution will allow). The first is the "Emergentia" program. "We have to find next-generational leaders within this tribe that goes beyond permission given by the super-structure. We don't need permission to create. We need to create a filter that is respectful and consistent with values." The vision is regionally based conversations around the pressing issues of today's culture (and briskly moving away from issues that are just about maintaining denominational structures of comfort or dead tradition). "Emergentia is the future. We need many of them. We are bringing in outside voices: stirring the pot; creating tensions; having original thoughts so that we don't have just patched thinking from the past and so we can stop trying to institute Midwest thinking into the Pacific Northwest. Help people to be relevant inside their context."[23] The second strategy is to bring education out of slow-moving and overhead-burdened institutions and into the local context through mobile and courageous education modules. It is called "Suma Dialogue."

> It is a new educational paradigm. Suma Dialogue has proctors come to the local context. Grades will be based on how they defend their position and interact around major theological issues. We are unleashing a conversation and observing how they exchange and interact.[24]

Suma Dialogue uses educational modules, and Pastor Wicks and his think tank have added ten modules specifically to unleash leaders into the new cultural realities.

Trying to build a next-generation add-on movement on top of a denominational structure (I use the word "structure" intentionally, as

---

22. Northwest Nazarene University is located in Nampa, Idaho. It is the designated Nazarene education and training institution for the churches of the Pacific Northwest.

23. Jim Wicks, interview by author, Portland, OR, November 29, 2010.

24. Jim Wicks, interview by author, Portland, OR, November 11, 2010.

opposed to "tradition" or "spirituality") is like trying to turn a tank into a sports car. While the idea has virtual inspiration (and would make for a great video game), in reality the tank chassis would eventually crush the project. As Pastor Wicks laments:

> We are facing a crisis if we don't have next-level leadership that is willing to confess a problem. How can we be right for the kingdom? How can we plant as many churches as possible for kingdom? How can we infuse our DNA into something else, some new movement? I don't know how we will survive. The super-structure does not provide for that sort of open-air thinking.[25]

This is an unfortunate reality and pragmatically speaking, this is why Bishop Todd Hunter has quipped on more than one occasion, "It is easier to give birth than raise the dead."

25. Jim Wicks, interview by author, Portland, OR, November 29, 2010.

# Chapter 17

# Do Small

THIS PAST TUESDAY (DECEMBER 1, 2010) at the Lents Commons in Southeast Portland, there was a gathering of sixty leaders from small faith communities around the city, most of which practice some form of hyper-local, communally based church life. It was the semimonthly story-telling roundtable for "Parish Collective–Portland." The group was quite varied in its church expressions. There were "communities" of no more than four people living in neighborhood homes. There was one twenty-five year veteran of communal living from North Portland. There were even a few pastors from more attractional-based Portland churches who came because, as one pastor stated publicly, "I am alone in my church, and it is so refreshing to be with people who think like all of you do."[1]

"Parish Collective is a growing group of churches, missional communities, and faith-based organizations which are rooted in neighborhoods and linked across cities: Edmonton, Vancouver, Seattle, Tacoma, Portland . . . Bellingham, Sacramento, San Francisco."[2] The organizing principle is a geographically based ecclesiology. It is a pressing passion that the hope of the mission of Jesus Christ may very much be found in getting a "smaller" vision: a clearly defined neighborhood, a walking-world, a parish. A mission that is too large ("we want to reach the world," "reach a generation" or even "reach our city") actually leads to impotence and inaction. It is little more than a virtual mission in an increasingly

1. Parish Collective, "Home Page." Quote from James Worley of Powell Valley Covenant Church's Lifechurch.tv contemporary service (located in Gresham, OR) on December 1, 2010 at the Parish Collective–Portland gathering at Lents Commons.

2. Ibid.

rootless virtual world. However, with a clearly defined parish, the community of faith knows what to be responsible for and where the bounds of that responsibility begin and end. As I wrote in a blog post for the Parish Collective:

> For a guy like me, my soul is simply too small to wrap itself around the whole world. I am indebted to religious leaders who delegate the world out in consideration of my limited soul-space. But even a goal like "Love Portland" is more than my mind can handle. A city like Portland is a divine circus of communities, dreams, economic forces, injustices, cultures, policies, sorrows, histories and, most importantly, stories. Just thinking about it all but crashes my spiritual operating system . . . I want to be a part of the stories of my time, be they found on a front-porch, in a dog park, at a neighborhood association meeting, in my kid's cafeteria, at a political rally, or simply across the table from a beautiful someone who, apart from intention, I would never otherwise know.[3]

The Parish Collective is "reaching backwards" to the parish-realities of old, when a city was divided into objective units (parishes), each unit contained one church (parish church), and that church was *responsible*. That spiritual community (clergy and lay alike) was responsible for the joys and injustices, the worshiping and caring, in fact all parts of the meaningful human life (christening, educating, marrying, burying, etc.).

Tim Soerens, one of the founders of the Parish Collective, a now three-year-old network, says:

> Within the context of the neighborhood we can work out the three pillars of the compassionate and justice-practicing church. Those three pillars are "community" based in a theology of the Trinity, "mission" based in participation in the *Misio Dei* and finally, a grounded personal and communal "identity" based in the *Imago Christi*.[4]

Once again, this network is defined more by an organizing principle than by any sort of unique theology.[5] It is the antithesis of "mega-church" or "church-growth" philosophies that reached their climax in the late twen-

---

3. Kriz, "Village Conspiracy."

4. Tim Sorens and Paul Sparks, the founders of Parish Collective, interview by author, Portland, OR, November 23, 2010.

5. Mainline, Charismatic, evangelical, non-Protestant, and emergent communities all participate equally in the life and leadership of the Parish Collective.

tieth century. The focus is not to grow as large as possible, nor is it to attract people from distances, which is only defined by the time consumers are willing to spend sitting in their car (as one parish leader said to me, "Everything changes when you get in your car").[6] The focus is to serve a very given place (clearly geographically defined), and from that bounded space, the community of faith will experience a truly multidimensional and integrated wholeness as all aspects of life are communally shared, from worship to neighborhood association meetings, from chance encounters in a local business to shared walks to and from children's schools.

This organizational style is gaining momentum in post-Christian urban centers. At last Tuesday's Parish Collective–Portland meeting, two dozen communities were represented and most of those had existed fewer than four years. Here is a map of Portland's eastside with some of those communities marked:

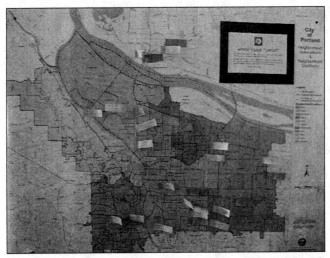

Figure 9. Parish Collective–Portland Communities. Source: Photo taken at the event.

The church is burdened today with a meaning deficit. One way of addressing this deficit is with the sort of integrated life that a parish philosophy presents (sustainability, service, shared life, simplicity), which is infusing meaning where previously many felt none existed.

This return to a parish orientation is birthing in harmony with many trends in secular society. In the urban center of Portland, there is

6. Quote from Eric Shreves, a leader in the "People of Praise," a Roman Catholic-founded intentional community rooted in the Kenton Neighborhood of Portland, OR.

a growing presence of sustainability values and urban homesteading.[7] Young families are increasingly localizing their lives. They are selling their cars, using bikes and metro services; they are buying local and patronizing neighborhood establishments (even when they cost "more"[8] than a suburban "big-box store").[9] My neighborhood in Portland's urban center has three urban-homesteading oriented stores with garden supplies, urban livestock, canning and food preservation resources, rainwater collection, and sustainable cooking services. Oxford University Press's 2007 word of the year was "locavore."[10] "The 'locavore' movement encourages consumers to buy from farmers' markets or even to grow or pick their own food, arguing that fresh, local products are more nutritious and taste better. Locavores also shun supermarket offerings as an environmentally friendly measure, since shipping food over long distances often requires more fuel for transportation."[11] Because of these shifting passions (and I mean *passions*, as whole communities are reorienting the very way they live, spend, work, serve, and schedule), one's local coffee shop, local pub, or local shopping hub have become subjectively meaningful—which begs the assumption that soon one's "local" church could follow in queue as a locus of subjective and integrated meaning. It is hard to explain the phenomenon of self-identification, but much of the population of post-Christian Portland identify themselves most passionately with their

7. Urban Homesteading, "Urban Homestead Definition": 1) a suburban or city home in which residents practice self-sufficiency through home food production and storage; 2) the home and garden of a person or family engaging in sustainable small-scale agriculture and related activities designed to reduce environmental impact and increase self-sufficiency; 3) a name describing the home of a person or family living by principles of low-impact, sustainable self-sufficiency through activities such as gardening for food production, cottage industry, extensive recycling, and generally simple living.

8. There are strong arguments that local shopping ultimately does not cost more since it requires less gas, less wear and tear on vehicles, and less time, which allow for other forms of productivity. These arguments are purely economic and do not even take into account quality of life, relationally driven commerce, or non-economically driven forms of life-investment (family, neighbor, volunteerism, church, etc.).

9. "Big-box store" is a euphemism for high-volume mega stores. The name is derived from the fact that most of these stores are found on huge lots and look like big boxes. Many stores meet the criteria of "big box," from Ikea to Home Depot. Walmart is the most notorious. This conglomerate system of product distribution is critiqued for at least three reasons: destruction of local economies, unjust product acquisition (including slavery and ecological destruction), and poor employee care.

10. Oxford University Press Blog, "Locavore."

11. Ibid.

"village" (another term used for a walking neighborhood), as opposed to the city as a whole.

Pastor Paul Sparks of Zoe Church in Tacoma and a founder of the Parish Collective says:

> The big thing I am proud of is not anything regarding numbers. Zoe members have started seven different small businesses that are their kingdom vocational callings. You can imagine the kind of social fabric that can create. It creates such amazing collaborative possibilities and irreplaceably significant to have the face of the church before the world (for bad or good): how we treat one another, social, governmental. Our best moments are beautiful moments, but our ugliness is also good for us . . . it is a mirror to our lives and shows the part of our lives that are untested and where our faith in Christ needs work.[12]

Tim Soerens's Cascade Neighborhood Church, uncompromisingly rooted in Seattle's South Lake Union, has never grown to more than twenty-five members. But of those attendees, over 90 percent are deeply involved in multiple justice and service missions in the neighborhood. Cascade Neighborhood Church has started three nonprofits.[13] Many of their Sunday gatherings appear more like community-action nonprofits than a church. Pastor Soerens insists that this is not a model of condescension,

> Popular terms like "contextual," "missional," and even "incarnational" can easily be "colonial." In my experience, there is not a lot of language about how we [the worshiping community] are going to be shaped and transformed by the world around us. In order to become truly "incarnational," then you must be reshaped by your context.[14]

As you have probably already guessed, this sort of church life is in many ways the most difficult. It is very difficult to maintain and takes a tenacity of conviction and propensity for risk. Many churches begin with the rhetoric of parish, but quickly betray that vision for streamlined growth and emotionalized worship services. One local Portland church, named after the specific downtown neighborhood in which they mission, seeks to reach their post-Christian "village." It is a wonderful church with a

12. Paul Sparks, interview by author, Portland, OR, November 23, 2010.

13. Cascade Neighborhood Church has also planted two other neighborhood-based churches in their three and a half years of existence.

14. Tim Soerens, interview by author, Portland, OR, November 23, 2010.

great heart for the city. I once asked a table of the church's leadership and committed congregants, "What percentage of your church attendants actually live your neighborhood?" The group stared at one another until one person meekly said, "Probably five percent." He was quickly corrected by an administrative staff member who said, "The percentage actually is much smaller than that."

Pastor Sparks's Zoe Church in downtown Tacoma was founded in 1989 and by the year 2000 had grown to over four hundred congregants. Then in the year 2000, Pastor Sparks, out of his growing conviction for a kingdom mission that is shaped by its context and geographically defined, began to change the vision and rhetoric of his church to embrace these parish ways. Within two years Pastor Sparks's church shrank from four hundred to fifteen.[15]

This is a story that I have heard time and again as pastors commit to convictions that infiltrate their congregants' freedom, comfort, pocketbook, and autonomy. In a world where the consumer is king and the appetites and declarations of that king are fed without temperance, the self-sacrifice and "smallness" of a parish philosophy swim against a very brisk cultural current.

## NEO-MONASTICISM

The close cousin of the parish orientation is the recent resurgence of monastic themes in what is often called "neo-monasticism." Nationally, the movement is linked to names like Shane Claiborne and Jonathan Wilson-Hartgrove. Locally in Portland and more broadly in the Pacific Northwest, there are no leaders' names of note apart from their tireless and selfless, often anonymous commitment to their small and devout communities of faith.

"New Monasticism" is one actual network of these intentional communities across the landscape of North America. They are based on the ancient ways of the monastic life, found in sources like the *Rule of St. Benedict*,[16] a way of "self discipline, and discipline always took the form of order—an ordered day, an ordered community, and ordered life."[17]

15. Paul Sparks, interview by author, Portland, OR, November 23, 2010. These statistics were received directly from Pastor Sparks.

16. Benedict and Timothy Fry, *Rule of St. Benedict*.

17. Kauffman, *Follow Me*, 19.

They are small, intentional, and geographical (if not "one-house") communities built on radical and often vow-based commitments. Those vows may include ancient themes like stability,[18] obedience,[19] relocation,[20] or hospitality.[21]

This is a revolutionary movement.

> . . . We are constantly tempted to form a church that will simply undergird the civil order. A new monasticism refuses that temptation. Given our fragmented world, the church is constantly tempted to import that fragmentation into its life. A new monasticism seeks to heal that fragmentation by rediscovering the *telos* of human life revealed in the gospel. . . . The new monasticism envisioned here is the form by which the church will recover its *telos*, the living tradition of the gospel, the practices and virtues that sustain that faithfulness, and the community marked by faithful living in a fragmented world.[22]

As stated before, these communities tend to be quite small and must remain so because of the high relational commitment and interdependency they foster. They also require an extremely narrow door of entry. Often such communities have a novitiate period of two years or longer, during which the proposed member explores and experiences the community's intense vows and the group has adequate time to discern the proposed member's place (if any) within the community's long-term life.

Church of the Servant King is the most famous such church on Portland's inner eastside. Pastored by Michael and Hilda Munk, they have faithfully practiced monastic living for two decades. In that time, their community has grown to five community houses of varying sizes. They focus on two core vows: stability and obedience. The community has several shared practices and insists upon communal living.

The monastic way stands as an anchor in a fragmented world. Its goal is not to "participate" in culture, but to stand against it like a rock in the shifting surf. The critiques are obvious, the expectations are so high, the way of entry is so narrow, and the lifestyle is often so sequestered that there is little impact on the society as a whole. That is not to say that such

18. Wilson-Hartgrove, *Wisdom of Stability*.

19. Stock, *Inhabiting the Church*, 57–86.

20. Perkins, *With Justice for All*, 60–105.

21. Chittister, *Wisdom Distilled*. See chapter 10.

22. Wilson, *Living Faithfully*, 78.

communities do not seek and participate with the kingdom of God in the world. Never. It is, however, a simple truth that society at large, along with the immediate neighborhood, often has no idea that such communities even exist.

# Chapter 18

# Free Faith (No "Brick and Mortar" Expressions)

A S COMMUNICATED IN THE introduction, people are quitting church. There is no mystery here and really no argument to the contrary. Churches are closing. Religious structures are resourcing a smaller and smaller percentage of the population.

Dave Olson, a researcher for the Evangelical Covenant Church, says that in recent years a significantly smaller number of Americans are "participating in the most basic Christian practices: the weekly gathering for worship, teaching, prayer, and fellowship."[1]

Julia Duin, in her book *Quitting Church*, consolidates several studies and states:

> Because the U.S. population is expanding, evangelical pollster George Barna estimates the number of unchurched Americans is growing by about one million each year. The fraction of Americans with no religious preference doubled during the 1990s from 8 to 14 percent, according to a 2001 City University of New York "American Religious Identification Survey." However, of that 14 percent, less than half (40 percent) were atheists; the other 60 percent were merely "religious" or "spiritual." In other words, plenty of people in this country are interested in spiritual matters. They are simply not going to church to feed this interest.[2]

These statements are indicative of an almost paradoxical dynamic. The unchurched are increasing. However, it appears that many people are not rejecting faith at all. What they are rejecting are the institutional con-

1. Smietana, "Statistical Illusion," 86.
2. Duin, *Quitting Church*, 13.

structs that have defined (or at least represented the primary stage of) the life of faith for much of religious history.

Several movements in contemporary society are nurturing faith and networking the spiritually committed, and are doing so outside tradition-al religious-institutional structures. There are leadership development networks, bible-study systems, and even online expressions.

By way of illustration, one particularly infamous network is most prominently known as "The Fellowship." This particular "network of friends" is so non-institutional that it hardly has a leadership structure. The only publicized expression (event) is the National Prayer Breakfast, which The Fellowship (also known as "The Family") has been overseeing for decades. Jeff Sharlet, in his critical and sensational expose in *Harper's Magazine,* said,

> The Family's only publicized gathering is the National Prayer Breakfast, which it established in 1953 and which, with congres-sional sponsorship, it continues to organize every February in Washington, D.C. Each year 3,000 dignitaries, representing scores of nations, pay $425 each to attend. Steadfastly ecumenical, too bland most years to merit much press, the breakfast is regarded by the Family as merely a tool in a larger purpose: to recruit the powerful attendees into smaller, more frequent prayer meetings, where they can "meet Jesus man to man."[3]

The vast majority of the network, which is loosely called The Fellowship, seeks to arrange and encourage small groups of authentic life, encourage-ment, and mutual faith mentoring. In contrast to Sharlet's commentary above, most of these groups are filled with the most unexceptional of folks, coming from any and every dimension of society. While it is true that there is, at times, an emphasis on societal leaders or business people, even those categories are misunderstood. Jim Eney, an Oregon minister affiliated with The Fellowship, serves (among other priorities) the State Capital Building as a resource and prayer partner. Jim's two days a week in Salem are spent as much with little-known aids and staff members as it is sitting with those who have a "vote" in the capital's hallowed halls. "I am just there to pray with people and talk about the love of Jesus."[4]

---

3. Sharlet, "Jesus Plus Nothing."
4. Jim Eney, interview by author, Portland, OR, December 7, 2010.

The Fellowship believes most strongly in the small group as the instrument of personal change. While it gives no all-encompassing critique of more structured religious institutions (churches), it has a steadfast commitment to these small and organic gatherings, which meet usually weekly in coffee shops, homes, or even workplaces. These groups are attractive because they are relationally driven and because they give greater freedom to leave religious pretense behind. In 1946, the founder of The Fellowship, Abraham Vereide, wrote:

> Man craves fellowship. Most of us want an opportunity to make our feelings known, to relate our personal experiences, to compare notes with others, and, in unity of spirit to receive renewal, inspiration, guidance, and strength from God. Such groups as we are thinking of have characterized every spiritual awakening. Jesus began with Peter and James and John. He had the twelve and the Seventy. At Bethany he established a cell . . . there you have the formula . . . faith embodied the same close informal fellowship . . . one common practice—gathering together in the name of Jesus.[5]

"The goal is to become One-Man [Woman]" as opposed to playing games for the sake of appearance. One of the mottos of The Fellowship is "Jesus plus nothing," meaning the goal is to remove the additional religious layers, which are often superimposed on top of simply following Jesus. They believe those additional layers have a shameful habit of becoming preeminent to the actual teachings of Jesus as taken from the Gospels.

An organization like The Fellowship provides an effective and life-changing work in the life of many individuals. I can say from personal experience that I have never found a better source of personal mentorship and spiritual development (apart from programs) than from individuals associated with The Fellowship, at least in its Oregon expressions.

The critiques of The Fellowship are many and Sharlet's previously listed quote is indicative of those critiques ("It is an elitist organization," "It exists to consolidate power"). And from the religious, it is accused of oversimplifying the Christian message and even hedging toward universalism.

My main concern for such systems is not that they are insignificant or ineffective (or heretical, for that matter). My concern is that they exist

---

5. Wikipedia, "The Fellowship." Original source is now out of print: Vereide and John Magee (chaplain to President Harry Truman) called "Together" (Abingdon Cokesbury), 1946.

in very tight veins of society. In truth, there is a secretiveness to them, as Sharlet claims. However, it is not in some malicious or "Illuminati"[6] sort of way. Instead, the secretiveness is to keep the introductions relationally driven and intimate. It is also to help foster a place of trust, so that even the dirty and shameful mistakes and addictions of life can be shared, prayed for, and ultimately forgiven and corrected. Unfortunately, because of this secretiveness, a group like The Fellowship (as an organization or association) has essentially zero visible presence in my neighborhood (or really any neighborhood on Portland's inner eastside). That is not to say Fellowship people are not there. They are, but you could not find them if you searched. Furthermore, because it resources the churched (or more accurately the de-churched or disillusioned church) through relational networks, interested non-Christians have no pathway to engage.

6. A term assigned to an often-imagined secret society that exists to rule the world.

# Chapter 19

# Going Ancient (Roman Catholicism and Eastern Orthodoxy)

ONE OF THE UNPREDICTABLE backlashes of post-Modernity, which is primarily a reaction against the post-Enlightenment cognitive construct often called "Modernity," has been the loss of *reliable truth*. Or to put it another way, with the surfacing of a more subjective orientation toward truth (or the loss of "absolute truth" as many theo-philosophers have framed it), many are seeking a new construct for personal and psychological assurance. Over the last couple of centuries, Western culture has taught its children that we can trust our minds: *cogito ergo sum* ("I think, therefore I am.") But with the rise of cognitive relativism and the deconstruction of propositionally driven ideologies/theologies, much of society longs for a new existential anchor. One place that some have gone to is objective church authority. Inspired by beliefs like "the one true Church" (and its close cousin "the original and purest Church"), "unbroken apostolic succession," and "absolute ecclesial authority," some are finding solace and comfort in submission to an ancient tradition. This is why books like *Why I Am Still a Catholic*[1] and Gillquist's *Becoming Orthodox*[2] have been so widely read.

Having watched several friends and spiritual confidants "convert" from free-church evangelicalism (emergent and otherwise) to one of these two traditions, I see that a major drive is ultimately, as suggested above, the need for authoritative assurance. This assurance is inevitably

1. Ryan and Ryan, *Why I Am Still a Catholic.*
2. Gillquist, *Becoming Orthodox.*

based in a historically argued, ecclesial-hierarchical, and absolute church construct. To oversimplify for clarity, the question is: "Why is it true?" The answer is: "Because *the* church says it is true." This authoritative appeal certainly works for the macro-questions: Is there a God? Is the Christian way true? Is there salvation and forgiveness? It also appeals in the far more nuanced questions of theological detail: What is the process of experiencing existential forgiveness? Can grace take on ontological forms? What is the means of soteriological assurance? This longing for clarity comes from a spiritual fatigue generated by philosophical inconsistencies from evangelical authorities or answers that hinge on subjective confirmation ("you will just know when it is right"). A portion of society is screaming, "Will someone just tell me what is right and how to believe?!"[3]

Another motivation for this ancient attraction is the longing for the unique sort of meaning that comes from the sign and symbol of historical forms. The simple reality that the system of faith and worship has been around so long, and because its processes (wording, liturgy, symbolism, structure, etc.) have been repeated and affirmed over so many centuries, makes these forms "feel" meaningful. This motivation is one that I can relate to and is why I have understood those who have come across my path who desire history (and maybe why I have known so many who have either converted or wrestled with conversion). So to find these assurances and meanings, they convert, and in my experience they convert in equal measure to Roman Catholicism or Eastern Orthodoxy.

The reality is that the group that actually embraces a conversion such as this is very small. It is small for a variety of reasons. First, it is small because this sort of conversion appeals to the sort of person who gets "stuck in their head." I am not talking about academic people necessarily (though they are found in this group). I am talking about the sort of folks who get internally handcuffed to questions and doubts. Their internal dialogue creates a sense of crisis that leads them to make a radical step of this kind. This step is radical because it requires a philosophical reprogramming. The same mind that can't let go of questions and doubts

---

3. This same longing, this assurance deficit, has also led to the occasional exceptional influence of theologically precise and authoritatively delivered philosophies of church. The most prevalent example currently would be the hyper-Reformed movement that has surfaced anew in recent years. To appeal to this psychological phenomenon, these ecclesiologies are conveyed in absolutes and defend a distinctly hierarchical authority structure.

now must agree to surrender its "vote" and, in a sense, give over decision making to a tradition. That may just sound like historical Christianity, but understand that this is a group that is ironically ruled by their cognitive processes. Second, to make this conversion, the individual must be willing to risk "losing their past." These converts are for the most part evangelical and mostly conservative evangelical. They risk alienating parents, friends, and former social and spiritual communities. It is my experience that this group, once the decision is made to convert, experiences at least three years of painful arguing to "prove" their decision to loved ones. And in the end they often establish a new social fabric with only their closest friends and confidants remaining close. Because of their natural religious fervor, they often come out of professional ministry positions in free-church models (or para-church models)[4] or leadership roles in whatever tradition they left.

My main critique of this trend is the limited viability it has to affect the broader population. For the most part, it happens in anonymous corners of Christendom. This is not Christian "conversion" in the ultimate sense. In fact, I don't know of anyone who has made such a conversion from a truly non-churched or non-Christian background (though I have no doubt that there are many examples). Also, Roman Catholicism and especially Eastern Orthodoxy have little emphasis (and certainly nothing comprehensive) on mission/evangelism to the greater culture. Roman Catholicism has a larger marketing problem as they carry a generally negative stereotype within the culture at large. Our study in North Portland revealed that Catholicism has the largest credibility gap with a 44.6 percent negative impression rating, and among those who offered some sort of impression (not neutral), only 12.4 percent had a positive rating.[5] This was among the worst impressions of the traditions we researched. Eastern Orthodoxy on the other hand has a predominantly neutral rating, neither positive nor negative. This fact does offer tremendous opportunity to the Orthodox Church in its varying nationalistic manifestations. However, it is also indicative of Orthodoxy's core issue: they have hidden themselves from the greater culture. In Portland, Orthodox churches exist in sequestered corners of the city. Their small congregations are mostly made

---

4. As Gillquist testifies through *Becoming Orthodox*. Gillquist comes out of a para-church ministerial background.

5. Evangelicals and Mormons rated the worst in our study of zip code 97217. To see the complete results of our study, see the appendix.

up of recent immigrants and social recluses. Their services are often not in English (totally or in part). Father George of St. Nicolas's church in Southwest Portland admits that his tradition has little to no emphasis on intentional mission to the city.[6] In fact, when I surveyed the content and "index of subjects" of Bishop Kallistos Ware's book, *The Orthodox Way*,[7] a highly regarded summary of the Orthodox faith, I found no entries or references to "mission," "evangelism," "outreach," "justice," "proclamation," "Great Commission," or any other missional term I could think of.

6. I interviewed Father George in February of 2010 for a group project on Eastern Orthodoxy for Dr. Carole Spencer's class at George Fox University: DMIN 541, Historical Models of Spiritual Formation.

7. Ware, *Orthodox Way*, 157–59.

# Chapter 20

# Final Thoughts

IN CONCLUSION, I WOULD like to restate what I said in this section's first pages: "It would be impossible to be exhaustive in examining and evaluating all such strategies, so I will choose a selection that are current in the mainstream Christian world, specifically focusing my comments on strategies that are currently active in Portland's urban center . . . I am asking an *effectiveness* question. In what ways does (or doesn't) each strategy actually draw citizens in our post-Christian society[1] into faith in Christ and church life? The purpose is not to criticize. In fact, many of my comments will be very complimentary."

I am proud of my brothers and sisters in the faith from each of the traditions and strategies listed here. I have walked with many of them as they compassionately labor for God's kingdom. Of that fact, I have little doubt.

As we examine the map of the church's work, it reveals the reality of our limited *real* influence on the society at large, particularly the inner-city, post-Christian society of a city like Portland, Oregon. Many of these strategies exist in what are effectively anonymous pockets. And those that do offer a more public or proclamational quality are mostly consolidating the last vestiges of suburban Christendom.

We live in a new world. No one strategy will be a cure-all.

I would like to suggest one movement that might help the church take a huge step in the right direction: Anglican liturgical churches that exist for the sake of others.

1. As opposed to simply more effectively consolidating the remaining vestiges of "Christian culture."

# SECTION 6

# A Hope in Eucharistic Liturgy

As long as you notice, and have to count the steps, you are not yet danc-
ing but only learning to dance. A good shoe is a shoe you don't notice.
Good reading becomes possible when you need not consciously think
about eyes, or light, or print, or spelling. The perfect church service
would be the one we were almost unaware of; our attention would have
been on God.[1]

C.S. Lewis

THERE IS AN OLD joke. It goes like this:

> A group of friends are hiking through the woods. They come upon
> a bear a ways up the path. The bear starts to charge and all the
> friends turn to run; all of them that is, except one. One man drops
> to the ground and starts to put on his running shoes.
> The man closest to him grabs him by the sleeve and says, "What
> are you doing? You will never outrun that bear!"
> The man on the ground calmly responds, "I don't need to out-
> run the bear. I only need to outrun you."

This joke is about survival, and it illustrates one definition of success. It
also illustrates the philosophy of the church's mission in America for some
time. Granted, that is a cynical interpretation. However, the statistics do
not lie. Some churches are growing, but they are filling their pews with
the diaspora of their church neighbors: mainline to evangelical, evangelical to mega church, mega church to emergent church, on and on it goes.

---

1. C.S. Lewis, *Letters to Malcolm*, 4–5.

And each time we reshuffle and redeal the congregational deck, many more of those precious cards simply slip off the table.

Maybe it is time to stop trying to outrun our friends.

Maybe it is time to face the bear.

The bear is our increasingly post-Christian world, with its post-Christian perspectives and post-Christian values. The bear is not evil. Let me say that again. *The bear is not evil.* It is a daunting, strong, resourceful, determined, and ultimately beautiful creation of the Most High. "God saw all that he had made, and it was very good."[2] The bear is on a quest and it is the same quest whether we (the church) stumble along its path or not. He wants to be fed. And he wants his meal to be satisfying—a meal that was made for his appetites, that nourishes his particular physiology—and not a meal that was made for some other sort of creature.

2. Gen 1:31a.

# Chapter 21

# Preliminary Thoughts

MANY TRADITIONS PRACTICE LITURGICAL worship. Among the liturgies there is much that is shared (see chapter 11). In an attempt to protect against overgeneralization, this book will make specific observations based on the Anglican Eucharistic liturgy. I encourage you to then apply these observations to your particular tradition.

## CLARIFYING THE CONTEXT

This book's purpose is to provide an essential dimension for the conversation about the Christian church and post-Christian culture. It is accomplishing that precious goal by tightly dialing the sociological and ecclesiological discussion onto a small and distinct population within a single zip code. From that vantage point, the goal is to offer one missing element, a particular structure and tradition, which will help woo many post-Christian people back to intimate and integrated worship and obedience of God in Christ. Also, while the implications of these conclusions are no doubt farther reaching, my specific concern and construct here is only the post-Christendom context we are currently living amongst in the urban centers of the Pacific Northwest—specifically, Portland, Oregon. From this point forward, to provide simplicity for you and sanity for me, I will refer to this specific context simply as "post-Christian culture." I am sure you can see the wisdom in this choice.

## CONTINUITY

One reality has already been consistently argued throughout this book, particularly in sections 2 and 3. That reality is this: Liturgical worship has tenaciously lasted the test of time, space, and culture. Its use in the ancient church is so clear and widespread that it would seem as if the liturgy has always been there. It has walked as the near constant companion of the church through her diverse and tumultuous history. It has thrived from periods of mass persecution to imperial mandate. It has thrived through the transitions from ancient to pre-modern to modern times and during the Middle Ages, Reformation, Renaissance, and Industrial Revolution. It thrived through the expanse of the Western Church and the Eastern Church. It has thrived from global North to global South. It has withstood communism and thrived within the Soviet block. It has survived innumerable wars (sometimes between Christian traditions) and thirteen hundred years of near-constant conflict with Islam, crossed centuries and continents, and planted and birthed within innumerable cultures and languages. So the question is this: How could we possibly believe that we are in some new frontier, so unique in all of the multidimensional streams of human expression, that we will inexplicably find these ancient ways meaningless? Is it now, after the cultures and generations of the human story have voted time and time again that the liturgy is meaningful and life-giving, that suddenly post-Christian humanity simply woke up, made of some new metal? Thinking people should begin their pursuit with what has most often been true.

## ANONYMITY IS OPPORTUNITY

I will make suggestions and arguments for new liturgical churches in post-Christian cultures, and I will be making these arguments from an Anglican perspective. One could wisely ask, Why Anglicanism? Why not the Presbyterian liturgy, or the Lutheran, etc.? Many of the unique features of Anglican structure and worship will be illuminated throughout this chapter. However, one preliminary idea will answer that important question. Anglicanism has a unique opportunity that other liturgical denominations do not: a chance to write its own press release. Anglicans are generally a mystery (anonymity) to the general public, and that provides a great opportunity. To demonstrate this anonymity, I will draw once again on our research here in zip code 97217.[1] The final section of our survey asked respondents their impression of a selection of Christian denominations/traditions. Each of the 193 residents was asked to rate twelve traditions[2] on a scale of 1–5 (one being strongly negative impressions, five being strongly positive impression, and three being an equal number of positive and negative impressions). The other option was "no impression" if the respondent hadn't had any real contact with the tradition (personally or publicly). For the twelve traditions, here is the number of "no impressions" logged:

### *Number of "No Impressions"*

| | |
|---|---|
| Roman Catholic | 28 |
| Charismatic | 96 |
| Emergent | 138 |
| Lutheran | 50 |
| Evangelical | 29 |
| Anglican | 92 |
| Baptist | 25 |

1. See the appendix.

2. These particular "traditions" were chosen for a number of reasons. First of all, as the survey indicates, it would be impossible to be exhaustive or even truly representative of the breadth of Christian traditions, so these are simply a sample of Christian traditions. They are listed in no particular order.

I've included "traditions" some might question. "Charismatic" and "Pentecostal" were both included because I did not know which term those outside of Christendom were more familiar with (I learned that they have more familiarity with Pentecostalism). I chose "Emergent" because it is a recurring topic in this book and though I assumed that it is more of an insider's term and would be little known outside of Christendom, which the survey confirmed, it also made for a good control case in our experiment. "Roman Catholic" and "Eastern Orthodox (Russian, Greek, etc.)" were included because they represent such a massive percentage of Christians globally and because they are referenced in this book. "Church of Jesus Christ and Latter Day Saints (Mormons)" was included because I wanted to test and see if they are perceived as poorly outside of Christendom as they have been within Christendom. It is also worth noting that there were no reports of respondents questioning, "Why were Mormons included in a list of Christian denominations?" We Christians need to accept that the Mormons are perceived as our brethren.

One possible criticism of this list is that it does not include "Episcopalians." After considerable thought, this was an intentional decision. I wanted to get an uncluttered impression of the term "Anglican" and I thought that would be best accomplished if it was not juxtaposed near the term "Episcopalian."

| Methodist | 50 |
|---|---|
| Eastern Orthodox | 65 |
| Pentecostal | 57 |
| Mormon | 20 |
| Presbyterian | 48 |

Of those that did have some specified impression (meaning they did not claim "no impression"), expressed on our one-to-five scale (one strongly negative and five strongly positive), here is the average numerical response:

*Average 1–5 Score*

| Roman Catholic | 2.4 |
|---|---|
| Charismatic | 2.2 |
| Emergent | 2.5 |
| Lutheran | 2.9 |
| Evangelical | 2.0 |
| Anglican | 2.8 |
| Baptist | 2.5 |
| Methodist | 2.9 |
| Orthodox | 2.8 |
| Pentecostal | 2.2 |
| Mormon | 2.0 |
| Presbyterian | 2.9 |

We can make some conclusions from this data. One application (forgive me this one-sided discussion) is that Christians in post-Christian contexts need, for the sake of mission, to avoid associating with the term "evangelical."[3] Most everyone has an opinion of the term "evangelical" (only twenty-nine "no impressions," which equals 15 percent); it also

---

3. Tomlinson, *Post Evangelical*, 16. "The post-evangelical impulse does not necessarily imply a move away from Christian orthodoxy or evangelical faith. Rather it demonstrates that to remain true to a tradition, we must come to terms with its changing cultural context in order to find an authentic expression of that tradition—'you have to change to stay the same.'"

records the second largest percentage[4] of "negative impressions" of any tradition (57.5 percent of respondents) and the lowest average ranking among those with impressions (2.0). It is clear, at least in 97217, that "evangelical" is not a well-regarded term.[5]

It is worth noting that among the one-to-five ratings, all the best-regarded denominations/traditions are liturgical traditions (with the exception of Roman Catholic): Lutheran, Presbyterian, Methodist, Eastern Orthodox, and Anglican.

There is another fact that separates Anglicanism from the other traditions, liturgical and non-liturgical. Let's look at the number of "no impressions" recorded for "Anglican." As you can see, there were ninety-two "no impressions" responses, the most of any tradition with exception to "emergent" and "charismatic," which are more Christian insider terms. Those ninety-two responses represent 47.4 percent. Also, Anglican received only 16.6 percent negative impressions (compare that to Roman Catholic 44.6 percent, Evangelical 61.1 percent, Baptist 42.0 percent, and Lutheran 23.3 percent). All of this means that the Anglican tradition can move through the post-Christian world with relatively little baggage. It has the ability to be both ancient and established[6] (something that will be important in post-Christendom as we will discuss later) and functionally mysterious to the average person. Therefore, Anglican churches have a chance to define themselves in the public sphere in a way that is relatively free of societal bias.

---

4. Only "Mormons" recorded more negative perceptions: 118 of 193 or 61 percent negative impression.

5. One could speculate and comment as to why the word "evangelical" has become so poorly regarded. America's recent political history has contributed to this decline. Whatever the reasons, the word does not translate into our post-Christian culture. The word "evangelical" is not a Bible word. It did not come from Jesus. In fact it is a fairly new term. From a church-insider point of view, I understand that the word is filled with wonderful connotations. However, a word is only valuable for what it communicates. Anyone who continues to use a word like "evangelical" in the public sphere (assuming it is received poorly and for that matter is inconsistent with the speaker's intent) is doing so for self-serving reasons, even if the intent is positive and honest.

6. A movement could label itself something new (like "emergent") and also have a relatively mysterious stigma. However, it is unique to be ancient and established and also enough of an unknown commodity to be able to write your own press release. The other tradition that could potentially claim the same is the Eastern Orthodox Church (if only they had a missional orientation and entrepreneurial structure).

## A LIMITED WINDOW

It is only responsible to point out that this bias-free window will have a limited lifespan. As the presence of Anglicanism grows, both through more and more Anglican churches being planted and because of news stories related to the Anglican Church, this currently clean canvas will be cluttered with images, impression, and opinions (both positive and negative). The plot line that offers the most potential drama is the ongoing relationship and comparison between Anglicanism and Episcopalianism. We are witnessing a season of sad separation between these historical ecclesial brothers. With separation comes pain. So far, most of the press has been on a local level, as historically Episcopalian churches choose as a local community to leave the Episcopal family and submit instead to Anglican leadership structures. These exits involve large amounts of money (especially when you consider historical properties and loss of annual dues), and relational severing with its correlated emotions (shame, anger, betrayal, etc.). One Episcopal church found on Portland's periphery, St. Matthew's, chose to leave their Episcopal heritage in May of 2010. A series of stories in the state newspaper, *The Oregonian*, followed the split throughout that month. Nancy Haught, a religion features writer for the paper wrote, "With a reputation as a conservative congregation, St. Matthew's had for sixty-six years included people who read the Bible almost literally and others who interpreted it from more liberal points of view. But over time, that range grew problematic. On March 21, a majority of St. Matthew's members voted to leave the church."[7] The issues listed were generally a divide between "liberal" and "conservative" theology, with divergent views of biblical authority and homosexuality as the most prevalent. This story came and went with little fanfare, but with the entrenchment of the Episcopal Church in America's story,[8] the prevalence and power of this national narrative will only grow. It is also responsible to note that this Episcopal/Anglican divide is helping set the pieces in place for a national (even international) debate on a theology of homosexuality. The conversation is escalating with the release of numerous

7. Haught, "Anglican Parish Splits."

8. It has been called our unofficial national church, since so many of the founding fathers were Episcopalians, resulting in, among other national distinctives, The United States National Cathedral being under the Episcopal Church.

books including *A Church at War: Anglicans and Homosexuality* by Stephen Bates,[9] *Church in Crisis: The Gay Controversy and the Anglican Communion* by Oliver O'Donovan,[10] and *Homosexuality and the Crisis of Anglicanism* by William L. Sachs.[11] Regardless of whether one feels this debate is important, the collateral damage will include more negative impressions of the Christian church as a whole, and specifically this burgeoning Anglican work and continuing Episcopal mission in North America.[12]

9. Bates, *Church at War*.

10. O'Donovan, *Church in Crisis*.

11. Sachs, *Homosexuality*. It is important to note that this debate is being chummed from both sides of the table. The books listed above are looking for both a more progressive anthropology (which includes sexuality and identity) and maintaining a conservative view. I would add to this list Hassett, *Anglican Communion in Crisis*.

12. Snook, "Reaching New People." 112. The tension between Anglicanism and Episcopalianism will most likely also receive additional fuel from the fact that Anglicanism is planting churches and growing in North America while, according to Snook, "Churchwide, the Episcopal church has not kept pace with population growth. New generations of young people are not finding their way to our church: the Episcopal Church is significantly older than the population at large, losing 19,000 member per year by virtue of our age structure alone. Overall our average Sunday attendance fell 10.5% from 2003–2007."

# Chapter 22

# Anglican Mission in Motion

THOUGH YOUNG AND LITTLE known, the Anglican movement is here.
The Anglican Mission[1] to the United States and particularly its post-
Christian urban centers has already arrived and is trekking forward. It has
vision, leadership, and determination. However, its arrival came along a
difficult road: a road through Rwanda.

The Right Reverend John Kabango Rucyahana wrote in the introduction to his book, *The Bishop of Rwanda*:

> In 1994, at least 1,117,000 innocent people were massacred in a
> horrible genocide in Rwanda, my homeland in central Africa. We
> are still finding bodies—buried in pits, dumped in rivers, chopped
> in pieces. Besides providing the details of the very sad story, my
> goal with this book is to tell an amazing, uplifting story. It is the
> story of the new Rwanda, a country that has turned to God, and
> which God is blessing.[2]

And which God is using to bless the world.

His book goes on to tell the tale of Rwanda's healing from one of the
greatest atrocities in human history: in one hundred days, over a million
souls were killed by soldier and neighbor, by bullet and machete, in hut,
hospital, and school. Into the wake of this great pain, church leaders, born
in Rwanda but living outside its borders, returned out of divine obedience
to love and serve their devastated land (leaders like Rev. John Rucyahana
and Rev. Emmanuel Kolini). They began by listening. Over time, through
a prayer-saturated story like few the world has ever known, they watched

1. Also called the Anglican Mission in America (AMIA).

2. Rucyahana, *Bishop of Rwanda*, xv.

144

a movement of forgiveness and reconciliation emerge all around them— Rwanda today is a modern parable of the Spirit in motion.

"There is no barrier that cannot be overcome and no division that cannot be healed. What could be worse than the violence that happened in Rwanda? If the Rwandan situation can be amended by repentance and forgiveness, and the people here can be reconciled enough to live together again, it can happen anywhere in the world."[3] Later, Rev. Rucyahana said,

> There cannot be any cruelty greater than the cruelty that was in Rwanda, and therefore there is no grace greater than the grace that is in Rwanda. It is a grace that frees people from great cruelty and allows them to share life. And that grace comes from the cross of Jesus Christ.[4]

This belief and passion for what "can happen anywhere in the world" turned the eyes of these Rwandan saints to other spiritual famines around the world. In 1997, "John Rucyahana stepped off the plane in Myrtle Beach. We did not know that day—none of us did—that the arrival of this Anglican bishop from the global South would mark the beginning of a massive correction in the United States."[5] And by the year 2000 the Anglican Mission had begun. Thaddeus Barnum records Rucyahana's declaration to The Mission:

> Go and do the work: preach the gospel, evangelize, start new churches, bring existing churches into the world, and send them into mission. Start with humility. . . . You have all the tools you need for this Anglican witness in Jesus Christ to grow . . . now go and preach the Gospel everywhere. Grow the church. We are part of you.[6]

This Anglican Mission has grown. "Established in 2000 as a missionary outreach of the Anglican Church of Rwanda, the Anglican Mission has focused on planting churches throughout North America, adding on average one new congregation every three weeks."[7] In January 2009, a fresh initiative was launched to focus specifically on urban centers of the West Coast. This initiative, called "Churches for the Sake of Others (C4SO)", is

3. Ibid., 221.
4. Ibid., 222.
5. Barnum, *Never Silent*, 66.
6. Ibid., 223.
7. The Anglican Mission, "Identity."

being led by church planting expert Todd Hunter, who was supernaturally called to serve the Mission and now functions as a missionary bishop.[8] Bishop Hunter's mandate is to plant churches, and particularly

> C4SO sees Jesus Christ as a transformer of culture and holds to an incarnational theology. We uphold the ancient creeds of the church with a strong missional emphasis upon the poor and needy. Missional engagement begins with church planters living within their context and listening to the people in their communities. In turn, the C4SO leadership will be listening to the individual churches that emerge. The overall purpose is to inspire followers of Jesus for the sake of others. My team is committed to engaging the post-modern, post-Christian culture and drawing the unchurched and dechurched to Christ by going where they are.[9]

This Anglican story answers any doubts about the organizational viability of Anglican church planting in post-Christian urban centers. It has vision, support, leadership, and authority. It also, in consideration of post-Christendom's critique, has credibility, for men and women who "have the right to speak" lead it.

8. Bishop Hunter tells his story in his book *The Accidental Anglican: The Surprising Appeal of the Liturgical Church.*

9. Churches for the Sake of Others, "Hear the Story."

# Chapter 23

# Anglican Liturgy and a Post-Christian Encounter with Truth

I WAS AT A gathering with Michael, a Masai warrior from Kenya, who recently received his PhD in indigenous theology from Asbury College.
"I am a follower of Jesus," he said. "I call myself a nomadic Christian." One
highly educated man present asked him, "Michael, have you killed the
lion?" He asked this because he had some knowledge of the Masai right of
passage, when boys are sent out to kill a lion. Michael responded, "There
are too few lions today and our land depends too much upon the lion for
us to kill them." Later, in the same gathering, Michael gave a traditional
blessing to a Lakota[1] brother named Richard. In his blessing, Michael exhorted Richard "to kill the lion." I was confused as to what Michael meant.
Then he continued, "Richard, kill the lion, and the lion that we must kill
is the lion of Modernity."

## SCRIPTURE

In early Christendom, the Bible was viewed as a mystical text, something
to be uncompromisingly revered. It came from the "church," and that is
really all that needed to be said

In later Christendom, particularly post-Enlightenment Modernity,
the Bible was viewed as a source of factual "truth." Now to what extent it is
the source of truth, that was the main topic of debate. Were the Scriptures
reliable only on the topics of faith and morality? Or did they also speak

---

1. The Lakota are members of the Sioux nation, originally from what is now called
the American upper Midwest.

147

universally to the topics of science, history, and society? And finally the dominant argument: Is the Bible a perfect book? And by "perfect" theologians meant was it error free. In the times of latter Christendom, these debates were fueled by secular materialism (or the absence of the spiritual dimension of reality) to textual criticism with initiatives like The Jesus Seminar. The Jesus Seminar was a group of New Testament scholars (led by Marcus Borg of Portland along with others) who came together to judge the words and actions of Jesus in the Gospels and to determine how historically authentic those items were. They voted on a four-step scale signified by colored beads: black for not authentic, gray for most likely not authentic, pink for possibly authentic, and red for most likely authentic. I give this brief description here of The Jesus Seminar because it is an excellent parable of the greater cultural phenomena of this era. The primary purpose of the individual in response to the Bible was to vote. And ultimately that opinion was about if and how to validate or invalidate the text. This is an important point, because I find that many people think that forces like The Jesus Seminar (and the popular voting that happens in general society) are "post-Christian" expressions, but they are not. In these moments, the Bible (Christianity) is still reacted to as a strong player in society and its cognitive constructs. The Bible is still an anxious document. No matter what part of the "Bible as truth" spectrum one might land on, the general tone is an anxious one. As Edwin Friedman says, "Differentiation is the lifelong process of striving to keep one's being in balance through the reciprocal external and internal processes of self-definition and self-regulation . . . with the minimum reactivity to the positions and reactivity of others."[2] When people are not differentiated, they respond as an "anxious presence." Emotions spike, becoming incongruent with the circumstances at hand. "Anxiety's major tone is seriousness, often an affliction in itself. It is always content-oriented."[3]

In post-Christendom, the anxiousness toward the Scriptures evaporates. Allow me to explain:

I served as a volunteer chaplain at Reed College from 2000 through 2003. If post-Christian culture (in its North American form) could be distilled into its purest form, what would be left over might just be in the shape and smell of Reed College. Why is that? Each year Princeton

2. Friedman et al., *Failure of Nerve.*

3. Friedman, *Generation to Generation,* 209.

Review[4] compiles approximately 122,000 survey results from students at 373 schools. An average of 325 students comment from each school. One popular category upon which these 373 schools are ranked is titled "Most Religious." Routinely, and expectedly, schools like Brigham Young, Wheaton, and Notre Dame[5] find themselves at the top of this list. At the list's bottom can routinely be found schools like Lewis and Clark College (also in Portland, Oregon), Vassar, Emerson, and yes, every year, Reed College is among the very last. 2011 was a banner year for Reed as it climbed to the unprecedented height of fifth from the last.[6] Additionally, Reed is one of the most academically stringent and robust campuses in the country. Loren Pope, former education editor for *The New York Times,* writes about Reed in *Colleges that Change Lives,* saying, "If you're a genuine intellectual, live the life of the mind, and want to learn for the sake of learning, the place most likely to empower you is not Harvard, Yale, Princeton, Chicago, or Stanford. It is the most intellectual college in the country—Reed in Portland, Oregon."[7] There may not be a better place in North America to both experience post-Christianity in all its integrated expressions and also to have thoughtful discussions, both impassioned and objective, about its personal and societal implications.

At Reed College, every incoming student must take Humanities 110: Introduction to Western Humanities. In this course students read a library's worth of the formative texts of Western society from the ancient Mediterranean up through the rise of the Roman Empire including Homer, Herodotus, Thycydides, Plato, and Petronius (I audited Humanities 110 one year and I assure you, it was even more daunting then you could imagine). Along with these other great texts, each student reads close to one fourth of the Bible, hears lectures on the profound contribution of the Judeo-Christian texts, and argues in conference[8] the necessary place

4. Princeton Review, "Home Page."

5. Ibid. The top five schools on the 2011 Princeton Review survey were Brigham Young University (Utah), Thomas Aquinas College (California), Wheaton College (Illinois), Hillsdale College (Michigan), and the University of Dallas (Texas).

6. Ibid. The bottom five schools on the 2011 Princeton Review survey were Sarah Lawrence College (New York), Bennington College (Vermont), Vassar College (New York), Eugene Lang College—The New School (New York), and Reed College (Oregon).

7. Pope, *Colleges that Change Lives*, 354.

8. "Conference" is a learning structure consistent throughout Reed's educational culture, in which in addition to sitting in larger lecture halls and learning from learned scholars, each student also meets with a small group of fellow students to argue and apply

of the Bible in society, in history, and in a complete intellectual construct. These students are nonanxious in their response to Scripture. It is not a threatening book. Nor is it a source of validation. It is a profound piece of history, philosophy, religion, and society, coequal with the other greatest texts of human history. It is to be honored and revered as such.

From the post-Christian cultural perspective, the Bible is an ancient, foundational, and transcendent book that for a thoughtful and complete life *needs* to be read (as opposed to *ought* to be read). Therefore, a spiritual paradigm in which people simply read the Scriptures regularly and consistently makes sense. What's more, people standing, honoring, and declaring the ancient text,[9] often without "contemporary editorializing," will find it having more import than it could have in Modernity. The Anglican liturgy, with its weekly declarative readings and daily offices, is positioned perfectly to fulfill this cultural priority.

Post-Christendom is not anxious about religion,[10] but it also does not want to be manipulated by an organizational agenda. In light of this it is important to ask: Who chooses which biblical passages are read at a given service? In the educational model of the free-church, it is a leader (Can I trust him?) or a committee of people (Secret committee? What is their agenda?). These people choose the sermon topics and passages to be read, as well as the pace and focus of those readings, and within Christian culture that is a reasonable process, since the pastor is revered

---

the texts within the peer-on-peer dialectic.

9. In section 7 I will make suggestions and give commentary about Scripture declaration for the post-Christian context. Specifically, I will add here, the Anglican tradition of walking to the center of the room to read the Gospel Reading and standing under a lamp to do so has transcendent beauty.

10. To further support this idea of post-Christendom being far less "anxious" about religion than her modernist predecessors, when we conducted our independent survey of zip code 97217, most everyone we stopped was more than content to give a few moments to answer questions about faith and religious perceptions. Those who did refuse always refused to answer *any* questions and always because of a time excuse: "I don't have time right now." The only times someone refused (this happened twice) to answer only a portion of the questions was in the "perceptions of Christian denominations/traditions" section and their reasoning was a desire for "peace among people" and "no desire to judge others." These people were more than happy, however, to comment about their own practices and beliefs.

In contrast to this, according to Wicker, 5 percent of the people approached in 2001 to take the American Religious Identification Survey refused to discuss their own religious beliefs/affiliation, while our survey revealed no one with similar hesitations. Wicker, *Fall of the Evangelical Nation*, 209.

as a benevolent CEO in charge of our spiritual development and product distribution. In contrast, a liturgical sacred experience appeals to a larger narrative. The passages being read were not decided by the pastor, and they were not chosen because there is a "building fund" to stimulate; the passages read each week were chosen in ancient times and affirmed again and again by innumerable cultures over generations. They are simultaneously shared across time and space by the people of God. These passages, read in a regular cycle, are the meta-narrative of the sacred.

## SYMBOL

Clifford Geertz, in his essay "Ethos, World View, and the Analysis of Sacred Symbols," comments on the unique role of sacred symbols. He says they "relate an ontology and a cosmology to an aesthetics and a morality, their peculiar power comes from their presumed ability to identify fact with value at the most fundamental level, to give to what is otherwise merely actual a comprehensive normative import. . . . The tendency to synthesize worldview and ethos . . . if it is not philosophically justified, it is at least pragmatically universal."[11] As Geertz goes on to say, sacred symbols both validate belief and motivate action. How do they do that? Their power "is made intellectually reasonable by being shown to represent a way of life by the actual state of affairs that the worldview describes, and the worldview is made emotionally acceptable by being presented as an image of an actual state of which such a way of life is an authentic expression."[12] The symbol's sacramental reality, embodied in its very real, meaning-filled presence, both affirms and inspires.

It has become old hat to say that symbols, such as sacred objects, have a meaning that transcends words. They embody an entire narrative. Think of a national flag, a peace symbol, or a wedding ring. A small, still object can contain a narrative that fills volumes.

In the Christendom of Modernity, sacred symbols were often replaced. New churches were given taupe walls and uncluttered stages. The aesthetic was reflective of the performance hall to ensure that it remained "multi-use." That is not to say that symbols don't remain. All those utilitarian choices are very important embodied symbols and they most certainly preach (removable chairs, bare walls, stain-resistant carpet, large

11. Geertz, *Interpretation of Cultures*.
12. Ibid.

sound-board, projection screens). Other meaning-filled symbols include the podium, the band, and the sound system. Ancient symbols were removed. The Baptist church of my youth, built in 1884, was colorless outside the cabernet carpet. It had a raised tower of a lectern. The single cross was reductionist in style and we were instructed that you "never leave Jesus on the cross." Communion was celebrated only once a month and only in an evening service, using small plastic cups (like cough syrup) and chalky pellets of bread (like aspirin). This symbolism taught me as young boy a lasting narrative: the Communion was a hassle (minimally practiced and relegated to an unimportant moment in the week), it was individual (taken alone in one's seat), disposable (using the most inexpensive and pragmatic of elements), and it existed to catalyze a sensation of moral guilt toward healing, for the message was to "get your heart right before you partake" and the elements looked and tasted like medicine. This anti-aesthetic reductionism leaves little for the post-Christian culture to embrace and from which to be inspired. A.W. Tozer warns us of the tendency of man. "Left to ourselves we tend immediately to reduce God to manageable terms. We want to get Him where we can use Him, or at least know where He is when we need Him. We want a God we can in some measure control."[13] Mark Galli reacts to this desire to control God with an understanding of worship beyond words, "Worship that doesn't in some way leave a large space for transcendence and mystery is not fully worship of the God of the Bible, who when asked to name himself—to explain his essence—said rather truculently, 'I am who I am.' The liturgy shines in the shadowy place called mystery."[14]

One reasonable, but waning, strategy of the twentieth-century American church was to provide religious alternatives to the trends of our times. For a time, this communications arms race "succeeded." There was enough money and momentum within Christendom to build more impressive concert halls and call them sanctuaries, buy competitive sound systems and use technology to graphically present the drama of worship. Within this era, Christian congregants were willing to give the church the benefit of the doubt, even though the technology and presentation was only a fraction of what they could find on MTV. They gave this benefit of the doubt because the soul of the congregant still needed the

13. Tozer, *Knowledge of the Holy*, 8.
14. Galli, *Beyond Smells and Bells*, 50.

church to work. This is simply not so with post-Christendom. There is no need to give the church the benefit of the doubt, and as a result much of churches' attempts at technology seem like a hollow shell. As if that were not enough, today's technological and entertainment culture has outpaced any hope the church might have had to compete.[15] The technology/entertainment arms race is over and the church has lost. And this fact, I believe, is a great gift.

Now we can get back to the priestly work of the church, we can get back to the transcendent. "We call this moment in the liturgy a sacrament, an outward sign of an invisible reality . . . the sharing of the bread and wine at the climax of the service—not only recalls something that happened, but re-presents it in a way that makes it a present reality."[16]

This brings a warning to faith leaders hoping to live and speak into this post-Christian reality. The worship curriculum must support the sacred symbols. The system itself must be presented as congruent with reality. The age of emotionalized half-truths and authoritatively dictated contradictions are coming to an end. The age of sacred symbols, congruently anchored, has come.

## SERMON

Related to the discussion of the Bible above, the sermon has a different impact and meaning in post-Christendom.

In the ancient world, the center of sacred space and focus of the congregation's gaze was the altar. In Modernity, particularly post-Enlightenment Modernity, the altar was replaced by the lectern at the church's center. The sermon became the climax of the service. It was given the most important place and often the largest percentage of time of any element of the sacred gathering.[17]

---

15. For just a sample of what I mean, consider this footage of some of the natal technology which is just getting off the ground. Keep in mind that these videos are already well over a year old at date of publication. YouTube, "Project Matal xBox 360 Announcemet" and YouTube, "Lionhead, Project Natal: Meet Milo." Not only is the technology baffling and eye-popping, it is interactive, communal, communicative, emotive, and adrenaline inducing.

16. Galli, *Beyond Smells and Bells*, 51–52.

17. It is worth noting that in latter evangelicalism the lectern was also removed and the band was moved to the stage's center. From church to lecture hall to performance hall.

People in post-Christian culture do not need an iconic someone to tell them what to believe and how to believe it. They are not particularly offended if someone does; they just don't need it. They feel what I call a "personality fatigue.[18]" What they are looking for is an authentic friend who will walk alongside them, express their own spiritual processes, and explain how the sacred might integrate with the world beyond the sacred gathering. Anglican liturgy gives the sermon an important place in the gathering, but not the most important. That is reserved for the Eucharist table (see "Symbol" above). The altar has returned. The transcendent and the ancient have been restored and given primacy. The sermon is an interlude amidst a greater narrative. The sermon is to translate this declared truth (declared by the entire liturgy: Word, symbol, confession, sacrament, and Table), revealing how everyone present may live sacredly in every niche of life and view of the world.[19] As Webber says, "It brings the Word of God to bear on our lives."[20]

It is noteworthy that we do not have a theological treatise from Jesus. He never wrote a theological text. Though he lived in a significant philosophical age, the ancient Greek culture, he never penned a philosophical tome. Instead we have four narratives. Jesus' life and teaching are delivered within a narrative. The liturgical orientation pulls us back to narrative: the narrative of the story read week by week over a three-year

18. We live in a world where personalities are elevated over content. Oprah is a personality. Katie Couric is a personality. Barak Obama is a personality. Tim Tebow is a personality. Rush Limbaugh is a personality. Advice, information, and entertainment (these three things are now impossible to separate from one another) are all delivered in the shape of a personality. And while we accept and participate daily in this reality, the church has an opportunity to provide the culture with a break from this personality inundation.

19. "The church, by focusing on its distinctive identity and vision, can be a depth-political presence of great consequence to society. The church's calling, we believe, is not to change society as such, but to be a steady and true witness of Christ's inauguration of the kingdom and his victory over the powers. The greatest service the church can do society—always, but certainly in an era of fragmentation—is to live out its distinctive story, to be a diacritical community, to present the promising contradiction personified by Jesus the Nazarene. If grace is real, if the gospel is truth, that is enough and more than enough." Webber and Clapp, *People of the Truth*, 123.

20. Webber, *Holy Eucharist*, 21. See chapter 17, section "Parish Orientation," to learn how post-Christian, Northwest culture is becoming far more localized (local living, local economy, urban homesteading, locavore) and looking to live and serve in their time and place. The sermon, as Webber says here, is the time to put some asphalt on the liturgical experience.

period, the narrative of the church calendar cycling through the spiritual seasons, the narrative of the Eucharist service with its lovely literary arc.

## ASSURANCE

Phyllis Tickle, in her book *The Great Emergence*, states that one of the core questions, which is as of yet unanswered, is where "the new Christianity of the Great Emergence [will] discover some authority base."[21] And to cut to the chase, that answer will be "something other than Luther's *sola scriptura*."[22]

As much as the church might love to think that she exists in a congruent state throughout time or that her ways are not reflective of greater cultural modes, it is simply not true. In the sixth century, Gregory the Great created a church that was run by monasteries, which was reflective of the fiefdom organization of the Dark Ages. In the eleventh century, after the Great Schism, the Roman Church placed authority in a single person, the pope and his throne-surrounding council of cardinals, reflective of an age of kings and lords. The Reformation's authority was in *sola scriptura*, which sounds like a commitment to an ancient text, but it ultimately places authority in the individual to interpret apart from priest and church. This same authority of the individual was seen in the doctrine of the "priesthood of all believers" and the birth of the democratic congregation and nation-state.

Wherever this "New Christianity," as Phyllis Tickle calls it, finds its authority base remains to be fully realized, but it will most assuredly find that base reflected in today's global realities.

Lesslie Newbigin begins to respond to this question when he calls the congregation the "Hermeneutic of the Gospel."[23] "How is it possible that the gospel should be credible, that people should come to believe that the power which has the last word in human affairs is represented by a man hanging on a cross? I am suggesting that the only answer, the only hermeneutic of the gospel, is a congregation of men and women who believe it and live by it."[24] Newbigin later says, "All human thinking takes place within a 'plausibility structure,' which determines what beliefs are

---

21. Tickle, *Great Emergence*, 150.

22. Ibid., 150–151.

23. Newbigin, *The Gospel in a Pluralist Society*, 223–33.

24. Ibid., 227

reasonable and what are not. The reigning plausibility structure can only be effectively challenged by people who are fully integrated inhabitants of one another." Newbigin is peeling back this new base of assurance and understanding, the source of the explanation. His brilliance is prophetic, but it is also limited by shifting time.

I affirm Newbigin's words as far as they go. However, these words were published in 1989 and the integrated changes of the last twenty-plus years are as vast as the Internet and wide as the world. He could not have imagined the nearness of the globe's other side. For the first time in human history, widely separated cultures can interact in real time. The hermeneutic is the real-time transcontinental critique of the believing community: east to west, south to north, "developing" to "developed," poor to rich. Falsehoods hide best in closed communities of the same: the same culture, the same race, the same class, the same demographic, the same literature, the same sages, the same education, the same politics, and the same ideology. In a closed community, everyone is working from the same experiences and perspectives, so they tend to have all the same values (worldview) and inevitably the same blind spots. This is what Tickle is getting at when she says about this emerging conceptualizing of the way of truth, "Whatever else such a conceptualizing may be, it is certainly and most notably global, recognizing none of the old, former barriers of nationality, race, social class, or economic status. It is also radical . . . and it is predictably our future both in this model as the relational, nonhierarchal, a-democratized form of Christianity entering into its hegemony and as an organization that will increasingly govern global life during the centuries of the Great Emergence."[25]

Therefore, one hermeneutical hope for the post-Christian is the integrated globalized life of the believing community. The Anglican Communion, particularly in the current format in North America, is better positioned than any other to facilitate this reality-sensation of truth and authority. No need to create a global network—Anglicanism is a real global network. When I say "real," I mean shared life, shared worship, and shared authority. In fact, it is one of the only functioning power structures on the planet in which authority flows freely and unapologetically from south to north. The Anglican Mission in North America is led by the Rwandan church and is dialogically integrated

25. Tickle, *Great Emergence*, 153.

with the national Anglican churches of the world: Africa, Asia, Australia, Americas, and Europe. Anglicans need to proclaim this actual global reality every chance they get as more and more churches are planted for the sake of post-Christian others.[26]

26. One of the most important elements that our 97217 research showed (see appendix) is how post-Christian culture has devout clarity. As discussed in chapter 2, 38 percent of respondents claim to attend church; however, when those same thirty-eight respondents were asked if they attend regularly (defined as "once a month"), all thirty-eight said they attend at least that often. Why is this important? One reason jumps out at me. It appears there is no cultural pull to pretend like one is a "good Christian." There is zero sense of obligation to claim something is true that is not. If there were, it seems there would have been at least a few people who would claim to attend church and then when asked to clarify would say "No, not that often" or "I know I should go more often" or would just admit their attendance is irregular. Instead, even though the number is small, every church attendee seems to be devout.

Therefore, as we discuss faith, truth, and assurance, we can be reasonably confident that *if* people in post-Christendom find a meaningful faith expression, as proposed in this book, they will stay and practice devotion.

# Chapter 24

# Anglican Liturgy and a Post-Christian Experience of Community

"It would only perpetuate the Enlightenment myth of 'the universal man' to suppose that the alternative to living the lie begins or ends with the inner life of individuals, regardless of whether we concern ourselves with what constitutes the requisite affections, attitudes, or beliefs. The possibility of life within the truth, with its 'existential dimension (returning humanity to its inherent nature),' its 'noetic dimension (revealing reality as it is),' and its 'moral dimension (setting an example for others),' requires the social practices of a certain type of community, or as Havel refers to it, 'a parallel *polis*.'[1] According to the New Testament, God assembles persons from every tribe and nation, tongue and people to be just such a community, so that it can display a holy madness in and for the sake of the world by living in the truth."[2]

## COMMON PRAYER AND COMMON WORSHIP

THE SCARIEST WORDS IN the English language are "alone" and "lonely."[3] "To affirm our identity with all God's people everywhere is to recover from historical amnesia and to discover our identity. We belong to

---

1. Havel and Keane, *Power of the Powerless*, 56–60.

2. Harvey, *Another City*, 137.

3. "Your way leads out of isolation, multiplies me and me into us. You call your people to put our heads and hearts together, to listen in concert." Srubas, *Oblation*. 5.

a great company of saints . . . We belong to them and they to us. Together we are one in Jesus Christ, brothers and sisters in the community of faith."[4]

Practically speaking, Anglican liturgy is a shared experience: readings are read in common voice, prayers are shared publicly, peace is delivered interpersonally, and Eucharist is approached communally. These experiences of human harmony stand in stark contrast to individualism experienced both inside the church (worship isolation) and outside the church ("my own thing in my own way"). It also contrasts the entertainment-like model of the attractional church, where congregants are ushered to their seats and get a chance to watch the artists, readers, and leaders perform the worship. This liturgical communality in itself is meaningful, but like all behaviors, it flows from and reflects a deeper theology. Zizoulas[5] shares in his theological treatise *Being as Communion* that the worshiping body "is liberated from individualism and egocentricity and becomes a supreme expression of community—the Body of Christ, the body of the Church, the body of the Eucharist. Thus, it is proved experientially that the body is not in itself a negative or exclusive concept, but the reverse: a concept of communion and love."[6]

This reality of liberated community appears time and again in the Eucharist liturgy. One does not take the Communion alone, but travels with the faith family to the "table" of the Lord. The elements are not taken in isolation, but received together from the hand and in the spoken blessing of a spiritual friend. It is also found in the giving and receiving of blessing, most specifically in the closing dismissal. "A benediction, given and received in faith, even in the most modest church, starts a river flowing with living water: from God, to his representative, to the people of God, and finally to the least, the last and the left out. Benediction finds its deepest fulfillment when blessing is practiced for the sake of others. . . Therefore, we repractice benediction by letting blessing—divine favor and power—flow through us to others."[7]

4. Webber, *Evangelicals*, 66.

5. Jean Zizioulas is an Orthodox scholar. He writes primarily for the Eastern Church and his thoughts here are in the context of an Eastern liturgical life.

6. Zizioulas, *Being as Communion*, 64.

7. Hunter, *Giving Church Another Chance*, 157–58.

## SHARING BELIEF

Another aspect of the shared worship is the common declaration of faith. This is most clearly seen in the reciting of the Creed. There will be few practices more challenging to many post-Christian people than to state aloud an exclusive statement of faith. However, there are a couple of aspects of the liturgical service that will serve the post-Christian believer well. First of all, the Creed is ancient (both the Apostles' and the Nicene), and therefore will be given the benefit of the doubt. The Creed is a simple Trinitarian declaration (mystical and God-centered) and it is devoid of denominational specifics and theological dogmatics more typical of a "theological statement of faith." Finally, there is a story in the life of Jesus (Mark 2 and Luke 5) in which Jesus heals a paralytic because of the faith of the paralytic's friends. As we consider the "experience of community," we need to increasingly consider the communal reality of faith (as opposed to an exclusively individualistic view). Jesus forgives sin and extends healing communally. The act of standing shoulder to shoulder and declaring the faith ("I believe in God the Father Almighty, maker of heaven and earth: And in Jesus Christ his only son our Lord") may very well infuse faith and healing.

## SHARING NEEDS/HURTS

One way to describe urban Northwest culture is to liken a person to an onion, made up of concentric layers, each layer deeper than the one before. The layers closest to the center of our personal onion tend to be the most tender and the most tied to our identity, which is made up of our precious affections and our lasting wounds. Now, if you were to describe your average middle-class American southerner as an onion, you could say the top few layers are just as open and free as can be. You can walk down the street of a southern town and total strangers will greet you with the most pleasant of smiles and respond just as quickly when you greet them. Once you get below those first few layers though, the onion gets a little tougher and less responsive. So, what can we say about the urban Northwesterner? Well, those first few layers are much, much crustier than the southerners'. As you walk down the street in Portland, no one says "hello," and if you did, the response would most likely come with a sideways stare and a furrowed brow. However, and here is the real beauty, if you manage to break through those first couple of layers (and they are surprisingly thin), you get the whole onion. I cannot tell you the number of times I have sat in a coffee shop and for whatever reason turned to make conversation with the isolated person at the adjacent table. They might ask me about what I am reading or I might comment on their pastry choice, and suddenly there is an epiphany of trust. Then it starts to flow: pain, spirituality, needs, passions, dreams, and wounds, as if we had been friends all of our lives.

Bishop Todd Hunter of Holy Trinity Church in Costa Mesa, California confessed to me recently that the most difficult part of the Eucharist service for his congregation is the Prayers of the People.[8] He said that it is hard to get people to talk about their real needs so they tend to speak of safer subjects, like a prayer for their great-aunt's illness. Bishop Hunter is not alone in this challenge.[9] We attend a small, dying Presbyterian church on Sunday mornings. It is populated by a handful of aging Presbyterians, and we often wonder how much longer it will exist. Each week, the prayers of the people is a pretty painful part of the service. The same four people speak up every week and the requests are inevitably about people far away and events to which the rest of the congregation has little contact.

I have a profound suspicion that post-Christian, urban Northwesterners are uniquely prepared to participate in this sort of prayer-focused life exchange. Even though it will not be easy to break through those first crusty layers, once a congregation has the epiphany of trust, real soulful requests and hurts will be shared and that sharing will confirm the transcendence of the Jesus-community.

## MAKING PEACE

Post-Christian people desire peace. They desire to live consistently as people of peace. They want to be more than peace lovers; they want to be peace makers.

For example, as we approached people to complete the 193 surveys of zip code 97217, we were surprised by the almost universal willingness to volunteer a few minutes to offer their beliefs and perceptions. In fact,

8. The Prayers of the People are usually led by a deacon or lay person and are often based upon some system of collecting the actual prayer needs of the gathered community.

9. Ruth Meyers speaks to both the historical challenge of the Prayers of the People and some contemporary ramification. Meyers, *Prayer Book*, 57–58.

only a few people ever said "no" and those that did always did so because of an urgent time constraint, insisting they were sorry that they did not have a few minutes to spare. The one area where we did get some push-back, and this was only by a few people, was in the survey's last section.[10] In this section, they were asked to offer perceptions of several Christian denominations/traditions. A few people were unable because they felt it required them to pass judgment on another person.

Historically, the parish worship service was one of the places, if not the only place, where the entire community came together, side by side, on an equal footing. It is an old saying that the ground is always level at the foot of the cross.[11] In the Eucharist, the whole of society share life. This sharing crystallizes in two moments. The final is the common sharing of Communion. However, the first is the Passing of the Peace.[12] It is here when the congregants parade around the worship space, look one another in the eye and say, "Peace be with you." In these moments of sacred human encounter, the spiritual family must release all wrongs and abuses and say, "All is well between us."

## PARTICIPATING IN AN ACTUAL GLOBAL AND HISTORICAL COMMUNITY

There is a famous African saying, "I am because we are, we are because I am."

"After this I looked and there before me was a great multitude that no one could count, from every nation, tribe, people, and language, standing before the throne and in front of the Lamb. They were wearing white robes and were holding palm branches in their hands. And they cried out in a loud voice: Salvation belongs to our God, who sits on the throne, and to the Lamb."[13] This vision compels Marva Dawn to say, "How glorious is this picture of all these people gathered together, from every ethnic group, all countries, every sort of culture, every tongue brought together

10. See appendix.

11. This saying is most often used in regards to the universality of our sinfulness; however, it also has profound implications societally in regards to class, generation, gender, race, and culture.

12. The Passing of the Peace: Now, "freed from sin, we are brought together in unity." It is a ritual of exchange and often includes blessing one another with the words, "Peace be with you."

13. Rev 7:9–10.

in the unity of God's reign! This promised future unity of everyone, forces us to ask now, How can we provide a foretaste of this gathering of all the people?"[14] Even more poignantly, if heaven is what is most real ("we look not at the things which are seen, but at the things which are not seen; for the things which are seen are temporal, but the things which are not seen are eternal"),[15] how can we not provide through worship an actual experience of that which is "most real" as a part of the rhythm of life? "Those who enter this particular earthly temple to worship God, ideally a diverse company, are a sign and promise of the gathering of the nations, of people of all ranks and races and lands to share in the unity that lies ahead of us in the culmination of the kingdom."[16]

Our newly globalized world has *virtually* given us the sensation of a universally connected humanity. The Anglican Liturgical Community *actually* provides an ontological integration with the ancient and the global. It is a profound gift to submit to the ecclesial and liturgical fathers of old (sections 2 and 3) and to submit to the global brethren, most specifically through the tested saints of the church of Rwanda (Mission in Motion).

14. Dawn, *Royal Waste of Time*, 270.

15. 2 Cor 4:18 (NASB).

16. Pfatteicher, *Liturgical Spirituality*, 185.

# Chapter 25

# Anglican Liturgy and Post-Christian Spirituality

ACCORDING TO OUR 97217 research results,[1] only 24.8 percent of respondents consider themselves "religious," while 74.6 percent self-identify as "spiritual." When asked to rate the importance of the "spiritual dimension of life on a scale of one to ten," the average response was 6.6. These statistics show a general-to-strong orientation toward a spiritual life. It was quite surprising that only 5.7 percent identified themselves as "atheist" or "agnostic" (compared to Barna's 16 percent).[2] In almost every category, our research showed that residents of 97217 are less religious than in Barna's data (e.g., fewer percentage of self-identifying "Christians," fewer churchgoers, etc.); however, when it comes to those who claim to have no spiritual/supernatural/transcendent beliefs at all (atheists and agnostics), the percentage here was a third of Barna's conclusions for the Portland area as a whole.[3] Post-Christians are "spiritual" and they are not non-religious, in the broadest sense of the term. They desire a spiritual life and one can only assume they would embrace meaningful outlets for those spiritual desires.

## PRACTICE

"Practice," in relation to spirituality, is an ancient term. It was used by early monastics to talk about the modes and habits of the truly devout life. It referred to regular and repeatable (if not constant) shared behaviors

---

1. See appendix.
2. Barna Group, "Diversity of Faith."
3. Christine Wicker claims the number to be 14 percent nationally. Wicker, *Fall*, 53.

exercised by the people of faith. I love the term "practice." I love it in part because, for whatever reason, it feels far less shackling then the word "discipline," a term I was given by my religious education. "Discipline"— how could it not have a pejorative connotation? And no matter how much discipline I did or how many hours I spent disciplining, I was sure to discover that I could be doing the disciplines better and more. I love "practice" because it assumes that I am not performing the act perfectly (be it prayer, service, or simplicity). In fact, it seems to indicate that perfection is not even the goal: "Did you say I'm not doing it perfectly? That's okay. I was only practicing."

Post-Christian people are seeking out "practices" as an integral part of life. For instance, they are searching for regular and practicable means to be sustainable: gardening, keeping chickens, riding the bus, and shopping locally.[4] When cornered and asked about the great crashing wave of consumption and waste in this world,[5] most post-Christian people will admit that their efforts are having little to no impact on the actual state of the environment. However, the very act of integrating sustainable patterns into their lives fills them with a sense of meaning, connectedness to the earth and their community, and makes them, for lack of a better term, a "better" person.

Stanley Hauerwas says in his book *After Christendom?*, "Christianity is not beliefs about God plus behaviors. We are not Christians because of what we believe, but because we have been called to be disciples of Jesus. To become a disciple is not a matter of a new or changed self-understanding, but rather to become part of a different community with a different set of practices."[6] It has become almost cliché within the church's postmodern discussion to say, "In the postmodern world, participation will precede conversion." This phrase is still true. However, what we need to understand is that participation *is* conversion, conversion in process. Participation is the spiritual practice.

Anglicanism has a profound opportunity to welcome people into this participatory life, and the historically established Eucharist liturgy provides both the stage and the story for that participation. Hauerwas

4. The Lenten season is an excellent and historical opportunity to infuse and practice simplicity and sustainability as an extension of the communal spiritual life.

5. I have heard that if the entire planet lived at the consumption rate of the average American today, it would take four and a half earths to sustain the population.

6. Hauerwas, *After Christendom?*, 107.

says, "I am sometimes confronted by people who are not Christians but who say they want to know about Christianity . . . After many years of vain attempts to 'explain' God as trinity, I now say, 'Well, to begin with we Christians have been taught to pray, 'Our Father, who art in heaven . . . '" I then suggest that a good place to begin to understand what we Christians are about is to join me in that prayer."[7]

Come join us as we pray.

"Liturgy is soul food. It nourishes our souls just as breakfast strengthens our bodies. It's sort of like family dinner . . . family dinner is about family, love, community . . . Liturgical theologian Aidan Kavanaugh says it well: 'The liturgy, like the feast, exists not to educate but to seduce people into participating in common activity of the highest order, where one is freed to learn things which cannot be taught.'"[8]

The liturgy provides not just a random practice, but practice according to a code. It is a spiritual code (based in humanity's history), and like all great codes, it does not originate with the individual but is received from and amongst those who have walked before.

## CONFESSION

It was a warm, spring afternoon. I was working, hammer in hand, with a small band of friends on the lawn, just off the great courtyard on the Reed College campus. We were building a renaissance-style confession booth, complete with dark interior, cramped quarters, and separation screen (as well as some fleurs-de-lis for decoration). Originally the plan had been to have the students confess their sins to us inside the booth as a mock drama of religion expression, but then we formed another plan. It was Reed's Renn Faire, an annual festival of ecstasy, experimentation, and raw experience, which ends each school year. This year was like any other: streaking students, rampant chemical use, and a bug-eating contest—just what every college student needs.

We were a small community of the Jesus-way on campus and we wanted to play along with the campus. There were certainly many activities that we were not willing to partake in. However, the great thing about

---

7. Ibid., 107–8. See Stone, *Evangelism After Christendom*, 24. "Nothing is more important for evangelism . . . than situating it both imaginatively and practically within an ecclesial bios, or form of life . . . [an] ecclesially grounded evangelism."

8. Claiborne et al., *Common Prayer*, 11.

Renn Faire is it makes space for others. And we had an idea. We wanted to be fully Christians and fully participants. Not an easy task. There are plenty of ways to be religious and out of harmony with the energy of an event like this, but we wanted to be religious and harmonious. In the end, the plan was to try to act like Jesus. So we built a booth. I climbed inside a monk's cowl and climbed inside the booth's clergy side. When the first person entered, giggling and adventurous, I nervously said:

> Welcome to the confession booth. This is where confessions are heard. With your permission I would like to begin. I would like to ask your forgiveness for the church. Would you forgive us for the Inquisition and the Crusades, for wars fought in history and today in God's name, for our role in racism and slavery? Would you forgive me, a foolish Christian, who claims to follow Jesus and yet my life looks little like his? Would you please forgive me?

What followed was nothing short of miraculous.

There is magic in a confession.[9] There was honor, sobriety, and joy in those Reed students' eyes when they got the chance to say, "I forgive you." Then there was the reciprocal dance of spiritual humility. Their pain, addiction, and experiences of abuse flowed as free as their tears. We would sit in a sacred moment together. We would talk about pain. We would talk about forgiveness. We would talk about Jesus. Throughout the weekend that seat was never empty, and every single student who entered the booth participated in the magic of confession and absolution.

The liturgy offers such magic. Each week the congregation stands together and in sacredness confesses:

> Most merciful God,
> we confess that we have sinned against you
> in thought, word, and deed,
> by what we have done,
> and by what we have left undone.
> We have not loved you with our whole heart;
> we have not loved our neighbors as ourselves.
> We are truly sorry and we humbly repent.
> For the sake of your Son Jesus Christ,

9. I believe this magic is self-evident. It is certainly evident in this story of confession to and with post-Christian Reed students. If that is not enough, this story of confession is the most quoted section of the bestselling book *Blue Like Jazz* by Donald Miller, and it was also part of the inspiration for the book *Lord, Save Us from Your Followers* (161–86) and the feature film by the same name.

have mercy on us and forgive us;
that we may delight in your will,
and walk in your ways,
To the glory of your Name. Amen.[10]

And then they get to hear those glorious words, "You are forgiven."

We have a small group that meets in our home, called "The Jesus Dojo."[11] It is a group of sojourners who want to take Jesus at his words and experiment accordingly. This past fall, we shared a month-long experiment in courageous confession,[12] meeting with the key people in our lives, asking them to answer probing questions about our manipulations, shortfalls, and blind spots. We then trained together in how to ask for forgiveness, ending in, "Would you please forgive me?" The conversations were often gut-wrenching, but in the end the euphoric stories of hearing those words, "I forgive you," were the stuff of fairy tales. Rob asked the repentance questions to his ex-wife, and she gave him over three hours of angry feedback. Then he asked her to forgive him, listing each of his failings, one by one. She did and followed up with, "Rob, you have set me free." When she said, "I forgive you," Rob said his life was changed forever.

Confession also exists as more than an individual experience. Both in taking responsibility for and living in solidarity with the universal condition, post-Christian people will long to confess on behalf of the world at large. Their natural activism, coupled with a less individualistic view of identity, will ensure this. "Contrition is also necessary to our world. The present escalating competition for the remaining, dwindling resources of planet earth—to name but one of the greatest crises we face and shall face for the foreseeable future—will surely lead to war and such destruction as can hardly be imagined unless the nations and those that inhabit them adopt different attitudes from those that now preoccupy them."[13] There is tremendous freedom to be found in acknowledging these imbalances and leaning into God to make things aright.

Where else will people go to experience magic like this? The liturgy provides a chance to experience confession and absolution as a rhythm

10. Webber, *Holy Eucharist*, 360.

11. Reimagine, "The Jesus Dojo."

12. We called it the "Be @ Peace Project." To learn more, see Kriz, "B @ Peace Project" and www.be-at-peace-project.

13. Wolf, *Anglican Spirituality*, 44. Also see Booty, "Contrition in Anglican Spirituality."

of life.[14] And who better to initiate this confessional revolution than a movement born out of and led by the people of Rwanda.

## FREEDOM TO JOURNEY

Stephen Sykes wrote in his essay "The Genius of Anglicanism" these words:

> When Anglicans reflect upon the history of the Church of England and of the Anglican Communion instinctively they find many things to regret and repent of, and some things which are more encouraging. This both-and at the heart of their corporate sense reflects, I would judge, the ecclesiology. . . . Its natural mode is to allow debate, disagreement, and conflict as a normal part of its life . . . and that structure will be appropriate to differing patterns of authority in different cultures at various times.[15]

It is both ironic and appropriate that in an article titled, "The Genius of Anglicanism," such a sincere and almost boastful emphasis would be placed on the traditions' shortcomings (things to regret and repent of). The commitment to open dialogue and free exchange, often called the *via media*, is based in the church's birth when she carefully navigated in the uncharted waters between historical Catholicism and new-wave Protestantism. The *via media* remains as a defining characteristic of Anglicanism and her liturgy to this day.

This same idea is what Bishop Todd Hunter refers to as a "sweet reasonableness" within Anglicanism. "Historically, Anglicanism does not bully but simply sets itself forth. It invites participation, contemplation and conversation. . . . This spirit is important to me because I have become weary of the increasingly dogmatic, angry, unkind, un-Christlike, argumentative, and dishonest spirit in much of the religious debate in America."[16]

Liturgically, this openness saturates all of Anglican worship expression. On an annual basis, the church twice practices "Ordinary Time." Joan Chittister reminds us that the church has intentionally cleansed the

---

14. The Lenten season also offers an annual opportunity to explore and practice confession.

15. Rowell, *English Religious Tradition*, 240. Essay by Stephen Sykes, "The Genius of Anglicanism."

16. Hunter, *Accidental Anglican*, 109.

calendar on at least three occasions, "purging them of various popular or cultural feast days."[17] She says, "The Liturgical year is designed to take us into deep contemplation. It is about immersion in the mysteries of the faith. It is about the life of Jesus as it intersects with our own."[18] About the two seasons of "Ordinary Time" she specifically reminds, "These two periods of time in the liturgical year, then, are contemplative times. They take us apart to think about what we have just seen of the faith (Advent and Lent) . . . It is an awesome context in which to begin the contemplation of the divine and the adventure of the spiritual development."[19]

Citizens of a post-Christian culture will ultimately find their spiritual bearing through participation (see "Practice" above) and belonging (see "Post-Christian Community" above), but that does not mean that they will not need a forum to freely and honestly express their questions and explore their evolving convictions. Remember, and I feel a bit foolish in saying this, but post-Christian people are "post-Christian": they do not have much experience with religious constructs and education.[20] Increasingly they are going to desire (and even demand) the space and opportunity to explore these as of yet uncharted ideological waters. An open and participation-filled liturgy offers wonderful space for the collective to contemplate and explore.

## THE GIFT OF TIME

"Come to me. Get away with me and you'll recover your life. I'll show you how to take a real rest. Walk with me and work with me—watch how I do it. Learn the unforced rhythms of grace."[21]

17. Chittister, *Liturgical Year*, 96.

18. Ibid., 95.

19. Ibid., 97.

20. For so long, American Christianity has been built on the assumption that everyone, whether they are devout Christian or not, has a basic understanding of Christianity. Therefore, the core issue was simply, "Will they choose to embrace or continue to ignore that which they already have an understanding of?" Here, the basic metaphor of the mission of the church was a "light switch," which existed in the heart of each person; the goal was to get the convert to "turn on" their switch. Today, when many do not have basic Christian education *and* have been raised in a globalized world of religious options, we need to change our metaphor from the light switch to something far more explorative and nuanced, like canoeing an uncharted river. An open and participation-filled liturgy offers wonderful space to contemplate and explore.

21. Matt 11:28b–29 (The Message).

The invitation of the liturgical church is a simple echo of Jesus' invitation. "Come," "get away," "take a real rest," "learn the unforced rhythms of grace." This happens through the sacred pause of the Eucharist service. It happens through the soulful cadence of the prayers and reading. It happens through the quiet of confession and encounter. It happens in the invitation to "take, eat . . ."

The almanac is a spiritual book. It is based as much in the rhythm of humanity as the passing of the seasons. As an urban-raised child of the modern world, I have never had to open an almanac. I have never had to plan for planting or prepare for harvest. My father, however, grew up on a ranch, and my mom, while living in town, worked every summer picking strawberries outside of Newberg, Oregon to help pay the family bills. This human connection to time and season has been taken from me by the patterns of the modern age.

> The liturgical year, with its great traversal from life to death to life again, carries us from one pole of time to the other with a sense of purpose and progress. It makes us aware of the presence of the kind of time that is not time, that is not our understanding of time, that is beyond time. The liturgical year wraps us in a kind of dual consciousness—of this early life and the life beyond. It reminds us that there is more to us than one kind of life alone, more than one dimension of time, more than one purpose in life.[22]

## ENCOUNTER WITH GOD

> A minster says words and performs actions, but at a deeper level, it is Christ who is presiding. We share in bread and wine, but the reality is that we are taking Christ into us. It looks like this is all occurring in time and space, when in fact the boundaries of time and space are being shattered, when for a few moments 'heaven and earth are full of [God's] glory.'[23]

In all my years in church growing up, I never once had the sense that Christ was presiding. It was clearly the pastor who was in charge and who we came to receive from. It was the choir or the band that offered us our spiritual experience. Sure, God was the object of our activities, but he was rarely the subject.

22. Chittister, *Liturgical Year*, 39–40.
23. Galli, *Beyond Smells and Bells*, 52.

In a brilliant rhetorical moment, Frank Schaeffer, while being interviewed by Terry Gross on National Public Radio's popular show *Fresh Air*, was asked why he doesn't leave faith altogether. Frank's response, "I'm stuck, because faith is just part of my life."[24] No longer do people feel "stuck." There is, however, the human hunger for the transcendent. "At the altar we are invited into what Jesus called heaven."[25] Ultimately, that hunger is to meet with God.

The Eucharist service begins with this sacred meeting, "Almighty God, unto whom all hearts are open, all desires known, and from whom no secrets are hid: Cleanse the thoughts of our hearts by the inspiration of the Holy Spirit, that we may perfectly love thee, and worthily magnify thy holy Name; through Christ our Lord, Amen." Frank Schaeffer, in that same interview, went on to say, "I found refuge in a liturgical tradition which is not centered around a guru. Our priests are interchangeable. They face the altar, not the people. They lead the people in a liturgy."[26]

The Eucharist service ends with the dismissal. "The Dismissal is a blessing. In worship, we actually bless God when we offer praise and worship . . . we bless God by doing what is pleasing to God—acknowledging and serving God. In contrast, when God blesses us, God confers on us a power to fulfill our calling in righteousness and holiness in Jesus Christ."[27] Where else will the people of post-Christendom be able to go to experience this holy exchange?

Both Advent/Christmas and Pentecost in the liturgical calendar offer additional emphasis on God's initiation to be with us.[28] It is worth

24. Schaeffer, "Keeping Abortion Legal."

25. Gallagher, *Sacred Meal*, 48.

26. Schaeffer, "Keeping Abortion Legal." James Giffiss expresses a similar experience: "The Eucharistic prayer of the 1928 Book of Common Prayer we used then taught me much about God and myself: 'And here we offer and present unto thee, O Lord, ourselves, our souls and bodies, to be a reasonable, holy, and living sacrifice unto thee; humbly beseeching thee that we, and all others who shall be partakers of this Holy Communion, may worthily receive the most precious Body and Blood of thy Son Jesus Christ, be filled with thy grace and heavenly benediction, and made one body with him, that he may dwell in us, and we in him.'"

27. Webber, *Planning Blended Worship*, 184.

28. Webber, *Worship Phenomenon*, 99–115. The Church calendar also celebrates the dynamic and diverse life of Christ. It welcomes the worshiper to explore different dimensions of Christ's life, ministry, and means of affection, as opposed to feeling like church (and our relationship with God) is always the same. This is but another impact of the calendar on the post-Christian person's encounter with God.

noting that immediately following both of these seasons of divine coming (Christ in Advent and Holy Spirit in Pentecost) are the seasons of contemplation and rest called "Ordinary Time." It is as if the experience of God's particular presence requires a sabbatical.

# Chapter 26

# A Worthwhile Journey

"THIS PARADOX MARKS EVERY Christian Eucharist. Gathered around the altar, our community is a sign of the Kingdom. We are the friends of God. But this same Eucharist challenges us to break down the walls around our little community and welcome in those who are excluded. Every Eucharist is the sacrament of our home in the Lord, and yet breaks down the walls that we build to keep out strangers. This is the necessary paradox of being . . . both a particular historical community and the sacrament of a community which transcends us and stretches out to embrace all of humanity."[1]

It is a significant thing to look soberly into the current life of the church and say, "This is not working." It is even more shocking to say, "It is true that we (the missional body of Christ) have not made the best decisions of late. There is hope. There is a profound hope."

In many ways it is counterintuitive to say that one of the most fruitful strategies the church can implement for the future is to reach to the ancient past. Just saying that makes me feel like some disheveled old guy, lost in a room of books, draped in a tweed jacket with patched elbows, fingering an unlit pipe, and staring at the world over a pair of wire spectacles. Even so, I am compelled to say it all the same.

I have been an innovator all of my life. I have created new missional models in some of the most extreme emerging cultures around the world. I am also the sort of person who, in many ways, is more comfortable outside a church than inside. And it is my innovator's heart that is screaming,

1. Pecklers, *Liturgy in a Postmodern World*, 143. Essay "Sacramentality of the Word" by Timothy Radcliffe.

"Follow the ancient ways!" I know that I am not the first to suggest such things. Robert Webber, Phyllis Tickle, and others have been saying them for years. The difference is that I am a post-Christian person. I was raised in a post-Christian culture, while all along the way maintaining a relationship with Christian churches and practicing Christian devotion. Today, in fact every day, I am living deeply rooted and in love with my post-Christian neighborhood and with my post-Christian neighbors. I am convinced that the Anglican Eucharistic liturgy provides a unique hope for my culture, for my people, for my cultural family.

This work was soulfully and compassionately compiled as evidence to that truth. We have researched (including original and revealing survey data), and the evidence is strong. The way of the worshiping people of Jehovah from ages past has been liturgical and Eucharistic, across cultures and generations and epochs. Time and time again the people of God have voted, and their vote has been, "It is meaningful." Today's post-Christian people are spiritual, and more so than even the most recent generations, they are looking for substance, clarity, and reverence, all encased in a much larger spiritual narrative. They, like all of humanity, want their lives to be marked by meaning. Anglican Eucharist liturgy provides just that. I pray that this generation will accept Jesus Christ's generous invitation to meet him at the Holy Table. Amen.

# SECTION 7

# Applying the Liturgy in Post-Modern Culture

THIS BOOK HAS PROVIDED a case for Anglican Eucharistic liturgy and its place in post-Christian culture,[1] specifically such culture as is manifesting in the urban centers of the Pacific Northwest.

The purpose of this section is to make some specific suggestions about how to creatively administer the individual steps and themes of the liturgy in a way that might communicate their greatest meaning within post-Christian culture. Section 4 described the theological and missional necessity of a contextualized expression of the church in every place and time, and also how this process of contextualization works hand in hand with historical liturgy. This section intends to apply that contextualization partnership (historical worship with current context) within my Pacific Northwest home.

This content has been saved for the end of the book because it will be fueled primarily by my subjective opinion (as a fully saturated Northwesterner with post-Christian cultural leanings) and missional creativity.

By way of review, Eucharist or "Holy Eucharist" is the Anglican name for its liturgical worship service. The word Eucharist is in many contexts synonymous with "Communion," as the name for the holy supper when Christian people come together at the table to break bread, to share the cup, and to answer Jesus' call to "remember Me," but in Anglicanism it refers to the entire liturgy culminating in Holy Communion. (See the step-by-step description of Holy Eucharist below.) It is the ongoing echo instituted by Christ in the upper room where his disciples were

---

1. See introduction for definition of this particular sort of post-Christian culture.

specifically exhorted to "do this in remembrance of Me"[2] and to do it "until He comes,"[3] a reference to his future return.

This section will provide a short description of each of the liturgical elements of the Holy Eucharist. In some cases, it will reprint an example of the specific liturgical wording of that element. Finally, and this is the primary purpose of this section, I will muse about creative suggestions for implementation and expression. The goal is to get the creative juices flowing.

I freely suspect that some of my suggestions will produce suspicious looks and furrowed brows among many Anglican traditionalists. I apologize to you beforehand. I also want to remind you of Cranmer's words:

> It is a most invaluable part of that blessed "liberty wherewith Christ hath made us free," that in his worship different forms and usages may without offence be allowed, provided the substance of the Faith be kept entire; and that, in every Church, what cannot be clearly determined to belong to Doctrine must be referred to Discipline; and therefore, *by common consent and authority, may be altered, abridged, enlarged, amended, or otherwise disposed of, as may seem most convenient for the edification of the people,* "according to the various exigency of times and occasions."[4]

I also invite you, both progressive and traditionalist, into this process. Bring both your critiques and creativity. Join the drama of improvisation.

---

2. Luke 22:19.

3. 1 Cor 11:26.

4. The Book of Common Prayer, "The Book of Common Prayer" (italics mine).

# Chapter 27

# Liturgy as Literature: Worship and the Literary Arc

BEFORE WE DISCUSS THE individual elements of the liturgical drama, it is important that we imagine them not primarily as separate elements but as perichoretic parts of a single piece of literature.

I hearken back to junior high school English class and recall the basic elements of literature:

Figure 10. Basic Literary Arc. Source: Created by author.

"Exposition" sets the stage and introduces the participating audience to the characters and setting of the drama that is about to be unleashed. "Conflict" sets the reality that all is not right and seeds hope in all present that something could be different. "Rising Action" speaks to the many coming and going dramatic turns that keep the audience engaged, reinforce the conflict, and build wonder for how this dissonance could be resolved. "Climax" is the moment of answer and elation; it is where the problem and the solution, which have been thus far separated and lost, come together. "Resolution" is where the dissonance is fully released and the collateral damage of the conflict resolves. It resolves through creating metaphoric "life" (the Shakespearean comedy) or "death" (the Shakespearean tragedy).

Not surprisingly all of these elements can be found in the famous introduction to Shakespeare's *Romeo and Juliet,* foreshadowing the perfectly orchestrated drama to come:

> Two households, both alike in dignity,
> In fair Verona, where we lay our scene, [exposition]
> From ancient grudge break to new mutiny, [conflict]
> Where civil blood makes civil hands unclean.
> From forth the fatal loins of these two foes [rising action]
> A pair of star-cross'd lovers take their life; [climax]
> Whose misadventured piteous overthrows
> Do with their death bury their parents' strife.[1] [resolution: in this case, death]

Inspiring dramas seem to follow this same arc, or one of her adaptations. One of her closest cousins simply introduces a preliminary climax to capture the crowd, but its purpose is to point to the greater climax to come. It looks like this:

Figure 11. Literary Arc. Source: Created by author.

---

1. Shakespeare and Gill, *Romeo and Juliet,* 141–42.

These simple diagrams illustrate the supernatural experience of the human heart when it encounters drama that is well expressed. Short story, Shakespearian play, or romantic-comedy film, it all remains the same. When this basic literary pattern is skillfully and artfully maintained, the story has a chance to transcendently speak to the human soul. "Truth" is the language of the head and "sign and symbol" is the language of the soul, but "story" is the language of the heart.

This is important because I believe that our worship formulas often miss this basic literary reality.[2] We often rely more upon the blunt tools of spectacle, personality, and entertainment as opposed to the subtle wooing of the literary arc.

Most of the evangelical, free-worship churches that I have attended over my life have an arc that looks something like this:

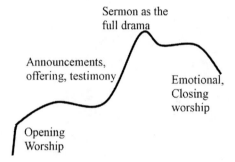

Figure 12. Literary Arc of an Evangelical Church Service (Observed).
Source: Created by author.

I have intentionally not used the traditional categories of literature (exposition, conflict, etc.) because I honestly don't know where they are in this sort of organization. Musically based worship, in this context, is responsible primarily to jump-start the room and to keep the engine revved up in part to set up and support the sermon. In my churches growing up, the sermon was everything, and it was actually responsible to embody the entire drama. The pastor had to set the scene, illustrate the conflict, and take the audience through the drama, climax, and call for a "resolution," all from a very limited palette: podium-based, cognitive monologue. Can we hope for something more?

2. A worship service, after all, is simply a piece of transcendent literature.

Before I try to reaffirm that the Anglican Eucharistic liturgy has a real opportunity to return to the influential heart-language of the literary arc, let me make an important disclaimer. One reason the liturgy has fallen out of vogue within much of the broader Christian community and culture is because we have lost the interconnected reality of the liturgical elements meaningfully conducted through the dramatic arc. Without that intentionality, the liturgical service becomes "dead" and free of heart-inspiration. It can end up feeling more like this:

Figure 13. Absence of Literary Arc. Source: Created by author.

It seems to reset a dozen times, there is no integration of elements, and then offers no "on-ramp" for the human heart. It is organized more like the music on a "Top 40" radio station than like a symphony. How can the human heart connect?

If the worship leaders are able to see the arc (i.e., stop treating the worship service as a set of mandatory pieces) and lead the congregation into the growing and resolving drama of the full Eucharist, then there is real hope to speak to the human heart. As I see it, such a service would utilize, as illustrated above, an "initial climax" and "ultimate climax" and might look something like this:

Figure 14. Proposed Liturgical Literary Arc. Source: Created by author.

Let me take a moment to explain a few elements of this integrated and literary perspective on the Anglican Eucharistic liturgy.

- The salutation is exposition. As with a Greek chorus, the audience is invited into the story, and as one of the characters they declare through their very presence that they are an essential character and then introduce the other characters and setting: "Blessed be God: Father, Son, and Holy Spirit. And blessed be His Kingdom now and forever. Amen."

- The Kyrie, as an example, declares to all the conflict—the separation of these core characters. This separation must be healed and crossed: "Lord, have mercy. Christ, have mercy. Lord, have mercy."

- The Collect reveals the particularity of each week's drama with its thematic prayer. The Collect is then followed by God getting to tell his story through the reading of the lessons, climaxing in the "hero" arriving on the scene to speak in his own words: the Gospel lesson (this is why the Gospel lesson needs to be set apart from the others).

- The sermon provides an intermission. Local and concurrent particularity is brought to the narrative. The rhetor here can tell an entire mini-narrative through the sermon (notice on the chart that the sermon exists in a mini curve of its own). However, this mini-narrative exists only in submission to the greater story.

- If act 1 is God telling his side through the lessons, in act 2 the people (his betrothed) get to wrestle through their story. Notice the undeniably human voice throughout act 2: the Creed ("We believe . . ."), Prayers of the People, Confession, and Passing of the Peace.

- The climax is found in the anticipated coming together of these two epic stories, God's and man's, as these thus far separated characters meet at the Table: Holy Communion. Here they fulfill the promise made by the hero in the initial climax.

- Now reconciled and renewed, the drama resolves with the "flying open of the church's doors" and the worshiping community stepping out in newness of life.

Post-Christian culture is *not* looking for church—at least not church "just because" or in just any form. Coaxing an audience with religious entertainment or dazzling personalities is a lot like producing a poorly constructed, widely criticized and low-budget action movie. Sure, the action-movie-zealot subculture will still buy tickets, but few others will come. However, a low-budget indie film with a whimsical and profound narrative arc will sneak up on people. These films are not widely circulated, nor do they have large marketing budgets. The hard part is getting people to see them; but once they do, these stories surprise and inspire us.

# Chapter 28

# Creative Suggestions for Administering the Elements of Holy Eucharist

B EFORE WE GET INTO the specific elements of the Eucharistic service, I have a couple of reminders. Among post-Christian and non-churched people it is more important than ever to provide a "tour guide" through the worship. Not for every element or throughout every week, but from time to time we need to take moments to educate about the importance and meaningfulness of the different Eucharistic elements. Bishop Todd Hunter often begins the Holy Communion by putting on his stole and saying, "I put on this stole just as Jesus wrapped a towel around himself in the upper room before the first Lord's Supper." Here is another example: in light of the literary discussion in the previous section, the congregation could be reminded before the Creed through the Peace section, "Having heard God's story just told to us through Holy Scripture, now let us respond by sharing our community's faith journey."

## SALUTATION

The salutation begins the conversation between God and his worshiping people. It draws priest and people into a dialogue and establishes the reason for being there. For example, "Blessed be God: Father, Son, and Holy Spirit. And blessed be his kingdom, now and forever. Amen."

The importance of the salutation, as stated above, is its role not only to welcome the audience but to declare the setting and characters for the drama that is about to unfold. In most churches, at least the ones that I have attended, the opening greeting seems to have two roles: first to

set the audience at ease and make them comfortable—especially the visi-
tor; and second to declare the church's brand. "Welcome to the Church
of the Ever-Journeying. Here at COEJ we strive to love people, love our
community, and find fresher ways to ever-journey." It is a far different
thing to set the people present not "at ease" but inside an epic story and in
their proper relationship to the other characters: "Blessed be God, Father,
Son, and Holy Spirit." Also to place the immediate congregation within
its greater context: "Blessed be His kingdom, now and forever." The
words of the opening prayer in the Book of Common Prayer even sound
Shakespearean in their cantor: "Almighty God, unto whom all hearts are
open, all desires are known, and from whom no secrets are hid; cleanse
the thoughts of our hearts by the inspiration of thy Holy Spirit, that we
may perfectly love Thee, and worthily magnify thy holy Name; through
Christ our Lord. Amen."

### Creative suggestions for the salutation:

- Ask members of the congregation to write alternate saluations. I
  would encourage these writers/artists to model the tone of a Shakespearean prologue.[1] I believe that even within such creativity it is
  essential to keep God and his kingdom at the center of Eucharistic
  salutation.

- Whether you use a historical salutation or a contemporary piece
  for the salutation, it doesn't hurt to have a flurry of the dramatic.
  Just be careful. The line between delightful/inspiring and cheesy is
  a dangerous tempter.

## GLORIA, KYRIE, OR TRISAGION

The Gloria, Kyrie, or Trisagion is the opening movement of the worship service in praise. "Lord, have mercy. Christ, have mercy. Lord, have
mercy."

The Gloria, Kyrie and Trisagion all end with an appeal for mercy.
They restate the core characters of the unfolding drama and set them in
relationship to one another. The tone is worshipful and is a call-out from
the audience to the divine with words like "holy," "praise," and "glorify."

---

1. An amusing example of which can be found toward the end of the film *Shakespeare
in Love.*

## THE COLLECT

The Collect is the "theme prayer of the day . . . and is intended to *collect* (hence the name) the prayers of the congregation around a single subject."[2]

The Book of Common Prayer is particularly helpful here because it includes a different theme prayer for each week that helps set up each week's lessons.

### Creative suggestions for the Collect:

- Ask members of the congregation to write their own theme prayers; however, these prayers should honor the specific structure of the Collect.

- Remember that the theme prayer introduces the God story, when his book is read and his ancient narrative retold. God is quite literally the main character of this act. Spatially it would make sense to embody that reality. Read the Collect from an elevated place. Recite with hands raised. Or, for the more daring, lightly strike a resonating instrument like a Tibetan gong bowl.

- Set up the Collect with a short reminder of that theme's importance. "In light of our world that is so full of pain and loneliness, let's read the theme prayer for today . . . "

## LESSONS (OLD TESTAMENT, PSALM, AND EPISTLE)

The lessons are the scriptural readings assigned to each Sunday on a three-year rotation. This ensures a thorough community review from the entire Bible every three years, and it is from these readings that the sermon is most often themed.

These lessons make up God's story. Among post-Christian people the lessons can also be read with a fair level of confidence[3] as is and without editorial, allowing the words to speak for themselves.

2. Webber, *Holy Eucharist*, 20.

3. See chapter 23 "Anglican Eucharistic Liturgy and a Post-Christian Encounter with Truth," subsection "Scripture."

*Creative suggestions for the lessons:*

- While the words of the lessons speak for themselves, people have a limited attention span. There are times when the readings may be shortened, though I would encourage reading at least a portion of every lesson.

- Space is our friend when we read the lessons. If the lessons are being read from the same place every week, the leadership is missing opportunities to both infuse spatial creativity and dramatic diversity.

  » Read each lesson from different corners of the room.

  » Read the lessons from within the congregation, with each reader "popping up."

  » If you have the space, read from a balcony or elevated place.

  » Have the readers stand side by side, reading each lesson into the next, like a classical Greek chorus.

- Some people have a knack for public reading. Their voices are dramatic, profound, inspiring, etc.; their inflections are perfect and they never make a mistake. However, this can embody an unspoken religious caste system. Post-Christian culture is increasingly looking for non-hierarchical religious orientation.[4] Therefore, having the Scriptures read by a child, a recent immigrant, or an undereducated adult can have a profound impact. *Remember, God's story is for all people and that reality ought to be embodied as it is proclaimed.*

- Spontaneously choose readers (or ask for volunteers) in the midst of the Eucharist service. This provides an organic feel and shows that our relation to the divine is not always prepackaged and often happens in the moment.

---

4. For more thoughts on authority and hierarchy see chapter 23 "Anglican Eucharistic Liturgy and the Post-Christian Encounter with Truth."

## GOSPEL READING

The Gospel reading is the same as "Lessons" above only it is the weekly reading from the Gospels. This reading "is given the highest honor"[5] of the lessons, is intended to be read by an ordained person, and is often read while standing within the congregation.

As explained above, I believe that the Gospel lesson, not the sermon, is the first climax of the service. Historically it was set apart in the liturgy and treated with more dramatic flair. There is a tradition to read the Gospel lesson from the center of the congregation. Sometimes a candle or lamp is lit above the head of the reader. This ancient tradition is so wonderful and meaningful that it is hard for me to think of other ways to demonstrate the importance of the Gospel lesson. I would encourage an elevated candle in the center of the room, auditorium, or sanctuary and to light the candle ceremoniously above the head of the lesson reader: a literal beacon of the Good News. Whatever ceremonial qualities are used, please maintain the tradition that sets the Gospel lesson apart and extends particular honor.

## SERMON

While the unmistakable climax of the Anglican service is Communion, the sermon still holds an important role. It is located in this first part of the liturgy and is intended to "bring the Word of God to bear on our lives."[6]

The sermon has a wonderful opportunity within the Anglican liturgy, an opportunity it does not have in many free-worship services. Since the message is embodied within the whole of the liturgy narrative, there is less weight and responsibility placed on the sermon to get everything "right." Also, as Webber said above, the sermon is to "bring the Word of God to bear on our lives."[7]

People in post-Christian culture do not need an iconic someone to tell them what to believe and how to believe it. They are not particularly offended if someone does, they just don't need it. As stated earlier in this book, they feel what I call a "personality fatigue."[8] What they are looking

5. Webber, *Holy Eucharist*, 20.

6. Ibid., 21.

7. Ibid.

8. We live in a world where personalities are elevated over content. Oprah is a per-

for is an authentic friend who will walk alongside them, express their own spiritual processes, and explain how the sacred might integrate with the world beyond the sacred gathering. The sermon is an interlude amidst a greater narrative. The sermon is to translate this declared truth (declared by the entire liturgy: Word, symbol, confession, sacrament, and Table) revealing how everyone present may live sacredly in every niche of life and view of the world.[9]

*Creative suggestions for the sermon:*

- I am new to the Anglican Way, but I would hope that this lowered expectation upon the sermon would free up the pastor in many important ways.

    » The pastor can be shockingly honest about his/her own struggles, journey, or doubts.

    » The pastor can use the sermon to simply point back to the other elements of the Eucharistic liturgy without needing to dazzle.

    » An entire sermon could be what I call a "thematic testimony." Many evangelicals are familiar with the "personal testimony," which is most often one's story of salvation. However, there is tremendous power in taking any theme or religious-philosophical question and telling one's lifelong journey of discovery. Such a story, well told, can easily fill fifteen minutes and should also follow the basic elements of the literary arc, as all

---

sonality. Katie Couric is a personality. Barak Obama is a personality. Tim Tebow is a personality. Rush Limbaugh is a personality. Advice, information, and entertainment (these three things are now impossible to separate from one another) are all delivered in the shape of a personality. And while we accept and daily participate in this reality, the church has an opportunity to provide the culture with a break from this personality inundation.

9. "The church, by focusing on its distinctive identity and vision, can be a depth-political presence of great consequence to society. The church's calling, we believe, is not to change society as such, but to be a steady and true witness of Christ's inauguration of the kingdom and his victory over the powers. The greatest service the church can do society—always, but certainly in an era of fragmentation—is to live out its distinctive story, to be a diacritical community, to present the promising contradiction personified by Jesus the Nazarene. If grace is real, if the gospel is truth, that is enough and more than enough." Webber and Clapp, *People of the Truth*, 123.

good storytellers do.

- Instead of a sermon, consider leading a discussion. If the purpose of the sermon is to "bring the word of God to bear on our lives" then it seems clear that the pastor cannot understand all the nuances of life outside the church. The "sermon" is an opportunity to validate and illuminate the experiences of the community in the journey of faith.

- Additionally, it would be powerful for the "pastor" to, instead of preaching, lead small group discussions along the topic of the Sunday liturgy. Encourage the congregation to get in small groups and have a led discussion around the theme topic. Then harvest the room for its best thoughts.

## THE CREED

The Creed is recited as our response to the Word, which has been read (lessons) and proclaimed (sermon). It affirms in common voice the belief that we have. Most often the Nicene Creed is read and it begins with the words, "We believe."

Nicene Creed

We believe in one God, the Father, the Almighty, maker of heaven and earth, of all that is, seen and unseen.

We believe in one Lord, Jesus Christ, the only Son of God, eternally begotten of the Father, God from God, Light from Light, true God from true God, begotten, not made, of one Being with the Father. Through him all things were made. For us and for our salvation he came down from heaven: by the power of the Holy Spirit he became incarnate from the Virgin Mary, and was made man. For our sake he was crucified under Pontus Pilate; he suffered death and was buried. On the third day he rose again in accordance with the Scriptures; he ascended into heaven and is seated at the right hand of the Father. He will come again in glory to judge the living and the dead, and his kingdom will have no end.

We believe in the Holy Spirit, the Lord, the giver of life, who proceeds from the Father and the Son. With the Father and the Son he is worshiped and glorified. He has spoken through the Prophets.

We believe in one holy catholic and apostolic Church. We acknowledge one baptism for the forgiveness of sins. We look for the resurrection of the dead, and the life of the world to come. Amen.[10]

Even with the growing loss of anxiety within the post-Christian culture toward Christianity and religious beliefs, the Creed could be one of the more challenging sections of the Eucharist. The exclusivity of the Creed, coupled with the tradition of swallowing the entire Creed "in one bite," may ask too much of the post-Christian person who is trying to discover and follow Jesus. Historically there has been real liturgical power in giving a communal oath—of declaring, for all to hear, the worshiping community's shared orthodox belief proclaimed in unison. This is still true. Here are some alternate proclamational perspectives.

### Creative suggestions for the Creed:

- In the story of the healing of the paralytic who is lowered down through the roof (Mark 2:1–12), it says in verse 5, "And Jesus, seeing their faith said to the paralytic, 'Son, your sins are forgiven.'" Jesus sets a precedent for healing and forgiveness that comes to a man through the faith of the surrounding community of love. Therefore, on some occasions the Creed could be recited "for the community" as opposed to "by the community," allowing those present to enter into the belief-declared through hearing and reflection. It is important to note, post-Christian people will by and large not be offended by a creed being read (even if they would feel awkward personally "taking the stand" and vowing along). Post-Christian people understand that sacred environments are sacred environments and will therefore have many specific (and even exclusive) traditions.

  » Ask a "chorus" to read the Creed in unison from the four corners of the room (representing all of humanity). Remind the audience to reflect on their own journey with God.

  » Show the Creed on screen, having it appear line by line slideshow style with accompanying images illustrating those beliefs.

  » Have a dozen "heralds" stand on crates around the room read

10. Webber, *Holy Eucharist*, 358.

the Creed in unison. Then encourage the community to affirm along with the heralds by raising their hands, standing,
or verbally offering an "amen" or "uh-huh" as their hearts respond. Note: I would be careful with having the Creed read
by a chorus of small children, which can give the appearance
of cultic manipulation. There are several other places in the
liturgy for child participation.

- Have the congregation read the Creed together, but explain beforehand that it is an ancient document, shared over centuries and
across cultures. Remind them that the Creed is not a document
intended to divide but to unify the human experience.

  » Remind the audience that on this very morning these same
  lines are being read by millions of people in hundreds of languages all across the globe. Help them connect faith to their
  globalized world.

  » Remind the audience that as they read it they can imagine
  the chorus of saints throughout history reading along with
  them. When else do modern people actually participate with
  history?

  » Point to the eschatological hope as we look forward to reading
  one day with humanity, being not "faith" but "sight."

- Specifically, give the audience permission to not read certain lines
or stanzas if they are "just not ready." This is a powerful thing to say
to a congregation of faith; it normalizes the *journey* of discovery
and belief. If done with generosity it indirectly tells the room that it
is okay if they don't believe it all, welcoming them to continue their
search within the community.

- Ask the audience to prayerfully look over the Creed, and then have
one person read it aloud and encourage each person to "proclaim
boldly" along with the reader the two or three phrases that are particularly meaningful to them on this morning. This allows people
to declare the specifics of their current faith narrative, and to do
so dramatically. It will also anecdotally indicate which creedal
ideas your particular congregation is drawn to (and which are less

inspiring or more challenging).11

> » Accomplish this same concept by having the audience declare phrases from the Creed aloud, in no particular order, "popcorn style." This would change the normal cadence of the Eucharistic service and give everyone a chance to process his or her most passionate beliefs.

> » The Creed could also be printed phrase by phrase, but in a nonlinear fashion. The phrases would be "scattered" around the page, maybe written in different fonts and styles. This would release a fresh encounter with the beliefs.

- Pause between lines or sections for an extended meditation. This could be very powerful for post-Christian people who need to ponder the tenants of Jesus-faith. Let the Creed breathe.

- Allow the community to write their own creeds. They could then be shared with the community.

- Instead of using a written creed, show a series of images on a screen and ask the community to vote on which image best illustrates their current dynamic with God. Those images would require some profound forethought. Show the images two times. On the third showing ask people to vote with a raised hand or a clap.

## THE PRAYERS OF THE PEOPLE

The Prayers of the People are usually led by a deacon or layperson and are often based upon some system of collecting the actual prayer needs of the gathered community.

Public prayer is something rarely if ever experienced by a post-Christian person. Entering into "prayer-request collection" can be foreign and awkward. One year into the Holy Trinity–Costa Mesa church plant, Bishop Hunter said that the Prayers of the People was the most challenging portion of the Eucharist for his congregation full of new practitioners of Anglicanism. Bishop Hunter is not alone in this experience.

Assure the audience that prayer is a way to bless one another and share life. Several studies show that people have great willingness to have

---

11. Take note of these "less popular" or "challenging" ideas and then look for opportunities in the future to woefully teach on those themes.

others pray for them, even if those individuals are not religious or even theists. I spent one summer in New York City where I participated with a ministry that simply stands on street corners and offers to pray for anyone's needs. These prayer stations are almost constantly occupied, and the response of passersby goes from gratitude to tears. The challenge is to assure the "audience" that it is safe to share.

### *Creative suggestions for Prayers of the People:*

- Begin the exercise in small groups of four to five and ask each person to provide something in his or her life that could be prayed for. Then harvest the room by asking congregants to share significant requests shared in their small group.

  » Tell people they cannot share their own requests, only a request they heard in their small group. This will open up a greater sampling of the room. It also provides another filter as to which requests are shared with the entire room and mediates the tendency for the same people and requests to be shared every week.

  » Encourage congregants to share requests from someone they just met.

- Establish a group of "request collectors," each responsible for a portion of the sanctuary (they could even begin the prayer collection process as people are taking their seats at the beginning of the service). At the appropriate time, these prayer requests could be proclaimed by the request collectors, each declaring the needs of their section of the congregation.

- Pose a handful of questions to the congregation and ask them to raise a hand if the question applies to them. "Who is currently experiencing illness?" "Who currently has scary financial issues?" "Who has a loved one in some sort of physical danger?" "Who has some sort of crisis of faith in their life today?" With each show of hands, exhort the congregation to take note of those near them while a short one- or two-line prayer is led by the worship guide. (Caring members of the congregation could briefly follow up with those "raised hands" during the Passing of the Peace.)

- Images are a powerful way to help people access and express their needs. A few sources of photo collections[12] are specifically designed and created to help people share their inner life. Place these photo collections on tables along the sides of the room and invite the congregation to go and examine the pictures. State a specific detail of life for which each person can seek a representative photo: a photo that represents their current emotional state, their current relationship with God, their connection to the church, and their connection to their own greater community. Then encourage them to share their picture with one other person in the room, even a stranger. That person can then pray for them as best as they know how.

## THE CONFESSION

The Confession is a prayer of repentance most often read together as a community. There are several historic examples. One of the most widely used includes, "Most merciful God, we confess what we have sinned against you in thought, word, and deed, by what we have done, and by what we have left undone." It is followed by a spoken absolution.

A fair amount of ink has already been spilt in this book discussing the place of confession in a post-Christian context.[13] In summary, confession has an opportunity for a profound rebirth within public worship. In fact, I believe that people want it, even if they don't know that they do. Confession and absolution are two things that people cannot experience anywhere else in the public sphere (and almost never do within the private sphere). "Ignore and move on" is the *modus operandi* of our culture and it is a sickness to the soul.

### Creative suggestions for the Confession:

- Post-Christian people will be moved by the return to confessing not only the "things I have done," but also "the things left undone."

---

12. Here are two of those photo collections: My Soularium (includes fifty 4"x6" images for $12.50), http://crupress.campuscrusadeforchrist.com/evangelism/soularium and Visual Explorer (includes 216 8"x10" images for $380) http://www.ccl.org/leadership/inHouse/tools.aspx.

13. Return to and review chapter 25, "Anglican Liturgy and Post-Christian Spirituality," subsection "Confession."

There is a just accusation of American Christianity and its focus on active "dos and don'ts," while forgetting the equally important passive "undones." Our culture feels this imbalance.

- Confess these done and undone things both as individuals but also communally as a part of humanity. There is a shift in the culture from a hyper-individualistic view of the world to an understanding of systemic and shared injustice. Post-Christian people (post-evangelical people) are seeing more clearly their solidarity with systems like racism, economic injustice, environmental destruction, consumerism, and classism. Where else can they go to declare their guilt aloud? Where else can they go and hear, "Almighty God have mercy on you, forgive you all your sins through our Lord Jesus Christ, strengthen you in all goodness, and by the power of the Holy Spirit keep you in eternal life, Amen"?[14] Or as one priest in a London parish says each week, "The Lord forgives you. Now forgive one another. Forgive yourself."

- As with other sections, a congregation could commission members to write their own prayers. However, I am often moved by the existing prayers of confession within the Anglican liturgy.

- The confession can also be used to allow people to reveal their current overall spiritual states (as opposed to listing the points of sin and guilt).

  » Have everyone hold up a hand and ask them, "On a scale of one to five, one being distant and five being near, where is your relationship to God?" Then have them turn and share with someone why they chose that number.

  » Use the photos again. Everyone could be encouraged to find a photo that best expresses their relationship with God and then share that image with someone.

## THE PEACE

Now, "freed from sin, we are brought together in unity."[15] The Peace is a ritual of exchange and often includes blessing one another with the words,

14. Anglican Mission in the Americas, *Anglican Prayer Book*, 53.
15. Webber, *Holy Eucharist*, 25.

"Peace be with you." The Peace is more than a "greet someone near you"; it is an opportunity to practice reconciled Christian community.

*Creative suggestions for the Peace:*

- Remind the congregation that in history the church service was the one place where classes met as equals—there are no lords or serfs in the house of the Lord. And when we give and receive the Peace, we are declaring that in a world of injustice, "we are right with one another, in Christ."

- Introduce the Peace by telling a short story of reconciliation. "The best stories of humanity are stories of reconciliation. They are stories of risk and interpersonal courage getting beyond passive to really engage, honoring the humanity in the other, seeking forgiveness."[16]

- Once again, use the photos with the question, "What image best illustrates your current relationship with this worshiping community?" Then share that image with one or two others as a bridge to going into deeper peace together.

## HOLY COMMUNION (GREAT THANKSGIVING, BREAKING OF BREAD, AND THE COMMUNION)

The Holy Communion is the unapologetic climax of the service. This section of the service begins with prayers that lead up to the breaking of the bread. These prayers include Eucharist prayers and the Lord's Prayer, which is recited by all. The Breaking of the Bread is marked primarily by silence. Then, "as God came to us in flesh and blood in Jesus of Nazareth, so now God comes to us here in the bread and wine."[17] The congregation comes forward to be served the bread and the wine.

Absolutely keep the Holy Communion as the climax of the service. This global-historical, symbol-saturated meeting with Christ and his sacrifice from within the collected church has maintained its power and significance over the centuries and across cultures for a very important reason. It is simply meaningful, designed before the creation of the world to speak to the human heart.

16. Kriz, "B @ Peace Project."
17. Webber, *Holy Eucharist*, 30.

## Creative suggestions for Holy Communion:

- Bring the altar off the "stage" and place it in the middle of the worshiping community, right in the center of the room. This geography would both support its centrality and express the equal footing for all followers.

- There are diverse examples of the types of "bread" that are used in the Eucharistic service. A post-Christian person like me has a hard time connecting with the otherworldly wafers used in many Anglican churches. They are stamped with the super-secret spiritual symbol and they most closely resemble Styrofoam in both texture and taste. For the bread and wine to retain meaning within a post-Christian context, I believe they should meet one of these two criteria:

  » Congruence with the elements' original form, which gives the worshiper historical transcendence. In the Jesus tradition, this would mean some sort of unleavened bread,

  » or they should be particularly congruent with the time and place in which they are served. Extreme examples would include cultures that use rice or even plantains for Christ's body. In the case of Portland, I would probably recommend some kind of hearty, multigrain bread from a local bakery. Even better, bread that is baked by members of the congregation. This local orientation brings to the worshiper the importance of *their* time and place while also communicating the incarnational nature of the gospel.

- Zwingli and Knox both set a tradition for the Eucharistic elements to be distributed by the worshiping community beyond just the ordained. This is still a challenging suggestion in many contexts; however, I am convinced that a greater connection happens when post-Christian people are not only the consumers[18] of the Eucharist but also participants in its administration.

---

18. Isn't a consumer mentality one of the greatest enemies of the gospel in our current cultural context? Aren't we also constantly struggling to shatter the perception that Christian life and ministry is not especially for the ordained but instead equally shared by all of God's people?

- Ornate vessels like a silver chalice communicate a certain sacredness. Vessels that have local and artisan roots bring another sort of grounded and incarnational sense. Try using locally made wooden plates or pottery. Even better, vessels worshipfully made by congregation members.

- One of the benefits of people coming to a "rail" to receive the elements is the opportunity to linger with Christ in a posture of worship. I recommend thinking through how to provide congregants with the opportunity to linger with Christ in the elements.

## THE BLESSING AND DISMISSAL

The blessing and dismissal is a closing blessing on the congregation and a sending out for the community to return to the world out of the renewal and sustenance of the Holy Eucharist. Send the congregation into the world with a renewed vision of reconciliation both in their souls and through their lives as they go as conduits of reconciliation.

*Creative suggestions for the blessing and dismissal:*

- Declare the dismissal with either enthusiasm or sobriety based on the theme of the week.

- Allow God to provide the "marking orders." In his book *Revolution*, George Barna wrote this about our changing culture, "Americans are used to controlling their lives. What makes Revolutionaries so bizarre is that they admit they do not have control of their lives and they are not seeking to attain control. Who else would you want controlling your life besides the God of Creation?"[19]

- I honestly question the use of a prolonged "coffee hour" as it distracts and dulls the moment of "sending into the world" that is so essential to fulfilling the drama of the Eucharist. Maybe a sending out to communal homes, where a shared meal happens within the neighborhoods would accomplish the same without dulling the sending.

The conversation has begun. These few ideas are shared here to inspire and release the people of God to communicate well, inspire the heart,

19. Barna, *Revolution*, 82.

and offer the great gift of the sacred encounter with God in Christ, by the power of the Holy Spirit. Amen.

# Appendix

*Survey Data for Zip Code 97217*

## INTRODUCTION

THE RELIGIOUS STATISTICS FOR the Pacific Northwest are widely chronicled.[1] They are regionally based, state based and in the case of Barna's *Markets 2011*,[2] even city based. My intent is to dial the discussion of religious identification, church attendance, and perceptions of the Christian church into tight focus. Here is my research, focused on a single zip code.[3]

I live in the 97217 zip code in the inner eastside of Portland. These addresses are technically "North" Portland, but the cultural dynamics are more defined by which side of the river you live on and how far your home is from the downtown waterfront. To determine how well the Barna numbers above (71 percent, 16 percent and 8 percent)[4] apply to my neighborhood, I decided to gather specific data. I initiated an independent survey of residents of the 97217 zip code.[5] For those with familiarity

1. Kinnaman and Lyons, *Unchristian*; Wicker, *Fall*; Duin, *Quitting Church*; and Olson, *American Church in Crisis*.

2. Barna Group, *Markets 2011* and *States 2011*.

3. Having spent quite some time researching, I have found nothing that takes research to this tight of a focus and on a population as small and specified as a single zip code. These numbers are a unique contribution to the understanding of urban Northwest culture and the emerging reality of a post-Christian nation.

4. In chapter 2, we discuss at length how Barna's statistics for Portland determine a 71 percent affiliation to Christianity, 16 skepticism of religion, and 8 percent identification with other religious traditions. This report seeks to derive specific numbers for zip code 97217.

5. I corresponded with David Kinnaman, President of Barna Group, regarding our

of Portland, this zip code covers the Overlook Neighborhood to the south and the Kenton Neighborhood to the north. It traverses Interstate 5 north of the Rose Quarter from Williams Avenue to the east and past Denver Avenue to the west.

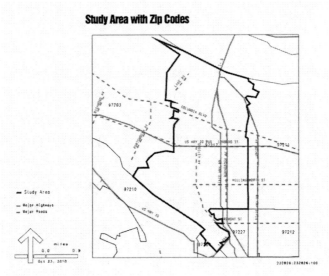

Figure 15. Study Area Definition: Zip Code 97217. Source: First View 2010 Prepared for Anglican Mission in America.

There were 193 individuals surveyed within zip code 97217. Every short interview was delivered face to face. Each volunteer interviewer was specifically trained in how to administer an objective interview, including the following polling rules: read the survey explanation and each question in a neutral way; read each question in the same tone, avoiding inserting personal emphasis or import; let the questions stand for themselves; and avoid "explaining further" as each interviewer risks inserting biased interpretations. (For instance, interviewers were coached not to define "spiritual" in the question, "Do you consider yourself a spiritual person?") Zip code 97217 has a total population of about thirty-one

research results. In his brief comments, he explained that our results were different from Barna's not only because of their geographic focus, but also because of our less sophisticated research methodology. He stated, "Typically intercept or face-to-face interviews even if done [in] what appears to be a random manner, do not always generate a representative sample." David Kinnaman, email correspondence with author, February 13, 2011.

thousand. One hundred and ninety three surveys represent a plus/minus 7 percent confidence interval with a 95 percent confidence level.[6]

Almost no one refused to participate when approached. Most everyone we stopped was more than content to give a few moments to answer questions about faith and religious perceptions. Those who did refuse always refused to answer all questions and always because of a time excuse: "I don't have time right now." The only times someone refused (this happened twice) to answer only a portion of the questions was in the "perceptions of Christian denominations/traditions" section and their reasoning was a desire for "peace among people" or having "no desire to judge others." These same individuals were more than happy, however, to comment about their own practices and beliefs. No one who had time to take the survey refused to discuss their own religious beliefs and practice. This is significant because according to Christine Wicker (in her book *The Fall of the Evangelical Nation*), 5 percent of the people approached in 2001 to take the American Religious Identification Survey "refused to answer the religion question."[7]

Individuals were surveyed on three important topics. The first topic dealt with how the respondent religiously self-identifies.

| |
|---|
| Do you consider yourself a "religious" person?  Yes  No |
| Do you consider yourself a "spiritual" person?  Yes  No |
| On a scale of 1-10 (10 being high and 1 being low), how important is the spiritual dimension of life? |
| What, if any, religion or spiritual tradition do you currently claim or practice? |

Figure 16. Survey for Zip Code 97217, Part 1.

6. Creative Research Systems, "Sample Size Calculator." The *confidence interval* (also called margin of error) is the plus-or-minus figure usually reported in newspaper or television opinion poll results. For example, if you use a confidence interval of 4 and 47% percent of your sample picks an answer, you can be "sure" that if you had asked the question of the entire relevant population between 43% (47-4) and 51% (47+4) would have picked that answer.

The *confidence level* tells you how sure you can be. It is expressed as a percentage and represents how often the true percentage of the population who would pick an answer lies within the confidence interval. The 95% confidence level means you can be 95% certain; the 99% confidence level means you can be 99% certain. Most researchers use the 95% confidence level.

7. Wicker, *Fall of the Evangelical Nation*, 209.

The second section dealt with further understanding if the respondent has ever attended a Christian church (worship) service.

| The next few questions are asking about attendance of a Christian church (any Christian tradition or denomination) |
| --- |
| Do you currently regularly attend a Christian church? Yes   No |
| If "yes", do you attend at least once a month on average? |
| If "no", have you ever regularly attended a Christian church? |
| Have you attended a Christian church in the last 6 months? |

Figure 17. Survey for Zip Code 97217, Part 2.

The third section dealt with discovering whether the respondent has negative or positive perceptions of a selection of Christian traditions and was measured using the following scale and list:

| On a scale of 1-5 how positive or negative are your impressions of each denomination/tradition?<br>    1 –strongly negative impressions<br>    2 –moderately negative impressions<br>    3 –equal number of neg. and pos. impressions<br>    4 –moderately positive impressions<br>    5 –strongly positive impressions<br>    OR –no real impressions one way or the other.<br><br>Reminder:  this list is only a sampling. | |
| --- | --- |
| Roman Catholicism | |
| Charismatic Churches | |
| "Emergent" Churches | |
| Lutheran | |
| Evangelical | |
| Anglican | |
| Baptist | |
| Methodist | |
| Eastern Orthodox: Russian, Greek, etc. | |
| Pentecostal | |
| Latter Day Saints (Mormons) | |
| Presbyterian | |

Figure 18. Survey for Zip Code 97217, Part 3.

I chose these particular traditions for many reasons. First of all, as the survey indicates, it would be impossible to be exhaustive or even truly representative of the breadth of Christian traditions, so these are simply a sample of Christian traditions. They are listed in no particular order.

There are some "traditions" included that some people might question. "Charismatic" and "Pentecostal" were both included because I did not know which term those outside Christendom were more familiar with (I learned they have more familiarity with Pentecostalism). I chose "emergent" because it is a recurring topic in this book and though I assumed that it is more of an insider's term and would be little known outside Christendom (as the survey confirmed), it also made for a good control case in our experiment. "Roman Catholic" and "Eastern Orthodox (Russian, Greek, etc.)" were included because they represent such a massive percentage of Christians globally and because they are referenced in this book. "Church of Jesus Christ and Latter Day Saints (Mormons)" was included because I wanted to test and see if they are perceived as poorly outside Christendom as they have been within Christendom. It is also worth noting that there were no reports of respondents asking, "Why were Mormons included in a list of Christian denominations?" We Christians may need to accept that the Mormons are perceived as our brethren.

One possible criticism of this list is that it does not include "Episcopalians." After considerable thought, this was an intentional subtraction. I wanted to get an uncluttered impression of the term "Anglican," and I thought that would be best accomplished if it were not juxtaposed near the term "Episcopalian."

Each person surveyed was categorized by a series of demographics. Those categories include the following: gender (male or female), approximate age (18–25, 26–45, or 46+), and race (Black, White, Hispanic/ Latino, Asian, or Other). These demographics were determined by the "eye test" of the surveying volunteer.

# SURVEY

## Here is the full survey for zip code 97217:

---

**Survey**

This survey is collecting research for a study of religious orientation and church attendance in urban contexts of the Pacific Northwest. This particular survey is focusing on zip code 97217.

**Questions:**
Do you live (or have you lived recently) in 97217 (show map)?     Yes    No    Near
_____

Do you consider yourself a "religious" person?     Yes     No

Do you consider yourself a "spiritual" person?     Yes     No

On a scale of 1-10 (10 being high and 1 being low), how important is the spiritual dimension of life?     1     2     3     4     5     6     7     8     9     10

What, if any, religion or spiritual tradition do you currently claim or practice? _____

The next few questions are asking about attendance of a Christian church (any Christian tradition or denomination.)
Do you currently regularly attend a Christian church?     Yes     No
   If "yes", do you attend at least once a month on average?     Yes     No
   If "no", have you ever regularly attended a Christian church?     Yes     No
Have you attended a Christian church in the last 6 months?     Yes     No

This study is collecting observations and critiques of contemporary Christian traditions. In this last section, I will name a number of religious denominations/traditions and ask you to respond in the following way:

On a scale of 1-5 how positive or negative are your impressions of each denomination/tradition?
    1 -strongly negative impressions
    2 –moderately negative impressions
    3 –equal number of negative and positive impressions
    4- moderately positive impressions
    5- strongly positive impressions
    OR- no real impressions one way or the other.

Reminder: this list is only a sampling.

| | 1 | 2 | 3 | 4 | 5 | No Impression |
|---|---|---|---|---|---|---|
| Roman Catholicism | | | | | | |
| Charismatic Churches | | | | | | |
| "Emergent" churches----------------- | | | | | | |
| Lutheran | | | | | | |
| Evangelical | | | | | | |
| Anglican----------------------------- | | | | | | |
| Baptist | | | | | | |
| Methodist | | | | | | |
| Eastern Orthodoxy (Russian, Greek, etc.) | | | | | | |
| Pentecostal | | | | | | |
| Latter Day Saints (Mormons) ------------- | | | | | | |
| Presbyterian | | | | | | |

F    M          18-25    25-45    45+          B    W    H    A    O

---

Figure 19. Full Survey for Zip Code 97217.

## SELECTIVE SUMMARY OF DATA

According to our results, only 24.8 percent of respondents consider them-selves "religious," while 74.6 percent self-identify as "spiritual." When asked to rate the importance of the "spiritual dimension of life on a scale of one to ten,[8]" the responses show an average of 6.6.

Now this is where the numbers get really fascinating. When asked, "What, if any, religion or spiritual tradition do you currently claim or practice?" only 25.8 percent claimed "Christian" of any sort or flavor (shattering Barna's 71 percent rating).[9] Only 19.2 percent of whites iden-tify as "Christians," in contrast to 78.6 percent of blacks. Conversely, only 5.7 percent self-identify as "atheist" or "agnostic" (compared to Barna's 16 percent), and 12.4 percent identify with religious systems other than Christianity (compared to 8 percent). And most shockingly, eighty re-spondents said "none" and nineteen others defined their faith in such individualistic terms as to not fall under any faith category.[10] That equals an alarming 51.3 percent of respondents as simply non-religious (Gallup says that Oregon is the most "non-religious" state with 18 percent iden-tifying as such statewide).[11] When asked, over 50 percent simply say they have no religious tradition or claim!

When asked about Christian church attendance, only thirty-eight respondents (19.7 percent) claim to attend church,[12] which is not a sur-prising number, especially after reading the religious affiliation numbers listed above. (Within that number, Blacks and Latinos attend church at a rate of about 65 percent according to this survey.) However, when those same thirty-eight respondents were asked if they attend regularly

8. Actual responses ranged from zero to ten.

9. I corresponded with David Kinnaman, President of Barna Group, regarding our research results. In his brief comments, he explained that our results were different from Barna's not only because of their geographic focus, but also because of our less sophis-ticated research methodology. He stated, "Typically intercept or face-to-face interviews even if done [in] what appears to be a random manner, do not always generate a repre-sentative sample." David Kinnaman, email correspondence with author, February 13, 2011.

10. "Atheists" and "agnostics" were not included here, nor were any responses that included any references to a deity of any sort.

11. Gallup is another highly regarded polling organization. 18 percent as "Non-Religious" is a 2004 statistic. Jeffery M. Jones, "Tracking Religious Affiliation."

12. Thirteen percent of those were of faiths other than "Christian." Therefore, those attending a "Christian church" is seemingly closer to 17 percent.

(defined as "once a month"), all thirty-eight said they attend at least that often. Why is this important? One reason that jumps out at me. It appears there is no cultural pull to pretend like one is a "good Christian." There is zero sense of obligation to claim something is true that is not. If there were, it seems there would have been at least a few people who would claim to attend church and then when asked to clarify would say, "No not that often" or "I know I should go more often" or would just admit their attendance is irregular. However, even though the number is small, every church attendee is devout. I would not have predicted this. Of the 80.4 percent who said they do not attend church, 66 percent of those said they had attended regularly at some point in their life (usually childhood).[13] This number was higher than I would have predicted.

## DATA ANALYSIS

The following data was compiled from 193 surveys.

### *Do you consider yourself a "religious" person?*
### *Answer "YES"*

| | | |
|---|---|---|
| Total religious "yes": | 48/193 | 24.9% |
| | | |
| Age 18–24 "religious" | 11/43 | 25.6% |
| Age 25–45 "religious" | 25/113 | 22.1% |
| Age 46+ "religious" | 11/32 | 34.4% |
| Male | 26/92 | 28.2% |
| Female | 16/92 | 17.4% |
| | | |
| White | 30/164 | 18.3% |
| Black | 9/14 | 64.3% |
| Asian | 2/8 | 25.0% |
| Latino/Hispanic | 1/6 | 16.7% |

13. This observation is anecdotal based on how people responded to the question, "If 'no,' have you ever regularly attended a Christian church?" Many people said something like "Yes, back when I was a kid."

## Do you consider yourself a "spiritual" person?
### Answer "YES"

| | | |
|---|---|---|
| Total spiritual "yes": | 144/193 | 74.6% |
| | | |
| Age 18–24 | 32/43 | 74.4% |
| Age 25–45 | 81/113 | 71.7% |
| Age 46+ | 26/32 | 81.2% |
| | | |
| Male | 63/92 | 68.5% |
| Female | 63/92 | 68.5% |
| | | |
| White | 126/164 | 76.8% |
| Black | 12/14 | 85.7% |
| Asian | 5/8 | 62.5% |
| Latino/Hispanic | 6/6 | 100% |

*On a scale of 1–10 (10 being high and 1 being low), how important is the spiritual dimension of life?*

### All Responses (193)

| | |
|---|---|
| 0 | 2 |
| 1 | 18 |
| 2 | 2 |
| 3 | 9 |
| 4 | 11 |
| 5 | 27 |
| 6 | 11 |
| 7 | 32 |
| 8 | 26 |
| 9 | 11 |
| 10 | 44 |

Average: 6.6

## Responses from Age Group 25–45 (113 respondents)

| 0 | 0 |
|---|---|
| 1 | 12 |
| 2 | 2 |
| 3 | 5 |
| 4 | 6 |
| 5 | 17 |
| 6 | 7 |
| 7 | 16 |
| 8 | 11 |
| 9 | 9 |
| 10 | 27 |

## Average: 6.5

| Age Group 18–24 | 6.3 |
|---|---|
| Age Group 46+ | 6.8 |
| | |
| Male | 6.3 |
| Female | 6.7 |
| White | 6.3 |
| Black | 8.4 |
| Asian | 5.9 |
| Latino/Hispanic | 7.5 |

*What, if any, religion or spiritual tradition do you currently claim or practice?*

| Christian | 50/193 | 25.9% |
|---|---|---|
| Catholic | 11/50 | 22.0% (of "Christians") |

## Christian by Sub-Group

| Age Group 18–24 | 7/43 | 16.3% |
|---|---|---|
| Age Group 25–45 | 31/113 | 27.4% |
| Age Group 46+ | 11/32 | 34.4% |
| | | |

| Male | 26/92 | 28.3% |
|---|---|---|
| Female | 20/92 | 21.7% |
| White | 28/146 | 19.2% |
| Black | 11/14 | 78.6% |
| Asian | 2/8 | 25.0% |
| Latino/Hispanic | 3/6 | 50.0% |

## Total breakdown:

| | |
|---|---|
| Buddhist | 5 |
| - Zen | 1 |
| Christian | 50 |
| - Catholic | 11 |
| - Baptist | 2 |
| - Bible | 1 |
| - Congregational | 1 |
| - Episcopal | 2 |
| - Evangelical | 2 |
| - Lutheran | 1 |
| - Methodist | 1 |
| - Non-denominational | 3 |
| - Orthodox | 1 |
| - Presbyterian | 1 |
| - United Church of X | 1 |
| Atheist | 7 |
| Agnostic | 4 |
| Mormon | 2 |
| JW | 1 |
| Taoism | 1 |
| Unitarian/Universalist | 6 |
| Independent (diverse) | 28 |
| - "Self" defined | 19 |
| Jewish | 6 |
| Muslim | 1 |
| Pagan | 2 |
| None | 80 |

*Do you currently regularly attend a Christian church?*

### Answer "Yes"

| All | 38/193 | 19.7% |
|---|---|---|
| Regularly | 38/38 | 100% |

### Of those who said "yes,"

| Muslims | 1 |
|---|---|
| Mormans | 2 |
| Unitarian | 1 |
| JW | 1 |

### Therefore, Christian church is: 17.1%.

| Age Group 18-24 | 7/43 | 16.3% |
|---|---|---|
| Age Group 25-45 | 21/113 | 18.6% |
| Age Group 46+ | 9/32 | 28.1% |
| | | |
| Male | 20/92 | 21.7% |
| Female | 15/92 | 16.3% |
| White | 18/146 | 12.3% |
| Black | 9/14 | 64.3% |
| Asian | 3/8 | 37.5% |
| Latino/Hispanic | 4/6 | 66.7% |

### Answer "No"

| All | 156/193 | 80.4% |
|---|---|---|
| Ever? | 103/156 | 66% |
| Last 6 Months | 20/156 | 12.8% |

*On a scale of 1–5 how positive or negative are your impressions of each denomination/tradition?*

1. strongly negative impressions

2. moderately negative impressions

3. equal number of negative and positive impressions

4. moderately positive impressions

5. strongly positive impressions

OR: no real impressions one way or the other.

Here are a few specific examples:

## Roman Catholic

| | |
|---|---|
| 1 | 140 |
| 2 | 46 |
| 3 | 55 |
| 4 | 19 |
| 5 | 5 |

| | | |
|---|---|---|
| Negative impression (1+2) | 86/193 | 44.6% |
| Neutral (3) | 55/193 | 28.5% |
| Positive impression (4+5) | 24/193 | 12.4% |
| No impression | 28/193 | 14.5% |

## Anglican

| | |
|---|---|
| 1 | 15 |
| 2 | 17 |
| 3 | 45 |
| 4 | 18 |
| 5 | 6 |

| | | |
|---|---|---|
| Negative impression (1+2) | 32/193 | 16.6% |
| Neutral (3) | 45/193 | 23.3% |
| Positive impression (4+5) | 24/193 | 12.4% |
| No impression | 92/193 | 47.4% |

## Evangelical

| 1 | 75 |
|---|---|
| 2 | 36 |
| 3 | 38 |
| 4 | 9 |
| 5 | 7 |

| Negative impression (1+2) | 111/193 | 57.5% |
|---|---|---|
| Neutral (3) | 38/193 | 19.7% |
| Positive impression (4+5) | 16/193 | 8.3% |
| No impression | 29/193 | 15.0% |

## Latter Day Saints (Mormons)

| 1 | 73 |
|---|---|
| 2 | 45 |
| 3 | 38 |
| 4 | 10 |
| 5 | 7 |

| Negative impression (1+2) | 118/193 | 61.1% |
|---|---|---|
| Neutral (3) | 38/193 | 19.7% |
| Positive impression (4+5) | 17/193 | 8.8% |
| No impression | 20/193 | 10.4% |

## Baptist

| 1 | 37 |
|---|---|
| 2 | 46 |
| 3 | 49 |
| 4 | 27 |
| 5 | 8 |

| Negative impression (1+2) | 83/193 | 42.0% |
|---|---|---|

| Neutral (3) | 49/193 | 25.4% |
|---|---|---|
| Positive impression (4+5) | 35/193 | 18.1% |
| No impression | 24/193 | 12.4% |

## Number of "No Impressions"

| Roman Catholic | 28 |
|---|---|
| Charismatic | 96 |
| Emergent | 138 |
| Lutheran | 50 |
| Evangelical | 29 |
| Anglican | 92 |
| Baptist | 25 |
| Methodist | 50 |
| Orthodox | 65 |
| Pentecostal | 57 |
| Mormon | 20 |
| Presbyterian | 48 |
| Nazarene | 44/78<br>Note: Only 78 surveys included "Nazarene" |

## Average 1–5 score

| Roman Catholic | 2.4 |
|---|---|
| Charismatic | 2.2 |
| Emergent | 2.5 |
| Lutheran | 2.9 |
| Evangelical | 2.0 |
| Anglican | 2.8 |
| Baptist | 2.5 |
| Methodist | 2.9 |
| Orthodox | 2.8 |
| Pentecostal | 2.2 |
| Mormon | 2.0 |
| Presbyterian | 2.9 |
| Nazarene | 2.7 |

97217 SURVEY OF RELIGIOUS PERCEPTION AND
CHURCH ATTENDANCE
SPREADSHEET KEY

B. Do you live in 97217: Y, N

C. Gender: M, F

D. Age: A(18–25), B(25–45), C(45+)

E. Race: B(Black), W(White), H(Hispanic), A(Asian), O(other)

F. Religious Person: Y, N

G. Spiritual Person: Y, N

H, How important is spiritual dimension: 1–10

I.  What, if any, spiritual tradition, claim, or practice:

  None
  Christian: (specific)
  Buddhist: (specific)
  Muslim: (specific)
  Jewish: (specific)
  Hindu: (specific)
  Pagan: (specific)
  New Age: (specific)
  Independent: (specific)
  Unitarian-Universalist (UU): (specific)

J.  Do you attend Christian Church: Y, N

K. If "yes" at least once a month: Y, N

L. If "no" ever regularly attended: Y, N

M. Have you attended a church in last 6 months: Y, N


How position or negative: 1, 2, 3, 4, 5, 6 (No Impression)

  N. Catholic

  O. Charismatic

  P.  Emergent

  Q. Lutheran

R. Evangelical

S. Anglican

T. Baptist

U. Methodist

V. Orthodox

W. Pentecostal

X. Mormon

Y. Presbyterian

Z. Nazarene

## RAW DATA SPREADSHEET

### Zip Code 97217 Survey of Religious Perceptions and Church Attendence

| Column1 | Live in 97217 | Gender | Age | Race | Religious? | Spiritual? | Spiritual Import | Spiritual Tradition | Attend Church | "yes": once a month | "No": ever attend? | church in last 6 mths | Roman Catholic | Charismatic | Emergent | Lutheran | Evangelical | Anglican | Baptist | Methodist | Orthodox | Pentecostal | Mormon | Presbyterian | Nazarene |
|---|---|---|---|---|---|---|---|---|---|---|---|---|---|---|---|---|---|---|---|---|---|---|---|---|---|
| 1 | y | m | A | H | N | Y | 9 | CHR:CHR FOLLOWER | N | | Y | N | 3 | 2 | 1 | 6 | 1 | 4 | 3 | 4 | 4 | 3 | 2 | 3 | |
| 2 | Y | M | B | W | N | N | 1 | NOTHING | N | | Y | N | 4 | 2 | 6 | 6 | 1 | 3 | 3 | 6 | 2 | 1 | 1 | 6 | |
| 3 | Y | F | B | W | N | Y | 10 | IND:UU | N | | Y | N | 2 | 6 | 6 | 5 | 6 | 6 | 4 | 4 | 3 | 6 | 2 | 2 | |
| 4 | y | F | B | W | N | Y | 5 | NONE | N | | Y | N | 2 | 6 | 6 | 2 | 2 | 2 | 3 | 6 | 6 | 6 | 4 | 3 | |
| 5 | y | F | B | W | N | Y | 7 | NONE | N | | Y | N | 3 | 1 | 6 | 3 | 1 | 4 | 1 | 3 | 3 | 1 | 1 | 3 | |
| 6 | y | M | B | W | N | Y | 10 | IND:SKEPTISISM | N | | Y | N | 3 | 1 | 6 | 3 | 1 | 3 | 3 | 3 | 5 | 3 | 2 | 3 | |
| 7 | Y | F | B | H | Y | Y | 10 | IND:JW | Y | Y | | Y | 1 | 6 | 6 | 6 | 6 | 6 | 6 | 6 | 6 | 6 | 6 | 6 | |
| 8 | Y | M | B | W | N | Y | 7 | IND:UU | N | | Y | Y | 1 | 6 | 6 | 3 | 2 | 6 | 2 | 3 | 2 | 6 | 1 | 3 | |
| 9 | Y | F | B | W | Y | Y | 8 | CHR:CATHOLIC | Y | Y | | Y | 4 | 4 | 6 | 4 | 3 | 4 | 3 | 4 | 4 | 3 | 3 | 4 | |
| 10 | y | F | A | W | N | N | 1 | CHR:LUTHERAN | N | | Y | N | 1 | 6 | 6 | 4 | 3 | 6 | 2 | 4 | 6 | 3 | 2 | 3 | |
| 11 | y | M | B | W | N | N | 1 | NONE | N | | Y | N | 1 | 1 | 1 | 2 | 1 | 1 | 1 | 2 | 1 | 1 | 1 | 2 | |
| 12 | y | M | B | W | Y | N | 6 | IND:UU | N | | N | N | 3 | 2 | 6 | 4 | 4 | 3 | 3 | 3 | 3 | 1 | 4 | 3 | |
| 13 | Y | F | B | | N | Y | 10 | IND:LIVING SLOWLY/PEACEFULLY | N | | N | N | 1 | 1 | 1 | 1 | 1 | 1 | 1 | 1 | 1 | 1 | 1 | 1 | |
| 14 | Y | M | B | W | N | Y | 5 | NONE | N | | Y | N | 3 | 3 | 4 | 6 | 3 | 6 | 2 | 6 | 4 | 6 | 4 | 6 | |
| 15 | Y | M | B | W | N | Y | 6 | NONE | N | | Y | N | 4 | 6 | 6 | 6 | 2 | 6 | 6 | 6 | 6 | 2 | 3 | 6 | |
| 16 | Y | F | B | W | N | Y | 9 | PAGAN:YOGA | N | | N | N | 6 | 6 | 6 | 2 | 2 | 3 | 2 | 6 | 4 | 6 | 2 | 6 | |
| 17 | Y | M | C | W | Y | Y | 10 | CHR | Y | Y | | Y | 3 | 5 | 5 | 4 | 5 | 4 | 4 | 4 | 5 | 5 | 1 | 5 | |
| 18 | Y | F | B | W | Y | Y | 8 | CHR:CONGREGATIONAL | N | | Y | N | 2 | 6 | 2 | 3 | 1 | 2 | 2 | 2 | 1 | 2 | 1 | 2 | |
| 19 | Y | F | B | W | Y | Y | 9 | CHR:EVAN | Y | Y | | Y | 4 | 5 | 6 | 4 | 5 | 4 | 4 | 4 | 4 | 4 | 3 | 4 | |
| 20 | Y | F | B | W | N | Y | 9 | NONE | N | | Y | N | 2 | 6 | 6 | 5 | 6 | 3 | 2 | 2 | 2 | 2 | 3 | 3 | |
| 21 | Y | F | B | W | N | Y | 8 | NONE | N | | Y | N | 2 | 2 | 2 | 2 | 1 | 2 | 2 | 2 | 2 | 2 | 2 | 2 | |
| 22 | Y | F | B | W | N | Y | 8 | CHR | N | | Y | N | 2 | 1 | 6 | 3 | 1 | 6 | 1 | 4 | 3 | 1 | 1 | 4 | |

| | | | | | | | | | | | | | | | | | | | | | | | | | | |
|---|---|---|---|---|---|---|---|---|---|---|---|---|---|---|---|---|---|---|---|---|---|---|---|---|---|---|
| 23 | Y | F | C | W | N | N | 0 | IND:ATHEIST | N | | N | N | 1 | 1 | 1 | 1 | 1 | 2 | 1 | 6 | 1 | 1 | 1 | 2 | |
| 24 | Y | F | B | W | Y | Y | 10 | CHR:CATHOLIC/NAT AME | Y | Y | | Y | 4 | 2 | 2 | 4 | 2 | 4 | 3 | 4 | 4 | 3 | 2 | 4 | |
| 25 | Y | F | C | H | N | Y | 6 | CHR:CATHOLIC | Y | Y | | Y | 3 | 3 | 3 | 3 | 3 | 3 | 3 | 3 | 3 | 3 | 3 | 3 | |
| 26 | Y | F | C | H | N | Y | 7 | CHR:CATHOLIC | Y | Y | | Y | 3 | 6 | 6 | 6 | 6 | 6 | 6 | 6 | 6 | 6 | 6 | 3 | 6 |
| 27 | Y | M | B | W | N | N | 1 | NONE | N | | N | N | 2 | 1 | 1 | 3 | 1 | 3 | 1 | 2 | 3 | 1 | 1 | 1 | |
| 28 | Y | M | C | W | Y | Y | 5 | IND:PRAY TO MYSELF | N | | Y | N | 3 | 6 | 6 | 4 | 3 | 6 | 4 | 4 | 4 | 4 | 4 | 4 | |
| 29 | Y | M | B | B | Y | Y | 5 | CHR | Y | Y | | Y | 6 | 6 | 6 | 6 | 6 | 6 | 6 | 6 | 6 | 6 | 6 | 6 | |
| 30 | Y | M | B | W | N | N | 2 | NONE | N | | Y | N | 3 | 2 | 6 | 3 | 2 | 6 | 2 | 6 | 3 | 2 | 3 | 6 | 6 |
| 31 | Y | F | B | W | N | Y | 8 | CHR:NON-DENOM | N | | Y | N | 2 | 6 | 6 | 3 | 1 | 6 | 2 | 3 | 6 | 1 | 2 | 3 | 6 |
| 32 | Y | M | B | W | Y | Y | 10 | CHR:CATHOLIC | Y | Y | | Y | 5 | 6 | 6 | 3 | 3 | 6 | 3 | 3 | 3 | 2 | 3 | 3 | |
| 33 | Y | F | A | W | N | Y | 5 | NONE | N | | N | N | 3 | 6 | 6 | 6 | 6 | 6 | 6 | 6 | 6 | 6 | 2 | 6 | |
| 34 | Y | F | B | W | N | Y | 10 | IND:MEHER BABA | N | | N | N | 2 | 6 | 6 | 2 | 1 | 2 | 2 | 2 | 3 | 3 | 4 | 2 | |
| 35 | Y | F | C | W | N | Y | 10 | NONE | N | | Y | N | 3 | 1 | 6 | 4 | 1 | 6 | 2 | 3 | 4 | 4 | 2 | 4 | |
| 36 | Y | M | A | W | N | Y | 7 | IND:AGNOSTIC | N | | Y | N | 2 | 1 | 6 | 4 | 1 | 4 | 3 | 5 | 2 | 1 | 2 | 4 | |
| 37 | Y | F | B | W | N | Y | 4 | IND:AGNOSTIC | N | | N | Y | 3 | 4 | 6 | 3 | 2 | 6 | 1 | 3 | 3 | 3 | 3 | 6 | |
| 38 | Y | F | A | W | N | Y | 10 | IND:LOVE | N | | Y | Y | 2 | 4 | 6 | 3 | 3 | 3 | 3 | 3 | 1 | 3 | 4 | 3 | |
| 39 | Y | F | C | W | N | Y | 7 | CHR:METHODIST | N | | N | N | 1 | 2 | 6 | 4 | 1 | 6 | 2 | 4 | 2 | 2 | 2 | 2 | 2 |
| 40 | Y | F | B | W | N | Y | 10 | BUD | N | | Y | N | 2 | 2 | 6 | 3 | 2 | 4 | 3 | 4 | 3 | 6 | 4 | 3 | |
| 41 | Y | F | B | W | N | Y | 3 | NONE | N | | Y | N | 3 | 6 | 6 | 3 | 1 | 6 | 3 | 3 | 3 | 3 | 1 | 3 | |
| 42 | Y | F | B | W | N | Y | 5 | NONE | N | | Y | N | 4 | 6 | 6 | 3 | 1 | 3 | 3 | 3 | 2 | 2 | 2 | 2 | |
| 43 | Y | M | B | W | N | Y | 10 | IND:UU | N | | Y | Y | 2 | 6 | 4 | 4 | 2 | 3 | 2 | 3 | 6 | 3 | 2 | 4 | 3 |
| 44 | Y | M | B | W | N | N | 7 | NONE | N | | Y | N | 2 | 6 | 6 | 4 | 2 | 3 | 6 | 6 | 3 | 2 | 1 | 3 | 6 |
| 45 | Y | M | B | W | N | Y | 10 | CHR | N | | Y | Y | 3 | 2 | 3 | 3 | 4 | 3 | 4 | 3 | 3 | 4 | 3 | 3 | |
| 46 | Y | M | B | W | N | Y | 7 | CHR:CATHOLIC | N | | Y | Y | 2 | 4 | 6 | 3 | 1 | 6 | 3 | 6 | 4 | 6 | 2 | 3 | 6 |
| 47 | Y | M | B | W | N | Y | 8 | CHR | Y | Y | | Y | 3 | 2 | 2 | 2 | 2 | 3 | 3 | 2 | 5 | 3 | 2 | 3 | 3 |
| 48 | Y | F | B | W | N | Y | 7 | IND:MY OWN | N | | Y | N | 1 | 6 | 6 | 6 | 1 | 6 | 1 | 6 | 6 | 6 | 1 | 6 | 6 |
| 49 | Y | M | A | A | N | N | 6 | NONE | N | | N | N | 6 | 1 | 6 | 2 | 1 | 2 | 2 | 2 | 6 | 1 | 6 | 6 | 6 |
| 50 | Y | F | B | W | N | Y | 5 | NONE | N | | N | N | 3 | 1 | 6 | 2 | 1 | 3 | 1 | 2 | 6 | 1 | 1 | 3 | |
| 51 | Y | F | B | W | N | Y | 5 | NONE | N | | Y | N | 1 | 1 | 6 | 2 | 1 | 1 | 2 | 3 | 6 | 1 | 1 | 3 | |
| 52 | Y | M | B | W | N | Y | 5 | NONE | N | | Y | N | 1 | 1 | 6 | 6 | 1 | 6 | 1 | 1 | 6 | 1 | 1 | 1 | |
| 53 | Y | M | B | W | N | Y | 10 | IND:TAOISM | N | | Y | N | 1 | 2 | 6 | 2 | 1 | 6 | 3 | 6 | 6 | 6 | 5 | 6 | 6 |
| 54 | Y | M | B | B | Y | Y | 8 | CHR | N | | Y | N | 1 | 5 | 6 | 6 | 3 | 6 | 5 | 2 | 6 | 6 | 5 | 1 | 6 |
| 55 | Y | F | B | W | N | Y | 6 | IND:CULTURAL CHR/YOG | N | | Y | N | 3 | 3 | 6 | 6 | 3 | 6 | 2 | 4 | 6 | 1 | 1 | 6 | 6 |
| 56 | Y | F | B | W | N | Y | 9 | IND:MEDITATION | N | | Y | N | 3 | 6 | 6 | 6 | 6 | 6 | 2 | 6 | 2 | 6 | 2 | 3 | 6 |
| 57 | Y | M | B | W | N | Y | 8 | NONE | N | | Y | Y | 4 | 6 | 6 | 3 | 3 | 3 | 3 | 3 | 3 | 3 | 3 | 3 | 3 |
| 58 | Y | M | B | W | N | Y | 4 | NONE | N | | Y | Y | 2 | 1 | 6 | 2 | 1 | 2 | 2 | 2 | 6 | 6 | 2 | 3 | |
| 59 | Y | F | C | W | Y | Y | 10 | JEWISH | N | | N | Y | 3 | 2 | 6 | 2 | 1 | 2 | 2 | 2 | 1 | 6 | 2 | 2 | |
| 60 | y | F | A | W | N | Y | 5 | NONE | N | | N | N | 2 | 3 | 3 | 4 | 4 | 3 | 4 | 3 | 4 | 6 | 2 | 4 | |
| 61 | Y | F | B | W | N | N | 3 | NONE | N | | N | N | 2 | 2 | 2 | 3 | 2 | 3 | 3 | 3 | 6 | 3 | 2 | 3 | |
| 62 | Y | M | A | W | Y | Y | 10 | NONE | N | | N | N | 4 | 6 | 6 | 6 | 1 | 6 | 6 | 6 | 6 | 6 | 1 | 6 | 6 |
| 63 | Y | F | B | W | N | Y | 10 | BUD | N | | Y | N | 3 | 2 | 2 | 4 | 1 | 5 | 2 | 6 | 6 | 1 | 1 | 3 | |
| 64 | Y | M | C | W | Y | Y | 10 | CHR:CHRIST | Y | Y | | Y | 1 | 6 | 6 | 3 | 5 | 6 | 5 | 4 | 1 | 5 | 1 | 5 | 5 |
| 65 | Y | F | A | W | N | Y | 7 | BUD | N | | N | N | 2 | 6 | 3 | 2 | 1 | 3 | 1 | 2 | 3 | 1 | 1 | 3 | 6 |
| 66 | Y | F | A | W | Y | Y | 10 | JEWISH | N | | N | N | 2 | 6 | 6 | 3 | 1 | 3 | 4 | 3 | 2 | 6 | 1 | 2 | 6 |
| 67 | Y | F | | | N | Y | 7 | IND:MY OWN MADE UP | N | | N | N | 2 | 6 | 6 | 6 | 3 | 6 | 4 | 6 | 6 | 6 | 3 | 6 | 6 |
| 68 | Y | M | A | W | N | Y | 10 | IND:BELIEVES IN GOD | N | | Y | N | 6 | 6 | 6 | 6 | 6 | 6 | 6 | 6 | 6 | 6 | 6 | 6 | 6 |
| 69 | Y | M | A | W | N | N | 0 | IND:ATHIEST | N | | Y | N | 1 | 3 | 6 | 2 | 1 | 1 | 1 | 3 | 2 | 1 | 1 | 1 | |
| 70 | Y | N | A | W | Y | Y | 8 | IND:MORMON | Y | Y | | Y | 3 | 3 | 6 | 3 | 6 | 3 | 6 | 3 | 6 | 6 | 5 | 3 | 6 |
| 71 | Y | M | B | W | Y | Y | 7 | CHR | N | | Y | N | 2 | 6 | 6 | 2 | 2 | 6 | 2 | 2 | 6 | 2 | 3 | 2 | 6 |
| 72 | Y | M | A | W | N | N | 5 | NONE | N | N | N | N | 1 | 6 | 6 | 2 | 1 | 3 | 3 | 3 | 3 | 1 | 1 | 3 | 6 |
| 73 | Y | F | B | W | N | N | 1 | IND:ATHIEST | N | | Y | N | 1 | 6 | 6 | 2 | 1 | 1 | 1 | 2 | 1 | 1 | 1 | 2 | 6 |
| 74 | Y | M | C | W | N | N | 1 | JEWISH | N | | N | N | 1 | 1 | 1 | 1 | 1 | 1 | 1 | 1 | 1 | 1 | 1 | 1 | |
| 75 | Y | F | C | O | Y | Y | 9 | CHR | Y | Y | | Y | 3 | 4 | 4 | 3 | 2 | 6 | 3 | 3 | 5 | 2 | 3 | 2 | |
| 76 | Y | M | C | W | Y | Y | 8 | IND:UU | N | | Y | N | 3 | 4 | 6 | 3 | 4 | 5 | 5 | 4 | 5 | 4 | 4 | 4 | 6 |
| 77 | y | M | B | B | Y | Y | 10 | CHR:BAPTIST | Y | Y | | Y | 4 | 3 | 6 | 3 | 3 | 3 | 5 | 5 | 4 | 6 | 3 | 6 | |
| 78 | Y | F | A | W | N | Y | 10 | IND:PERSONAL | N | | Y | N | 3 | 3 | 3 | 3 | 3 | 3 | 3 | 3 | 3 | 3 | 3 | 3 | 3 |
| 79 | Y | M | B | W | N | N | 4 | NONE | N | | N | N | 2 | 6 | 6 | 6 | 1 | 6 | 1 | 3 | 6 | 2 | 3 | 4 | 6 |
| 80 | Y | F | A | B | N | Y | 7 | PAGAN:WICKEN | N | | Y | N | 6 | 5 | 6 | 6 | 6 | 6 | 4 | 6 | 6 | 2 | 1 | 6 | 6 |

| # | | | | | | | # | Religion | | | | | | | | | | | | | | | | | | |
|---|---|---|---|---|---|---|---|---|---|---|---|---|---|---|---|---|---|---|---|---|---|---|---|---|---|---|
| 81 | Y | F | A | W | N | Y | 3 | IND:PEACE & LOVE | N | | Y | N | 1 | 3 | 1 | 1 | 1 | 6 | 1 | 6 | 2 | 6 | 1 | 1 | 4 |
| 82 | Y | M | A | W | N | Y | 4 | IND:PEACE & LOVE | N | | Y | N | 2 | 6 | 6 | 6 | 1 | 6 | 2 | 6 | 3 | 6 | 6 | 2 | 6 |
| 83 | Y | M | A | B | Y | N | 5 | CHR:BIBLE | Y | Y | | Y | 6 | 6 | 6 | 6 | 6 | 6 | 5 | 6 | 6 | 6 | 6 | 6 | 6 |
| 84 | Y | M | B | W | N | N | 7 | NONE | N | | Y | N | 3 | 1 | 6 | 6 | 1 | 6 | 3 | 3 | 1 | 6 | 2 | 3 | 6 |
| 85 | Y | F | B | W | N | N | 1 | NONE | N | | Y | N | 3 | 2 | 1 | 3 | 2 | 3 | 2 | 3 | 3 | 1 | 2 | 3 | |
| 86 | Y | | B | O | Y | N | 9 | CHR:CATHOLIC | N | | Y | N | 5 | 3 | 6 | 6 | 3 | 3 | 3 | 3 | 3 | 3 | 3 | 3 | 3 |
| 87 | Y | M | | | Y | Y | 7 | CHR | Y | Y | | | 6 | 6 | 6 | 6 | 6 | 6 | 4 | 6 | 5 | 6 | 6 | 6 | |
| 88 | y | M | C | B | Y | Y | 10 | CHR | Y | Y | | | 3 | 6 | 6 | 3 | 6 | 6 | 3 | 3 | 6 | 3 | 3 | 3 | |
| 89 | Y | | A | W | Y | Y | 7 | CHR | Y | Y | | | 6 | 6 | 6 | 6 | 6 | 6 | 3 | 6 | 6 | 4 | 6 | 6 | 6 |
| 90 | Y | | A | W | Y | Y | 7 | CHR | Y | Y | | | 6 | 6 | 6 | 6 | 6 | 6 | 4 | 6 | 6 | 4 | 6 | 6 | 3 |
| 91 | Y | | A | W | Y | Y | 8 | CHR | N | | N | N | 6 | 6 | 6 | 6 | 6 | 6 | 4 | 6 | 6 | 4 | 6 | 6 | 3 |
| 92 | Y | | B | W | Y | N | 9 | IND:GOD | N | | N | N | 6 | 6 | 6 | 6 | 6 | 6 | 4 | 6 | 6 | 3 | 1 | 6 | 3 |
| 93 | Y | F | A | W | N | Y | 8 | NONE | N | | Y | N | 4 | 6 | 3 | 6 | 3 | 4 | 4 | 4 | 2 | 2 | 3 | 3 | |
| 94 | Y | F | A | W | N | Y | 10 | IND:UU | Y | Y | | | 6 | 6 | 3 | 2 | 3 | 4 | 4 | 4 | 2 | 2 | 3 | 3 | |
| 95 | Y | M | B | A | N | Y | 5 | NONE | N | | Y | N | 3 | 6 | 6 | 6 | 3 | 6 | 6 | 6 | 3 | 6 | 5 | 4 | |
| 96 | Y | M | A | W | N | N | 4 | NONE | N | N | N | N | 2 | 2 | 2 | 3 | 3 | 2 | 3 | 5 | 3 | 3 | 2 | 3 | |
| 97 | Y | M | A | W | N | Y | 7 | IND:BASIC | N | N | Y | N | 2 | 2 | 4 | 5 | 1 | 1 | 3 | 4 | 1 | 1 | 1 | 5 | |
| 98 | Y | M | A | W | Y | Y | 8 | NONE | N | N | N | N | 1 | 1 | 1 | 1 | 1 | 1 | 1 | 1 | 1 | 1 | 1 | 1 | |
| 99 | Y | M | B | B | Y | Y | 10 | CHR:NON-DENOM | Y | Y | | Y | 5 | 5 | 5 | 5 | 5 | 5 | 5 | 5 | 5 | 5 | 5 | 5 | |
| 100 | Y | M | B | W | Y | Y | 10 | CHR | N | | Y | Y | 4 | 2 | 6 | 3 | 1 | 3 | 4 | 4 | 4 | 3 | 1 | 4 | 4 |
| 101 | Y | F | A | O | Y | Y | 10 | CHR:EVAN | Y | Y | | Y | 4 | 3 | 6 | 4 | 5 | 3 | 4 | 5 | 1 | 4 | 1 | 4 | 6 |
| 102 | Y | M | B | W | N | N | 1 | IND:ATHIEST | N | | Y | N | 1 | 1 | 1 | 1 | 1 | 1 | 1 | 1 | 1 | 1 | 1 | 1 | 1 |
| 103 | Y | M | A | | N | N | 1 | NONE | N | | Y | N | 1 | 6 | 6 | 1 | 1 | 6 | 1 | 1 | 6 | 1 | 1 | 1 | 6 |
| 104 | Y | F | B | A | N | Y | 5 | NONE | N | | Y | N | 2 | 3 | 6 | 2 | 2 | 6 | 1 | 2 | 2 | 2 | 2 | 2 | 2 |
| 105 | Y | F | B | W | N | N | 1 | NONE | N | | N | N | 6 | 6 | 6 | 1 | 3 | 6 | 3 | 2 | 6 | 1 | 3 | 2 | |
| 106 | Y | M | B | W | N | N | 4 | NONE | N | | Y | N | 3 | 6 | 6 | 4 | 2 | 6 | 3 | 3 | 3 | 6 | 3 | 3 | |
| 107 | Y | F | A | W | N | Y | 7 | IND:CHRISTIAN HOLIDAY | N | | Y | N | 6 | 6 | 6 | 6 | 6 | 6 | 6 | 6 | 3 | 6 | 3 | 4 | 6 |
| 108 | Y | M | C | B | Y | Y | 10 | CHR | N | | Y | Y | 3 | 3 | 3 | 3 | 5 | 3 | 3 | 3 | 3 | 3 | 3 | 3 | 6 |
| 109 | Y | F | C | W | N | Y | 8 | NONE | N | | Y | N | 1 | 1 | 2 | 1 | 1 | 6 | 1 | 2 | 6 | 1 | 2 | 6 | 1 |
| 110 | Y | M | C | W | N | N | 4 | NONE | N | | Y | N | 2 | 1 | 3 | 6 | 3 | 6 | 3 | 6 | 6 | 1 | 3 | 6 | 6 |
| 111 | Y | M | B | B | N | N | 10 | CHR | Y | | | Y | 4 | 3 | 4 | 3 | 1 | 6 | 4 | 2 | 5 | 1 | 2 | 6 | 6 |
| 112 | y | M | A | A | Y | Y | 8 | IND:MORMON | Y | Y | | | 3 | 6 | 6 | 3 | 3 | 6 | 4 | 4 | 3 | 3 | 5 | 4 | 6 |
| 113 | Y | F | B | W | Y | Y | 5 | NONE | N | | Y | N | 6 | 6 | 6 | 6 | 6 | 6 | 6 | 6 | 6 | 6 | 6 | 6 | 6 |
| 114 | Y | M | B | W | Y | Y | 9 | CHR:CATHOLIC | Y | Y | | Y | 4 | 1 | 3 | 4 | 3 | 4 | 4 | 4 | 4 | 2 | 2 | 4 | 3 |
| 115 | Y | F | B | W | N | N | 6 | NONE | N | | Y | Y | 2 | 6 | 6 | 6 | 2 | 6 | 6 | 6 | 3 | 1 | 1 | 6 | |
| 116 | Y | M | B | W | N | Y | 7 | NONE | N | | Y | N | 2 | 6 | 2 | 3 | 2 | 3 | 3 | 3 | 6 | 6 | 2 | 3 | 2 |
| 117 | Y | M | B | W | N | N | 7 | IND:AGNOSTIC | N | | Y | N | 3 | 1 | 3 | 4 | 1 | 4 | 1 | 4 | 3 | 1 | 2 | 4 | 6 |
| 118 | Y | F | B | A | N | Y | 10 | CHR:CATHOLIC | Y | Y | | Y | 4 | 6 | 6 | 3 | 3 | 3 | 2 | 3 | 3 | 2 | 1 | 3 | 3 |
| 119 | Y | M | C | W | N | Y | 6 | NONE | N | | Y | N | 3 | 6 | 6 | 4 | 3 | 3 | 4 | 4 | 4 | 3 | 1 | 3 | 3 |
| 120 | Y | F | C | W | N | N | 3 | NONE | N | | N | N | 3 | 6 | 6 | 3 | 3 | 6 | 3 | 3 | 3 | 3 | 3 | 3 | 3 |
| 121 | Y | F | C | W | N | Y | 5 | NONE | N | | Y | N | 2 | 6 | 6 | 3 | 3 | 3 | 3 | 3 | 3 | 3 | 3 | 3 | 6 |
| 122 | Y | F | B | | N | N | 3 | NONE | N | | Y | N | 1 | 6 | 6 | 3 | 1 | 6 | 1 | 4 | 2 | 1 | 1 | 3 | 6 |
| 123 | Y | M | B | B | Y | Y | 10 | CHR:NON-DENOM | Y | Y | | Y | 3 | 3 | 6 | 3 | 4 | 6 | 4 | 4 | 6 | 3 | 2 | 3 | |
| 124 | Y | F | B | B | N | Y | 6 | NONE | N | | N | N | 6 | 6 | 6 | 6 | 6 | 6 | 6 | 6 | 6 | 6 | 6 | 6 | 6 |
| 125 | Y | F | C | B | N | Y | 10 | NONE | N | | Y | N | 6 | 6 | 6 | 6 | 6 | 6 | 6 | 6 | 6 | 6 | 6 | 6 | 6 |
| 126 | Y | F | C | W | N | N | 1 | NONE | N | | Y | N | 3 | 2 | 6 | 3 | 2 | 3 | 2 | 3 | 6 | 2 | 2 | 3 | 2 |
| 127 | Y | M | C | W | N | N | 4 | NONE | N | | Y | N | 2 | 2 | 2 | 2 | 1 | 2 | 2 | 2 | 2 | 2 | 1 | 2 | 2 |
| 128 | Y | M | B | W | N | N | 1 | NONE | N | | Y | N | 6 | 6 | 6 | 6 | 6 | 6 | 6 | 6 | 6 | 6 | 6 | 6 | 6 |
| 129 | Y | M | B | W | N | N | 5 | IND:ATHIEST | N | | Y | N | 6 | 6 | 6 | 6 | 1 | 6 | 6 | 6 | 3 | 3 | 1 | 6 | |
| 130 | Y | M | C | W | N | Y | 5 | NONE | N | | Y | N | 2 | 6 | 6 | 3 | 2 | 3 | 3 | 3 | 3 | 2 | 1 | 3 | |
| 131 | y | M | B | H | N | Y | 7 | MUSLIM | Y | Y | | Y | 3 | 1 | 6 | 5 | 4 | 6 | 4 | 3 | 1 | 1 | 3 | 4 | |
| 132 | Y | F | B | W | N | Y | 7 | JEWISH | N | | N | N | 6 | 6 | 6 | 6 | 2 | 6 | 6 | 6 | 6 | 6 | 3 | 6 | |
| 133 | Y | M | A | W | N | Y | 5 | NONE | N | | N | N | 2 | 6 | 6 | 2 | 2 | 3 | 2 | 2 | 2 | 2 | 1 | 2 | 2 |
| 134 | Y | M | B | W | N | Y | 5 | JEWISH | N | | N | N | 2 | 6 | 6 | 3 | 1 | 3 | 1 | 3 | 6 | 1 | 1 | 3 | 6 |
| 135 | Y | F | C | W | N | Y | 8 | IND:NO NAME | N | | N | N | 2 | 6 | 6 | 3 | 2 | 6 | 6 | 6 | 6 | 2 | 4 | 6 | |
| 136 | Y | F | B | W | N | Y | 10 | BUD | N | | Y | Y | 3 | 6 | 6 | 3 | 2 | 3 | 3 | 4 | 3 | 4 | 4 | | |
| 137 | Y | M | B | W | Y | Y | 6 | CHR:PRESB | Y | Y | | Y | 3 | 3 | 4 | 3 | 3 | 3 | 3 | 3 | 3 | 3 | 3 | 5 | 3 |
| 138 | Y | M | B | A | Y | Y | 7 | CHR:CATHOLIC | Y | Y | | Y | 4 | 2 | 2 | 4 | 4 | 4 | 4 | 4 | 4 | 4 | 2 | 4 | 4 |

| ID | | | | | | | | Religion | | | | | | | | | | | | | | | | | |
|---|---|---|---|---|---|---|---|---|---|---|---|---|---|---|---|---|---|---|---|---|---|---|---|---|---|
| 139 | Y | F | C | W | N | Y | 8 | NONE | N | | Y | N | 1 | 3 | 4 | 3 | 2 | 3 | 2 | 3 | 3 | 2 | 2 | 3 | 3 |
| 140 | Y | F | C | W | N | Y | 7 | NONE | N | | Y | N | 3 | 6 | 6 | 4 | 3 | 3 | 3 | 3 | 3 | 3 | 1 | 3 | 3 |
| 141 | Y | M | B | W | N | N | 1 | NONE | N | | N | N | 1 | 6 | 6 | 2 | 1 | 2 | 2 | 2 | 1 | 1 | 1 | 2 | 1 |
| 142 | Y | M | B | W | N | N | 5 | NONE | N | | N | N | 1 | 6 | 6 | 6 | 1 | 6 | 1 | 6 | 6 | 6 | 1 | 6 | 6 |
| 143 | Y | F | A | W | Y | Y | 5 | JEWISH | N | | N | N | 6 | 6 | 6 | 2 | 6 | 6 | 4 | 4 | 4 | 6 | 4 | 4 | 6 |
| 144 | Y | M | B | W | Y | Y | 6 | IND:PERSONAL | N | | Y | N | 6 | 6 | 6 | 6 | 6 | 6 | 6 | 6 | 6 | 6 | 6 | 6 | |
| 145 | Y | F | B | B | Y | Y | 7 | CHR | Y | Y | | | 6 | 6 | 6 | 6 | 6 | 6 | 4 | 4 | 6 | 5 | 6 | 6 | 6 |
| 146 | Y | M | B | W | N | Y | 10 | NONE | N | | Y | N | 1 | 2 | 6 | 2 | 1 | 2 | 1 | 1 | 2 | 1 | 1 | 2 | |
| 147 | Y | F | A | O | N | N | 4 | NONE | N | | Y | N | 6 | 6 | 6 | 6 | 6 | 6 | 6 | 6 | 6 | 6 | 6 | 6 | |
| 148 | Y | F | B | O | N | Y | 8 | CHR:BAPTIST | N | | Y | N | 1 | 6 | 6 | 5 | 5 | 5 | 5 | 5 | 6 | 5 | 5 | 5 | |
| 149 | Y | M | B | W | N | N | 3 | IND:RUBEN SANDWICHE | N | | Y | N | 1 | 1 | 6 | 1 | 1 | 6 | 1 | 1 | 1 | 1 | 1 | 1 | |
| 150 | Y | M | B | W | N | Y | 5 | NONE | N | | Y | N | 3 | 1 | 1 | 1 | 1 | 6 | 1 | 1 | 3 | 1 | 1 | 1 | |
| 151 | Y | F | B | O | Y | Y | 10 | CHR:ORTHODOX | Y | Y | | | 6 | 6 | 6 | 6 | 6 | 6 | 6 | 6 | 5 | 6 | 6 | 6 | |
| 152 | Y | F | B | W | N | N | 1 | NONE | N | | N | N | 2 | 6 | 6 | 3 | 1 | 6 | 1 | 3 | 3 | 1 | 1 | 2 | |
| 153 | Y | M | B | W | N | N | 1 | CHR:CATHOLIC | N | | Y | Y | 3 | 6 | 6 | 3 | 1 | 6 | 3 | 6 | 6 | 6 | 1 | 6 | |
| 154 | Y | M | A | A | N | N | 5 | NONE | N | | N | N | 3 | 2 | 6 | 4 | 1 | 2 | 2 | 3 | 5 | 1 | 1 | 3 | |
| 155 | Y | F | C | W | N | N | 3 | NONE | N | | Y | N | 1 | 2 | 2 | 3 | 2 | 2 | 6 | 3 | 6 | 2 | 2 | 3 | |
| 156 | y | F | B | W | N | Y | 10 | IND:NOT DEFINABLE | N | | Y | N | 3 | 6 | 6 | 6 | 1 | 6 | 2 | 3 | 6 | 6 | 6 | 6 | |
| 157 | y | M | B | W | N | Y | 10 | NONE | N | | N | N | 1 | 6 | 6 | 3 | 1 | 6 | 2 | 3 | 3 | 6 | 2 | 4 | |
| 158 | Y | M | A | H | N | Y | 6 | IND:AGNOSTIC | N | | N | N | 1 | 1 | 1 | 1 | 1 | 1 | 1 | 1 | 1 | 1 | 1 | 1 | |
| 159 | Y | M | B | W | N | N | 2 | IND:BEING A COOK | N | | N | N | 5 | 1 | 1 | 1 | 1 | 1 | 1 | 1 | 1 | 1 | 1 | 1 | |
| 160 | Y | F | B | W | N | Y | 7 | NONE | N | | Y | N | 2 | 6 | 6 | 3 | 2 | 6 | 2 | 6 | 6 | 6 | 2 | 6 | |
| 161 | Y | F | A | W | N | Y | 7 | IND:MEDITATION | N | | Y | N | 6 | 2 | 6 | 2 | 2 | 3 | 1 | 3 | 3 | 1 | 2 | 1 | |
| 162 | Y | M | B | W | N | Y | 4 | IND:ATHIEST | N | | Y | N | 2 | 1 | 6 | 3 | 1 | 3 | 3 | 3 | 2 | 1 | 1 | 2 | |
| 163 | Y | F | B | W | N | Y | 5 | NONE | N | | Y | Y | 1 | 3 | 6 | 4 | 2 | 4 | 3 | 4 | 1 | 1 | 1 | 3 | |
| 164 | Y | F | B | W | N | Y | 5 | NONE | N | | N | N | 3 | 6 | 6 | 3 | 2 | 3 | 2 | 3 | 3 | 2 | 2 | 1 | |
| 165 | Y | F | B | W | N | | 5 | NONE | N | | N | N | 3 | 6 | 2 | 6 | 1 | 6 | 3 | 6 | 3 | 2 | 6 | | |
| 166 | Y | F | A | | | N | N | 1 | NONE | N | | Y | N | 6 | 6 | 6 | 1 | 1 | 1 | 1 | 1 | 3 | 6 | 1 | 1 |
| 167 | Y | M | C | | Y | Y | 10 | NONE | N | | Y | N | 3 | 3 | 3 | 3 | 3 | 3 | 3 | 3 | 3 | 3 | 3 | 3 | |
| 168 | y | F | B | W | N | N | 4 | NONE | N | | Y | N | 2 | 1 | 6 | 3 | 1 | 6 | 2 | 2 | 6 | 1 | 1 | 3 | |
| 169 | Y | F | B | W | N | N | 3 | NONE | N | | N | N | 3 | 6 | 6 | 3 | 1 | 6 | 2 | 3 | 6 | 1 | 1 | 3 | |
| 170 | Y | F | A | W | N | Y | 10 | IND:MEDITATION | N | | N | N | 3 | 6 | 6 | 2 | 2 | 6 | 2 | 2 | 3 | 2 | 1 | 1 | |
| 171 | Y | F | B | B | N | Y | 10 | CHR | Y | Y | | Y | 4 | 6 | 6 | 4 | 4 | 6 | 5 | 4 | 6 | 5 | 3 | 4 | |
| 172 | Y | F | B | A | N | N | 1 | IND:ATHIEST | N | | N | N | 3 | 1 | 2 | 2 | 1 | 2 | 2 | 2 | 2 | 2 | 1 | 2 | |
| 173 | Y | M | A | | | N | Y | 8 | NONE | N | | Y | N | 1 | 6 | 6 | 4 | 1 | 3 | 2 | 3 | 2 | 6 | 1 | 3 |
| 174 | Y | | | | N | Y | 7 | NONE | N | | N | N | 3 | 6 | 6 | 3 | 3 | 3 | 4 | 3 | 3 | 6 | 2 | 6 | |
| 175 | Y | M | A | | N | N | 1 | NONE | N | | Y | N | 1 | 1 | 6 | 3 | 1 | 6 | 1 | 6 | 4 | 2 | 1 | 6 | |
| 176 | Y | M | A | W | N | Y | 3 | NONE | N | | N | N | 1 | 6 | 6 | 6 | 1 | 1 | 1 | 1 | 6 | 1 | 1 | | |
| 177 | Y | F | A | W | N | Y | 8 | NONE | N | | N | N | 2 | 6 | 6 | 6 | 2 | 6 | 2 | 6 | 6 | 6 | 1 | 6 | |
| 178 | Y | M | B | W | N | Y | 7 | NONE | N | | Y | N | 1 | 6 | 6 | 1 | 1 | 4 | 2 | 2 | 4 | 4 | 1 | 4 | |
| 179 | y | | | W | N | Y | 7 | NONE | N | | N | N | 3 | 3 | 3 | 3 | 3 | 3 | 3 | 3 | 3 | 3 | 3 | 3 | |
| 180 | Y | | | | N | Y | 7 | NONE | N | | N | N | 2 | 2 | 6 | 2 | 2 | 2 | 2 | 2 | 2 | 2 | 1 | 2 | |
| 181 | Y | F | B | W | N | Y | 7 | IND:BELIEVES IN GOD | N | | N | N | 4 | 6 | 6 | 4 | 4 | 4 | 2 | 4 | 4 | 6 | 2 | 4 | |
| 182 | Y | M | B | W | N | Y | 9 | IND:ECHARTTOLLE | N | | Y | Y | 1 | 6 | 6 | 2 | 1 | 1 | 1 | 1 | 1 | 1 | 1 | 1 | |
| 183 | Y | M | B | O | N | Y | 9 | BUD:ZEN | N | | N | N | 2 | 3 | 3 | 6 | 2 | 6 | 6 | 6 | 2 | 6 | 1 | 2 | |
| 184 | Y | F | B | W | N | Y | 10 | IND:CHURCH OF NATURE | N | | N | N | 6 | 6 | 6 | 6 | 6 | 6 | 6 | 6 | 6 | 6 | 6 | 6 | |
| 185 | Y | M | C | W | N | Y | 8 | NONE | N | | Y | N | 1 | 1 | 2 | 1 | 1 | 1 | 1 | 1 | 1 | 1 | 1 | 1 | |
| 186 | Y | M | B | W | N | Y | 10 | IND:ONENESS/LOVE | N | | Y | Y | 2 | 1 | 4 | 3 | 3 | 6 | 3 | 3 | 2 | 2 | 3 | 3 | |
| 187 | Y | M | B | W | N | Y | 10 | CHR | Y | Y | | Y | 2 | 3 | 4 | 4 | 4 | 6 | 2 | 3 | 6 | 2 | 1 | 4 | |
| 188 | Y | M | B | W | N | Y | 10 | CHR | Y | Y | | Y | 2 | 3 | 4 | 4 | 2 | 3 | 2 | 3 | 2 | 3 | 2 | 3 | |
| 189 | Y | F | B | W | N | Y | 8 | IND | N | | N | Y | 1 | 6 | 6 | 3 | 6 | 6 | 2 | 3 | 6 | 6 | 2 | 3 | |
| 190 | Y | F | C | W | Y | Y | 8 | CHR:UNITED CHURCH OF | Y | | Y | | 4 | 3 | 6 | 4 | 3 | 3 | 4 | 4 | 4 | 3 | 3 | 4 | |
| 191 | Y | F | C | W | Y | Y | 8 | CHR:EPISC | Y | Y | | Y | 2 | 6 | 6 | 4 | 3 | 5 | 3 | 4 | 3 | 3 | 5 | | |
| 192 | Y | M | C | W | Y | Y | 8 | CHR:EPISC | Y | Y | | Y | 2 | 3 | 3 | 4 | 3 | 5 | 3 | 4 | 5 | 3 | 3 | 5 | |
| 193 | Y | F | B | W | Y | Y | 8 | CHR | N | | Y | Y | 3 | 2 | 6 | 4 | 3 | 4 | 4 | 4 | 4 | 2 | 3 | 4 | |

Figure 20. Raw Survey Data for Zip Code 97217.

# Bibliography

Barna, George. *Revolution*. Wheaton, IL: Tyndale House, 2005.

Barna Group. "About Barna Group." Barna Group. Online: http://www.barna.org/about.

———. "Barna Report: Markets 2011 and States 2011." Barna Group. Online: http://www.barna.org/research/barna-reports/reports-markets-and-states-2011.

———. "New Barna Report Examines Diversity of Faith in Various U.S. Cities." Barna Group. Online: http://www.barna.org/faith-spirituality/435-diversity-of-faith-in-various-us-cities.

Barnum, Thaddeus. *Never Silent: How Third World Missionaries Are Now Bringing the Gospel to the U.S.* 1st ed. Colorado Springs: Eleison, 2008.

Bat Kol Institute. "Home Page." Bat Kol Institute. Online: http://www.batkol.info/.

———. "A Sabbath Evening Table Celebration." Bat Kol Institute. Online: http://www.batkol.info/wp-content/uploads/2011/01/BK_Sabbath_Meal_2_0.pdf.

Bates, Stephen. *A Church at War: Anglicans and Homosexuality*. London: I.B. Tauris and Co. Ltd, 2006.

Benedict, and Timothy Fry. *The Rule of St. Benedict in English*. 1st ed. Vintage Spiritual Classics. New York: Vintage Books, 1998.

Bettenson, Henry Scowcroft. *Documents of the Christian Church*. World's Classics. Galaxy Edition. New York: Oxford University Press, 1947.

Bicycling. "America's Top 50 Bike-Friendly Cities." *Bicycling*. Online: http://www.bicycling.com/news/advocacy/2-portland-or.

Black, Kathy. *Culturally-Conscious Worship*. St. Louis, MO: Chalice Press, 2000.

Bradshaw, Paul F. *The Search for the Origins of Christian Worship: Sources and Methods for the Study of Early Liturgy*. New York: Oxford University Press, 1992.

———. *Eucharistic Origins*. Oxford; New York: Oxford University Press, 2004.

Bread & Wine. "Home Page." Bread & Wine. Online: http://www.breadandwine.org.

Brown, Raymond Edward. *The Birth of the Messiah: A Commentary on the Infancy Narratives in Matthew and Luke*. 1st ed. Garden City, NY: Doubleday, 1977.

Bureau of Labor Statistics. "Economic News Release: Regional and State Employment and Unemployment Summary." United States Department of Labor. Online: http://www.bls.gov/news.release/laus.nro.htm.

Calvin, John. *Institutes of the Christian Religion*. Albany, OR: Sage Software, 1996.

Carlton, Clark, and Dmitri Royster. *The Faith: Understanding Orthodox Christianity (An Orthodox Catechism)*. The Faith Series. Salisbury, MA: Regina Orthodox, 1997.

———. *The Faith: Understanding Orthodox Christianity (an Orthodox Catechism)*. The Faith Series. Salisbury, MA: Regina Orthodox, 1997.

Catholic Church, et al. *The Missal in Latin and English Being the Text of the Missale Romanum with English Rubrics and a New Translation*. New York: Sheed & Ward, 1949.

Chan, Simon. *Liturgical Theology: The Church as Worshiping Community*. Downers Grove, IL: InterVarsity Academic, 2006.

Chapman, Mark D. *Anglicanism: A Very Short Introduction*. Very Short Introductions. New York: Oxford University Press, 2006.

Chittister, Joan. *Wisdom Distilled from the Daily: Living the Rule of St. Benedict Today*. 1st HarperCollins pbk. ed. San Francisco: HarperSanFrancisco, 1991.

———. *The Liturgical Year*. The Ancient Practices Series. Nashville Thomas Nelson, 2009.

Churches for the Sake of Others. "Hear the Story and See the Vision." C4SO. Online: http://www.C4SO.org.

Claiborne, Shane, et al. *Common Prayer: A Liturgy for Ordinary Radicals*. Grand Rapids, MI: Zondervan, 2010.

Creative Research Systems. "Sample Size Calculator." Creative Research Systems. Online: http://www.surveysystem.com/sscalc.htm#two.

Cyprian. "Epistle Lxii, Section 4." In *Ante-Nicene Fathers, Vol. 5*, 5, 777–78: Sage Software, 1996.

Daniélou, Jean. *The Bible and the Liturgy*. University of Notre Dame. Liturgical Studies. Notre Dame, IN: University of Notre Dame Press, 1956.

Davies, J. G. *The New Westminster Dictionary of Liturgy and Worship*. 1st American ed. Philadelphia: Westminster, 1986.

Dawn, Marva J. *A Royal Waste of Time: The Splendor of Worshiping God and Being Church for the World*. Grand Rapids, MI: William B. Eerdmans, 1999.

Dictionary.com. "Liturgy." Dictionary.com. Online: http://dictionary.reference.com/browse/liturgy.

Dix, Gregory. *The Shape of the Liturgy*. New York: Seabury, 1982.

Douglas, Mary. "The Eucharist: Its Continuity with the Bread Sacrifice of Leviticus." *Modern Theology* 15, no. 2 (1999): 209–24.

Driscoll, Mark. "Vision of Acts 29." Acts 29 Network. Online: http://www.acts29network.org/about/vision/.

Duin, Julia. *Quitting Church: Why the Faithful Are Fleeing and What to Do About It*. Grand Rapids, MI: Baker, 2008.

Eusebius. *Ecclesiastical History*. New York: Fathers of the Church, 1953.

Finch, R. G. *The Synagogue Lectionary and the New Testament: A Study of the Three-Year Cycle of Readings from the Law and the Prophets as a Contribution to New Testament Chronology*. London: Society for Promoting Christian Knowledge, 1939.

Flax, Peter. "The Best of Running." *Runner's World*. Online: http://www.runnersworld.com/article/0,7120,s6-239-281--13339-6-1X2X3X4X5-6,00.html.

Flemming, Dean E. *Contextualization in the New Testament: Patterns for Theology and Mission*. Downers Grove, IL: InterVarsity Press, 2005.

Freeman, Curtis W. "Where Two or Three Are Gathered: Communion Ecclesiology in the Free Church." *Perspectives in Religious Studies*, no. 31, 3 (2004): 259.

Friedman, Edwin H. *Generation to Generation: Family Process in Church and Synagogue*. The Guilford Family Therapy Series. New York: Guilford, 1985.

Friedman, Edwin H., et al. *A Failure of Nerve: Leadership in the Age of the Quick Fix: An Edited Manuscript*. Bethesda, MD: Edwin Friedman Estate/Trust, 1999.

Gallagher, Nora. *The Sacred Meal*. The Ancient Practices Series. Nashville: Thomas Nelson, 2009.

Galli, Mark. *Beyond Smells and Bells: The Wonder and Power of Christian Liturgy*. Brewster, MA: Paraclete, 2008.

Geertz, Clifford. *The Interpretation of Cultures: Selected Essays*. New York: Basic, 1973.

Gillquist, Peter E. *Becoming Orthodox: A Journey to the Ancient Christian Faith*. 1st ed. Brentwood, TN: Wolgemuth & Hyatt, 1989.

Gopal, Prashant. "America's Unhappiest Cities." *Bloomberg Businessweek*. Online: http://images.businessweek.com/ss/09/02/0226_miserable_cities/1.htm.

Grassi, Joseph A. "St. Paul the Apostle, Liturgist." *Worship* 34, no. 10 (1960): 610–13.

Grenz, Stanley J. *A Primer on Postmodernism*. Grand Rapids, MI: William B. Eerdmans, 1996.

Harvey, Barry. *Another City: An Ecclesiological Primer for a Post-Christian World*. Christian Mission and Modern Culture. Harrisburg, PA: Trinity, 1999.

Hassett, Miranda Katherine. *Anglican Communion in Crisis: How Episcopal Dissidents and Their African Allies Are Reshaping Anglicanism*. Princeton: Princeton University Press, 2007.

Hauerwas, Stanley. *After Christendom?: How the Church Is to Behave If Freedom, Justice, and a Christian Nation Are Bad Ideas*. Nashville: Abingdon, 1991.

Haught, Nancy. "Anglican Parish Splits from Episcopal Congregation in Northeast Portland." OregonLive.com. Online: http://www.oregonlive.com/news/index.ssf/2010/05/anglican_parish_splits_from_ep.html.

Havel, Václav, and John Keane. *The Power of the Powerless: Citizens against the State in Central-Eastern Europe*. Armonk, NY: M.E. Sharpe, 1985.

Hefling, Charles C., and Cynthia L. Shattuck. *The Oxford Guide to the Book of Common Prayer: A Worldwide Survey*. New York: Oxford University Press, 2006.

Hiebert, Paul G. *Anthropological Insights for Missionaries*. Grand Rapids, MI: Baker, 1985.

Hippolytus. "The Apostolic Tradition of Hippolytus of Rome." Online: www.bombaxo.com, http://www.bombaxo.com/hippolytus.html.

Holmes, Urban Tigner. *What Is Anglicanism?* Wilton, CT: Morehouse-Barlow, 1982.

Hunter, Todd D. *The Accidental Anglican: The Surprising Appeal of the Liturgical Church*. Downers Grove, IL: InterVarsity, 2010.

———. *Giving Church Another Chance: Finding New Meaning in Spiritual Practices*. Downers Grove, IL: InterVarsity, 2010.

Hustad, Donald P. "The Psalms as Worship Expression: Personal and Congregational." *Review & Expositor* 81, no. 3 (1984): 407–24.

Imago Dei Community. "About: What We Believe: Mission and Values." Imago Dei Community. Online: http://www.imagodeicommunity.com/about/mission-and-values/.

———. "Home Page." Imago Dei Community. Online: http://www.imagodeicommunity.com.

Jones, Alan W. *Common Prayer on Common Ground: A Vision of Anglican Orthodoxy*. Harrisburg, PA: Morehouse, 2006.

Jones, Cheslyn, et al. *The Study of Liturgy*. New York: Oxford University Press, 1978.

———. *The Study of Spirituality*. New York: Oxford University Press, 1986.

Jones, Jeffrey M. "Tracking Religious Affiliation, State by State." Gallup. Online: http://www.gallup.com/poll/12091/tracking-religious-affiliation-state-state.aspx.

Jungmann, Josef A. *The Early Liturgy to the Time of Gregory the Great.* Translated by Francis A. Brunner. Notre Dame, IN: University of Notre Dame Press, 1959.

Kauffman, Ivan J. *Follow Me: A History of Christian Intentionality* New Monastic Library. Eugene, OR: Cascade, 2009.

Kidd, B. J. *Documents Illustrative of the Continental Reformation.* Oxford: The Clarendon Press, 1911.

Kinnaman, David, and Gabe Lyons. *UnChristian: What a New Generation Really Thinks About Christianity—and Why It Matters.* Grand Rapids, MI: Baker, 2007.

Kipen, Nicki. "The Top Ten Greenest Cities." *Move.* Online: http://www.move.com/home-finance/real-estate/general/top-greenest-cities-in-us.aspx.

Klauser, Theodor. *A Short History of the Western Liturgy: An Account and Some Reflections.* 2d ed. Oxford; New York: Oxford University Press, 1979.

Kriz, Tony. "B @ Peace Project." Tony Kriz. Online: http://tonykriz.com/?p=360.

Kriz, Tony. "A Village Conspiriacy." Parish Collective. Online: http://parishcollective.ning.com/profiles/blogs/tony-kriz-a-village.

Levy, Francesca. "America's Safest Cities." *Forbes.* Online: http://www.forbes.com/2010/10/11/safest-cities-america-crime-accidents-lifestyle-real-estate-danger.html.

Lewis, C. S. *Letters to Malcolm: Chiefly on Prayer.* 1st American ed. New York: Harcourt, 1964.

Littell, Franklin H. "The Historical Free Church Defined." *Brethren Life and Thought* 50, no. 3–4 (2005): 51–65.

Marchetti, Nino. "Draft Beer Town: Portland." *DRAFT Magazine.* http://www.draftmag.com/beertowns/detail/Portland.

Martin, Ralph P. *Carmen Christi: Philippians II 5–11 in Recent Interpretation and in the Setting of Early Christian Worship.* Rev. ed. Grand Rapids, MI: William B. Eerdmans, 1983.

Merchant, Dan. *Lord, Save Us from Your Followers: Why Is the Gospel of Love Dividing America?* Nashville: Thomas Nelson, 2008.

Metzger, Marcel. *History of the Liturgy: The Major Stages.* Collegeville, MN: Liturgical, 1997.

Metzger, Paul Louis. *The Word of Christ and the World of Culture: Sacred and Secular Through the Theology of Karl Barth.* Grand Rapids, MI: William B. Eerdmans, 2003.

Meyers, Ruth A. *A Prayer Book for the 21st Century.* Vol. Three Liturgical Studies. New York: The Church Hymnal Corporation, 1996.

Miller, Donald. *Blue Like Jazz: Nonreligious Thoughts on Christian Spirituality.* Nashville: Thomas Nelson, 2003.

Mosaic. "Church Planting." Mosaic. Online: http://www.mosaicportland.org/mission/church-planting/.

Murray, Stuart. *Post-Christendom: Church and Mission in a Strange New World.* Carlisle, United Kingdom: Paternoster, 2004.

Newbigin, Lesslie. *Unfinished Agenda: An Autobiography.* Grand Rapids, MI: William B. Eerdmans, 1985.

———. *Foolishness to the Greeks: The Gospel and Western Culture.* Grand Rapids, MI: William B. Eerdmans, 1986.

———. *The Gospel in a Pluralist Society.* Grand Rapids, MI.: William B. Eerdmans, 1989.

Niebuhr, H. Richard. *Christ and Culture.* 1st ed. New York: Harper, 1951.

O'Donovan, Oliver. *Church in Crisis: The Gay Controversy and the Anglican Communion*. Eugene, OR: Cascade, 2008.

Olson, David T. *The American Church in Crisis: Groundbreaking Research Based on a National Database of over 200,000 Churches*. Grand Rapids, MI: Zondervan, 2008.

OregonLive.com. "Results by Precinct for the 2010 Oregon Governor Election." OregonLive.com. Online: http://blog.oregonlive.com/mapesonpolitics/2010/12/precinct_results.html.

Oxford University Press Blog. "Oxford Word of the Year: Locavore." Oxford University Press Blog. Online: http://blog.oup.com/2007/11/locavore/.

Parish Collective. "Home Page." Parish Collective. Online: http://www.parishcollective.org/.

Pecklers, Keith F. *Liturgy in a Postmodern World*. London; New York: Continuum, 2003.

Perkins, John. *With Justice for All: A Strategy for Community Development*. 3rd ed. Ventura, CA: Regal, 2007.

Pfatteicher, Philip H. *Liturgical Spirituality*. Valley Forge, PA: Trinity, 1997.

Pope, Loren. *Colleges That Change Lives: 40 Schools That Will Change the Way You Think About Colleges*. 2nd rev. ed. New York: Penguin, 2006.

Pramis, Joshua. "America's Best Cities for Summer Travel." *Travel + Leisure* by American Express Publishing Corporation. Online: http://www.travelandleisure.com/articles/americas-best-cities-for-summer-travel/31.

Princeton Review. "Home Page." princetonreview.com. Online: http://www.princetonreview.com/.

Prins, A. A. *The Booke of the Common Prayer, 1549*. Amsterdam: M. J. Portielje, 1933.

Quenot, Michel. *The Icon: Window on the Kingdom*. Crestwood, NY: St. Vladimir's Seminary Press, 1991.

Randall, Ian M. "Mission in Post-Christendom: Anabaptist and Free Church Perspectives." *Evangelical Quarterly* 79, no. 3 (2007): 227–40.

Red Sea. "Home Page." Red Sea. Online: http://www.redseachurch.org/.

Reimagine. "The Jesus Dojo." Reimagine. Online: http://www.reimagine.org/node/32.

Roberts, Alexander, et al. *The Ante-Nicene Fathers. Translations of the Writings of the Fathers Down to A.D. 325*. Buffalo, NY: The Christian Literature Publishing Company, 1885.

Robertson-Textor, Marisa. "The World's Best Street Food." *Budget Travel*. Online: http://www.budgettravel.com/btdyn/content/article/2010/05/10/AR2010051004077.html.

Rorty, Richard. *Philosophy and the Mirror of Nature*. Princeton, NJ: Princeton University Press, 1979.

Rowell, Geoffrey. *The English Religious Tradition and the Genius of Anglicanism*. Wantage: Ikon, 1992.

Rucyahana, John. *The Bishop of Rwanda*. Nashville: Thomas Nelson, 2007.

Ryan, Kevin, and Marilyn Ryan. *Why I Am Still a Catholic*. 1st ed. New York: Riverhead, 1998.

Sachs, William L. *Homosexuality and the Crisis of Anglicanism*. Cambridge, UK; New York: Cambridge University Press, 2009.

Schaeffer, Frank. "Pro-Life—and in Favor of Keeping Abortion Legal: An Interview with Frank Schaeffer." npr.com. Online: http://www.npr.org/templates/story/story.php?storyid=97998654.

Schmemann, Alexander. *The Historical Road of Eastern Orthodoxy*. 1st ed. New York: Holt, 1963.

————. *Introduction to Liturgical Theology.* Library of Orthodox Theology No. 4. London: Faith Press; Portland, MA: American Orthodox, 1966.

Schmidt, Richard H. *Glorious Companions: Five Centuries of Anglican Spirituality.* Grand Rapids, MI: William B. Eerdmans, 2002.

Schnackenburg, Rudolf. *The Gospel According to St. John.* New York: Seabury, 1980.

Schwantes, Carlos A. *The Pacific Northwest: An Interpretive History.* Lincoln: University of Nebraska Press, 1989.

Segal, Judah Benzion. *The Hebrew Passover, from the Earliest Times to A.C. 70.* London: Oxford University Press, 1963.

Senn, Frank C. *Christian Liturgy: Catholic and Evangelical.* Minneapolis: Fortress, 1997.

Shakespeare, William, and Roma Gill. *Romeo and Juliet.* New ed. Oxford School Shakespeare. Oxford: Oxford University Press, 2008.

Sharlet, Jeff. "Jesus Plus Nothing: Undercover among America's Secret Theocrats." *Harper's Magazine.* March, 2003.

Smietana, Bob. "Statistical Illusion." *Christianity Today.* April, 2006.

Snook, Susan Brown. "Reaching New People Through Church Planting." *Anglican Theological Review* 92, no. 1: 111–16.

Srubas, Rachel M. *Oblation: Meditations on St. Benedict's Rule.* Brewster, MA: Paraclete, 2006.

Stock, Jon. *Inhabiting the Church.* Eugene, OR: Cascade, 2007.

Stone, Bryan P. *Evangelism after Christendom: The Theology and Practice of Christian Witness.* Grand Rapids, MI: Brazos, 2007.

Sweet, Leonard I., and Andy Crouch. *The Church in Emerging Culture: Five Perspectives.* El Cajon, CA: Youth Specialties, 2003.

Tachiaos, Anthony-Emil N. *Cyril and Methodius of Thessalonica: The Acculturation of the Slavs.* Crestwood, NY: St. Vladimir's Seminary Press, 2001.

Taylor, Howard, et al. *Hudson Taylor's Spiritual Secret.* Grand Rapids, MI: Discovery House, 1990.

The Anglican Mission, "Identity," The Anglican Mission, Online: http://www.theamia.org/identity/.

The Anglican Mission in the Americas. *An Anglican Prayer Book.* Philadelphia, PA: Preservation Press of the Prayer Book Society of the U.S.A., 2008.

The Book of Common Prayer. "The Book of Common Prayer." anglican.org. Online: http://justus.anglican.org/resources/bcp/formatted_1979.htm.

The Community of Asideo. "Welcome to Asideo." The Community of Asideo. Online: http://www.communityofadsideo.com/Adsideo/Home.html.

The Evergreen Community. "Home Page." The Evergreen Community. Online: http://www.evergreenlife.org/.

The Table. "Home Page." Wikipedia. Online: http://www.thetablepdx.com.

Theology and Worship Ministry Unit for the Presbyterian Church. *Book of Common Worship: Pastoral Edition.* Louisville, KY: Westminster/John Knox, 1993.

Thiong'o, Ngugi Wa. *Decolonizing the Mind: The Politics of Language in African Literature.* Oxford: James Currey, 2009.

Thompson, Bard. *Liturgies of the Western Church.* 1st Fortress Press ed. Philadelphia: Fortress, 1980.

Tickle, Phyllis. *The Great Emergence: How Christianity Is Changing and Why.* Grand Rapids, MI: Baker, 2008.

Tomlinson, Dave. *The Post Evangelical*. Rev. North American ed. El Cajon, CA: Emergent YS/Zondervan, 2003.

Tozer, Aiden Wilson. *The Knowledge of the Holy. The Attributes of God: Their Meaning in the Christian Life*. 1st ed. New York: Harper, 1961.

Tucker, Ruth. *From Jerusalem to Irian Jaya: A Biographical History of Christian Missions*. Grand Rapids, MI: Zondervan, 1983.

Urban Homesteading. "Urban Homestead Definition." Urban Homesteading. Online: http://urbanhomestead.org/urban-homestead-definition.

US Election Atlas.org. "2004 Presidential General Election Results–Oregon." Online: http://www.uselectionatlas.org/RESULTS/state.php?f=0&year=2004&fips=41.

Village, Emergent. "A Growing, Generative Friendship." Emergent Village. Online: http://www.emergentvillage.com/.

Ware, Kallistos. *The Orthodox Way*. Yonkers, New York: St. Vladimirs Seminary Press, 1995.

Webber, Christopher. *The Holy Eucharist, Rites I and II*. Harrisburg, PA: Morehouse, 1997.

Webber, Robert. *God Still Speaks: A Biblical View of Christian Communication*. Nashville: Thomas Nelson, 1980.

———. *Evangelicals on the Canterbury Trail: Why Evangelicals Are Attracted to the Liturgical Church*. Waco, TX: Word Books, 1985.

———. *Planning Blended Worship: The Creative Mixture of Old and New*. Nashville, TN: Abingdon, 1998.

Webber, Robert, and Rodney Clapp. *People of the Truth: The Power of the Worshiping Community in the Modern World*. 1st ed. San Francisco: Harper & Row, 1988.

Webber, Robert E. *The Worship Phenomenon*. Nashville: Abbott Martyn, 1994.

Weil, Louis. "The Holy Spirit: The Source of Unity in the Liturgy." *Anglican Theological Review* 83, no. 3 (2001): 409–15.

———. *A Theology of Worship* The New Church's Teaching Series V. 12. Cambridge, MA: Cowley, 2002.

Wharton, James A. "Obedience and Sacrifice: Some Reflections on Worship from the Old Testament Side." *Austin Seminary Bulletin (Faculty ed.)* 85, no. 3 (1969): 5–25.

White, James F. *Introduction to Christian Worship*. 3rd ed. Nashville: Abingdon, 2000.

Whiteman, Darrell L. "Contextualization: The Theory, the Gap, the Challenge." *International Bulletin of Missionary Research* 21, no. 1 (1997): 2–7.

Wicker, Christine. *The Fall of the Evangelical Nation: The Surprising Crisis inside the Church*. 1st ed. New York: HarperOne, 2008.

Wikipedia. "Anglican." Wikipedia. Online: http://en.wikipedia.org/wiki/Anglican.

———. "Emerging Church." Wikipedia. Online: http://en.wikipedia.org/wiki/Emerging_church.

———. "The Fellowship." Wikipedia. Online: http://en.wikipedia.org/wiki/The_Fellowship_%28Christian_organization%29.

———. "Great Schism." Wikipedia. Online: http://en.wikipedia.org/wiki/Great_Schism.

———. "Hudson Taylor." Wikipedia. Online: http://en.wikipedia.org/wiki/Hudson_Taylor.

———. "Justin Martyr." Wikipedia. Online: http://en.wikipedia.org/wiki/Justin_Martyr.

———. "North-South Divide." Wikipedia. Online: http://en.wikipedia.org/wiki/Global_south.

———. "Postchristianity." Wikipedia. Online: http://en.wikipedia.org/wiki/Post-Christianity.

————. "Saints Cyril and Methodius." Wikipedia. Online: http://en.wikipedia.org/wiki/Cyril_and_Methodius.

Wilson-Hartgrove, Jonathan. *The Wisdom of Stability: Rooting Faith in a Mobile Culture.* Brewster, MA: Paraclete Press.

Wilson, Jonathan R. *Living Faithfully in a Fragmented World: Lessons for the Church from Macintyre's After Virtue.* Christian Mission and Modern Culture. Harrisburg, PA: Trinity, 1997.

Witvliet, John D. "The Former Prophets and the Practice of Christian Worship." *Calvin Theological Journal* 37, no. 1 (2002): 82–94.

Wolf, William J. *Anglican Spirituality.* Wilton, CT: Morehouse-Barlow, 1982.

YouTube. "Project Natal: Meet Milo." YouTube. Online: http://www.youtube.com/watch?v=HluWsMlfj68

————. "Project Natal Xbox 360 Announcement." YouTube. Online: http://www.youtube.com/watch?v=p2qlhoxpiom.

Zizioulas, Jean. *Being as Communion: Studies in Personhood and the Church.* Contemporary Greek Theologians No. 4. Crestwood, NY: St. Vladimir's Seminary Press, 1985.

Zunkel, C. Wayne. "Countering Critics of the Church Growth Movement." *Christian Century* 98, no. 31 (1981): 997–98.